A Visitor's Britain

A Visitor's Britain

Exploring Culture Past and Present

Edited by
Martin Upham and Patricia Tatspaugh

AHA International

British Library Cataloguing in Publication Data
A catalogue record for this book is available from the British Library

ISBN 0–9538971–0–9

Produced for the publisher AHA International by
Chase Publishing Services, Fortescue, Sidmouth, Devon EX10 9QG
Printed and bound in the European Union

Contents

Colour Plates

Acknowledgements

We are grateful to the Rose E Tucker Charitable Trust and Mr Tom Stoel, Trustee, for a grant and to Dr Robert Selby, executive director, AHA International, and the executive board of the Independent Liberal Arts Colleges Abroad (ILACA) for its support of this volume. From the book's inception our ever-generous colleagues Maggie Kovacevic and Christine Owen have encouraged, cajoled, and aided us. We are grateful to them for numerous contributions. We are also grateful to our colleagues in the USA study-abroad community for their advice and encouragement. Finally, it is our pleasure to record our indebtedness to Erica Groat of Word Processing Plus, whose computer wizardry and good sense continue to guide us through this self-publishing venture and to Carole Machin of AHA International for help and advice beyond the call of duty.

Martin Upham and Patricia Tatspaugh

Contributors

Henry Davis (Lecturer and Examiner in International and European Studies at the Faculty of Continuing Education, Birkbeck College; European Studies Convenor at SOAS, University of London). US London Programmes taught include those of AHA International, AIFS, FIE, Central University of Iowa, New England and Elon.

Michael Doorley (Associate Lecturer, Open University and professor, American University in Dublin). Previously taught at the University of Illinois.

Jean Elliott (Senior A-level adviser in Modern English Literature). US London Programmes taught include those of AHA International, Notre Dame, Delaware, and Hollins. Under her stage name of Ellie Dickens, Jean Elliott is a professional actor and playwright.

Harry Eyres (Regular contributor to *The Spectator*, former *Times* theatre critic and author of several books on wine). US London Programmes taught include those of AHA International, Elon and Lewis and Clark. Harry Eyres edits the daily poetry column for the *Express*.

Peter Grosvenor (Assistant Professor of Political Science, Pacific Lutheran University). US London Programmes taught include those of AHA International, Lewis and Clark and Elon.

Karen Kleeh-Tolley (Professor of Sociology, St Lawrence University). Director of the St Lawrence London Programme, 1997–98, 1999–2000.

Carole Machin (London Resident Director, AHA International). US London Programmes taught include those of AHA International, Guilford (North Carolina), AIFS and Elon.

David Smith (Professor of History, University of Puget Sound). Visiting Director of the AHA London Programme. He is currently undertaking research into refugees in the British-occupied zone of Germany.

Alan Walker (Anglican priest). Formerly Chaplain at the University of Westminster and lecturer at the University of Rome; writer and presenter of BBC Radio series on church music, history and the liturgy. US London

Programmes taught include those of AHA International, the College of St Benedict/ St John's University, Elon and Florida State.

Patricia Tatspaugh (London Resident Director AHA International, 1992–99). Taught British literature to US undergraduates in America, writes about British theatre and performance history and was associate editor of a multi-volume *History of British Political Thought.*

Martin Upham (Freelance writer and lecturer). His publications include *Tempered – Not Quenched* (1997), *Trades Unions of the World* (1996), and contributions to the *Cassell Dictionary of Modern Britain* (1995); former Research Officer, Iron & Steel Trades Confederation and a parliamentary candidate. US London Programmes taught include those of AHA International, St Lawrence, Illinois Wesleyan, Notre Dame and Hollins.

Preface

Martin Upham

This book arose out of discussions among members of the British faculty of the Independent Liberal Arts Colleges Abroad (ILACA) at the end of the 1990s. As the teacher of the core course, 'Britain Today', I felt great dissatisfaction at the absence of books I could sensibly recommend to my students. The purpose of a core course on a study-abroad programme is to act as a gateway to British life and culture, and to provide some kind of context for the more specialised study students would undertake while pursuing their course options. The books available tended either to deal with Britain in an excessively compartmentalised way, or simply to omit key aspects of the British experience. What was needed, we felt, was a compilation of essays that ignored conventional separations of subject but offered an authoritative *tour d'horizon*, a companion for students as they experienced Britain for the first time.

Acting on the old maxim that if you want something done it's better to do it yourself, we set about organising just such a volume. We drew primarily upon the richest resource available to us, namely the experience and knowledge of our colleagues on the ILACA programme, to commission essays; we supplemented their proposed contributions with others from the pens of teachers who, like them, had a strong background in study-abroad programmes. The result is this volume of essays, which, for the most part, arises from the actual experience of teaching a particular course to study-abroad students from the United States, though it must be said that the teaching experience of the authors impressively spans students of almost every age and many nationalities. Perhaps one should add that it is truly transatlantic in conception and execution: the book team includes six English authors, but they are joined by one from Ireland, a Welshman and an Englishman living and teaching in the United States, and by two Americans with very considerable experience of running study-abroad programmes in England! On a personal note, I confess that it was only after trying to agree with my fellow-editor, Pat Tatspaugh, on points of style that I first understood the true significance of Bernard Shaw's dictum:

England and America are two nations divided by a common language...

The British-American convergence responsible for this volume was not intended to produce a uniform approach. Far from it: one of the original intentions certainly has been achieved, since students can on the following pages read, unusually in one volume, British perspectives from the standpoint of modern and contemporary history, political science, religious studies, fine art, English literature, sociology, film and theatre studies. *A Visitor's Britain* is meant to be a joyful celebration of the fact that, though we have to cut the world up into little pieces in order to study it, human experience is one. Readers will be reminded of this as they turn the following pages, where they will encounter subjects out of their conventional, some would say natural, order.

What then of the essays themselves? The first two reach into the national contrasts within Britain. We begin with Jean Elliott's examination of the English character through the prism of the twentieth-century novel. The word 'English' is deliberately used here, as in the essay itself, to refer to the nation that dominates, demographically and perhaps culturally, the United Kingdom of Great Britain and Northern Ireland (UK). 'English' and 'British' are not synonyms. They express differences that are objective and deeply felt. The novel, the death of which was once discussed, certainly remains a favourite art form. As Elliott shows, there is a massive output from England alone, in which the dilemmas, complacencies and passions of personal and public life are discussed from every possible angle.

And that is only the English novel. Some of the most prominent contemporary British writers of fiction have not been English at all – Allan Massie and James Kelman to name but two (fantastically contrasting) examples. Some of the objective differences between the nations of the United Kingdom can be traced in Michael Doorley's discussion, the second essay in the book. The Irish, Welsh and Scots could be forgiven for ruefully observing that their national experiences have sometimes been roughly shaped by 'Englishness'. It has at times been very unpleasant to share an island with a nation of such pronounced warlike tendencies. Today the United Kingdom of Great Britain and Northern Ireland is an example of what is increasingly rare in the world: a multinational state. The view of some recent historians is that the end of the British Empire means also an end to the glue that bound these nations together, and that separation, not union, will mark their future. There has been speculation (assisted of course by other historians) that the English might rediscover themselves if they emerge as a single nation unscreened by 'Britain'. The Scots, Welsh and Irish are conveniently described as the Celtic nations, a label which expresses something of their past, but each is nationally distinct. Scottish nationalism (a sentiment wider than support for the political party that bears the name) is on the upbeat, and has gained a political reality with the election of a Scottish parliament. Students who visit Scotland, as all sensible ones will, will find themselves in a country which is linguistically, culturally, politically, even spiritually different with perhaps two world cities in Edinburgh and Glasgow. For the moment, Scotland remains part of the UK but is there another country in the world that, though not independent, is so self-evidently a nation?

Wales is different. It too is a nation, but the majority of its inhabitants seem less sure than the Scots that they want to assert their distinctiveness by political means. In recent centuries, most of the Welsh who do want to be more different have chosen cultural vehicles to say so. As recently as twenty years ago Welsh nationalism in the political sense seemed to dwell on the margins; as recently as 1997 the nation was evenly split over whether to accept more self-government. The country's National Assembly (the world's newest parliament) has only with difficulty found a distinct voice. Yet when students visit Wales they will meet a growing sense of certainty: the British state was not (in the twentieth century) a barrier to the good health of a Welsh-based culture and this seems to have assisted nationalism to gain the allegiance of the English-speaking majority. The old traditions are still in evidence but Cardiff, with its huge building projects, is at last starting to look like a capital city. An independent Wales may still be unthinkable; it is no longer impossible to envisage greater self-confidence as the country explores its own destiny.

It is, thankfully, a time of relative tranquillity in Northern Ireland. Here, as Michael Doorley explains, there are two nationalisms at work. One (the 'Nationalist' variety) thinks in terms of uniting the Irish nation that inhabits the island of Ireland; the other ('Unionism') cleaves to the United Kingdom and proudly asserts its Britishness. The Anglo-Irish Peace Accord heroically describes these conflicting universes as the 'two traditions' of Northern Ireland, and they may yet come to settle into the peacefulness that the phrase implies. Students should visit Ireland too. If they go to Dublin they will see a city that has much architecturally in common with Georgian Bath or Edinburgh, yet is the capital of an independent state, which is at last embracing modernity. If they go to Belfast, they will find sights familiar from the cities of the English North and Midlands. Belfast is the capital only of a territory of the UK, but the peace process has released energies there that are starting, literally, to find concrete expression.

The next two essays discuss some renowned aspects of contemporary Britain. Peter Grosvenor takes readers through a painful yet pleasurable half-century for the British, decades marked by straitened economic circumstances, decolonisation and political failure, but also by the construction, perhaps by accident, of a society which is, by and large free and tolerant, and (quite deliberately) of institutions of which the people remain proud, like the Welfare State and the National Health Service (NHS). Politically, the British tend to elect right-wing governments for long periods of office and then put in a government of the left for a rather briefer spell of modernisation. Radicalism of the left brought the mixed economy, the welfare state and an altered constitution; radicalism of the right created a much more individualist society but also one that came to terms with a diminished international status.

The people elect the government, and the people are the subject of Karen Kleeh-Tolley's dissection of British society. In Elliott's essay, the English obsession with class is charted in detail. Kleeh-Tolley traces social class by means of its economic manifestations. Britain, not England alone, is socially divided.

The most grotesque extremes of wealth and poverty have gone but they have been replaced by something else, a two-thirds/one-third society. The prime minister, Tony Blair, once envisaged a society where the large and growing majority were (like him) 'middle-class'. This argument was intended to persuade members of his own party to abandon a class-based ideology, but there can be little doubt that this country, which a century ago was numerically dominated by an industrial proletariat, has been transformed into an increasingly white-collar and service-dependent society. The British continue to work the longest hours in Europe, but the majority who have some money to spend are enjoying themselves as never before.

Mr Blair's government has been fertile in initiatives directed towards those who fall into the 'one-third' category where multiple deprivations reproduce themselves through bad housing, joblessness, low educational attainment, poorer health and culturally impoverished lives. How effective these plans will be remains to be seen. But social change is slow and it is vital that students from abroad who rightly enjoy the metropolitan excitements of London don't remain unaware of the continuing darker side of British society. Talk to the paper seller from whom you buy your copy of *The Big Issue*; take a stroll round a council estate; speak to a teacher. On average, the British are better off than ever before, but participation in this greater national wealth is very unequal.

It is not only novelists and sociologists that write about class; dramatists too are fascinated. Many students will have been attracted to London by its stage, the subject of Harry Eyres' essay. London is, happily, bursting with theatre: you could go to different productions each night of the week and not see the same play twice. It is tempting to present the theatre as a simple reflection of society, and as Eyres shows the post-war shift in dramatic style from drawing-room comedy to social realism did match, even anticipate, other contemporary changes. Go to the theatre today and you will see plays grappling with every possible theme and tapping on the capital's huge reservoir of actors, designers and playwrights to do it. Yet there is more, for drama in London has demonstrated its robustness over four centuries. One great resource of the London stage (not used anything like as much as it might be) is its own past and above all Shakespeare; the willingness and ability of the stage to return to such sources of inspiration is evidence of its self-confidence.

Compared with London's flourishing stage, the British film industry is a pygmy. It is as old as any in the world, yet for its entire lifetime it has struggled to escape from the shadow of foreign domination. 2000 brought yet another state-led attempt to revive the British film and we can only hope it succeeds. But Ken Nolley's essay demonstrates how hard it has been to construct a genuinely national cinematic voice. It is easy to complain about the impossibility of rivalling Hollywood; certainly, there is little chance of it when actors, scriptwriters and directors speak the same language. But many wounds have been self-inflicted: a narrowness of vision, a lack of interest in national history yet, paradoxically, the use of themes which do not interest foreign audiences. It is surprising that a country with such depth of acting and directing does not find more success on the screen. Nolley shows that, despite this patchiness, the British film industry has achieved memorable successes. These continue to occur, but often in an Anglo-American form, as with the Oscar-laden *American Beauty*, directed by Sam Mendes, known hitherto for his work at the Donmar Warehouse in London.

As the theatre essay shows, a favourite modern stage theme is (as it was for Shakespeare) politics. My essay discusses not so much politics as the framework thereof. The structure of British government is anomalous: past and present, continuities and changes dwell side by side. Britain can seem dominated by its past, but what is less easily understood is the political system's capacity for change. The electorate can alter everything just by throwing a switch at the polls. They don't often choose to do so: radicalism seems to exhaust the British (or at least the English) quite quickly. Usually it is policy that changes while the context remains constant. But 1999 saw the inauguration of a Scottish parliament, a Welsh Assembly and a Bill of Rights, not to mention a decision to expel most of the hereditary peers from the House of Lords. 2000 brought the election in London of Britain's first executive mayor. For once it is the context that is changing; the government that is leading this constitutional revolution has been much more cautious in other fields.

The altered circumstances, which have led the electorate to vote in a 'modernising' government, owe much to Britain's relationships with other countries. Of all the shifts which occurred in the second half of the twentieth century the altered global status of Britain is perhaps the most dramatic. As Henry Davis shows, in fifty years the British have yielded up an empire (and replaced it with a voluntary Commonwealth), abandoned national aloofness (perhaps) for participation in the European Union (EU) and sought, intermittently, a joint identity with the United States. Yet each of these processes reverberates at home. One consequence of the empire is a multi-racial society at least in the towns and cities; the extent of future national engagement with the EU is perhaps the most towering decision that now faces politicians and voters alike; the robustness of a distinct *British* culture when the Anglo-Saxon world is so dominated by the United States is of considerable concern. Davis rebuts temptations to construe all this as a catalogue of failure. The trail of decolonisation, though not unmarked by blood, was arguably less gory a trail than that left by other former imperial powers; many Britons are at least thinking seriously about the prospect of a closer European union; the preposterous government attempt to relaunch the country as 'Cool Britannia' has happily collapsed into giggles all round, leaving some hope that high culture might be taken seriously.

High culture points in the direction of fine art. The twentieth-century British achievement in painting and sculpture has been considerable as Carole Machin shows and the illustrations testify. But art, no less than the novel, poses problems that are peculiar to the British and that have their origins in insularity, not only physical but spiritual. Just how has Britain engaged with trends and developments in art that had their origins on the mainland continent of Europe? At times, it seems that national artistic renewal has needed to be kick-started by an impulse from abroad; and yet there are national traditions – portraiture above all – which have persisted almost regardless of circumstances and subject. In her first essay, Machin asks if there can be a British art in the modern period. Students are invited to explore this question for themselves, aided by the matchless resources of the galleries she has helpfully listed at the end of her essay. With perfect timing for our purposes, London's art spaces have put themselves on display with refurbishment at the Courtauld, Dulwich and Wallace collections, an extension to the National Portrait Gallery and above all the new Tate Modern, the largest modern art gallery in the world. They join Tate Britain, the National Gallery, Hayward Gallery and the Royal Academy.

There follows a contribution different from the others in the book. In her second contribution Machin has sought to illustrate in the most literal sense why it is that British buildings are as they are. While a superficial glance at a building, for example a thatched cottage or a Georgian terrace, leaves the observer with a sense that this is perhaps something unique to the country, the very basic explanation can remain hidden. Often the reason behind architectural style lies simply in the availability – or scarcity – of materials. Climate, the need for comfort and function also dictate. And buildings express enduringly the openings and closures created by politics and international cultural developments. So much that is distinct about the structures of the sixteenth and seventeenth centuries can be explained by the Protestant Reformation. How different from the twentieth when the new Scottish parliament building has been designed by a Dane celebrated for his work in Spain! In her drawings, Machin has offered an invaluable preparation for the sights students will see as they travel round Britain. Again, one only needs to look up: the London skyline and that of many provincial cities is beginning to change as new buildings crowd the old. Lottery money and private capital are vying to alter many familiar perspectives: a whole series of seriously tall buildings was sanctioned for London in summer 2000. It has happened before – after the Great Fire of 1666 for example – but has it ever happened so fast? How will a nation that is used to grumbling about new buildings then growing to love them react?

To return to our theme, Alan Walker's subject matter addresses one explanation for English – perhaps British – separateness. The Reformation of the sixteenth century cut off England from many contemporary European intellectual currents or at least delayed their impact. But English Christianity is old (and British, arguably, older); indeed it defines the character of the state itself. It has become a commonplace that this is now a secular age but, as Walker demonstrates, the decline of Christianity may not mean the decline of belief: one of the consequences of the shift to a multi-ethnic society is a shift to a multi-faith society. Moreover, there was some evidence that the arrival of the year 2000 led some in the nation to think about its Christian past. The erection of the Millennium Dome near the Prime Meridian in Greenwich provoked comment; many people pondered the paradox of the secular celebration of an unmistakably Christian anniversary.

And so to history and David Smith's survey of the rise of the modern state. He begins at the great turning point for the English, the Reformation, an event to which can be attributed the nation-state, literacy and democracy. He ends with the lonely and exhausting heroism of World War Two. As he explains, the notion of a peaceful evolution of feudal into modern society is something of a myth; popular pressure was constantly felt. But there are strong continuities and the student here only for three months can still be served wonderfully by the built environment and the evidence it provides of the past. Visit St Margaret's, Westminster, where Henry VIII married Katherine of Aragon; stand outside the Banqueting House in Whitehall, where Charles I was executed (or outside Burford Church, where the Leveller leaders lost their lives four months later); explore the eighteenth-century courtyard of Somerset House and look up at the rooms where British naval supremacy was plotted; ponder on the Victorian Gothic style of the Palace of Westminster, which witnessed the parliamentary duels of Gladstone and Disraeli; explore twentieth-century urban re-development with a political message in London's and Cardiff's docklands.

Students from abroad who think about English identity will readily volunteer another component, the subject of the afterward to this book. It is impossible, and pointless, to summarise Elliott's tribute to Shakespeare. The reader can only marvel at the way one man has shaped a country's speech, perception of its past and identity. He is not just a matter for English students but central to the way the country expresses itself even in a time of change. Shakespeare's Globe, immediate neighbour to Tate Modern, and the achievement of an American, Sam Wanamaker, is a rigorous re-creation of the theatre for which Shakespeare wrote his plays. During 2000, you could see his plays performed in every conceivable space, including an early Hitchcock film studio. He is there waiting for you.

Of course, this book is only a partial examination of Britain. Huge areas of endeavour and achievement have been omitted. The British twentieth-century achievement in music (by contrast to the sad nineteenth century) has been colossal; it has surely been matched by poetry and each is worthy of an essay on its own. In popular music, pre-eminently an American art form, the British contribution, if not of the first rank, has also been considerable. And what of the literary contributions of the Welsh, Scots and Irish novel?

Despite these omissions, it is the hope of the authors that this volume will prove a stimulating introduction to British life and culture. The student who reads, and thinks, about (say) the English attitude to foreigners will learn something from reading about the novel, about Britain in the World, and about religion; if he or she is interested in class divisions then there are discussions of them from sociological, historical and literary perspectives. There is much else besides, and students are encouraged to challenge the authors on the views they express in these pages.

And in every essay, there is the same tension between old and new that is to be found in each field of British culture. That's what makes the place so interesting: read, reflect and explore!

1

The 'Englishness' of Modern English Fiction

Jean Elliott

In the preface to his book *The Situation of the Novel* (1970), Bernard Bergonzi observes: '... I have become increasingly aware that to write about modern English fiction is also, in some measure, to attempt to define what it means to be English at the present time.' Bergonzi explores this topic in the chapter entitled 'The Ideology of Being English', and in it he quotes the American scholar Norman Podhoretz, who described his experience of studying in England with an English professor: 'The more I listened to him ... the more uneasily aware I became of the Englishness of English literature.' Similarly, in teaching English literature to visiting American students, I too have become increasingly aware of 'the Englishness of English literature'. Throughout this essay I shall be using the word 'English' in a very specific, and admittedly very narrow way, so I must begin by trying to define my use of that term.

English versus British

First, visiting Americans should remember to make a clear distinction between 'British' and 'English'. 'British' is an adjective that can cover a wide variety of races and societies, not just within the British Isles, but of those whose origins lie in the far-flung quarters of what was once the British Empire. Great Britain consists of three different countries: England, Scotland, Wales, which with Northern Ireland make up the United Kingdom; and, with the coming of devolution, the boundaries of these countries are becoming firmer. You should note that the Republic of Ireland is a quite separate country, not part of Great Britain, though it is in the same island as Northern Ireland, where many consider themselves to be British. Be very careful how you refer to an Irishman. He may indeed be Irish, or he may crossly inform you that he is 'British'. A Scotsman *might* not mind being referred to as British, but he will certainly object to being called English. Doris Lessing recalled that after living in London

1

for two years, she was eventually introduced to an Englishman. ('London is full of foreigners,' she explained to her friend from South Africa.) In the pub with him later, she expressed her delight at meeting the English at last:

> He drew himself up. His mild blue eyes flashed ... 'I am not,' he said, with a blunt but basically forgiving hauteur, 'English. I have a Welsh grandmother.'
> (*In Pursuit of the English*, 1960)

I am not, of course, using the word 'English' to mean a language either. English is spoken by millions of people all over the world, and novels in English are written by many different races and cultures. The Booker Prize, probably the most prestigious prize in Britain for a work of fiction in English, makes a heroic attempt to define the limits of its eligibility by accepting submissions from authors who are citizens of Britain, the Republic of Ireland, the Commonwealth, South Africa, Pakistan or Bangladesh (i.e. what was once, more or less, the British Empire). Thus, Canadian and Australian authors qualify, but not Americans (the 'colony' of America having been lost too long ago to count, presumably!). In fact, very few winners of the Booker Prize for Fiction in English have actually been 'English'. I may as well add to the confusion by noting that the winner of the 1989 Booker Prize, *The Remains of the Day*, is a superbly 'English' novel – English in its precise observation of detail, its nostalgic yearning for a distant glorious past, narrated by a quintessential Englishman, precisely aware of every subtle class signifier, and totally incapable of expressing emotion. And this novel was written by Kazuo Ishiguro who, although he has lived in England since he was six, is, by origin and birth, Japanese.

There are numerous collections of Scottish short stories (stories by Scots writers), Irish stories (by Irish writers) and Welsh stories (by Welsh writers). Collections of English stories, however, have been far more eclectic, often meaning stories written in English by any nationality under the sun. In a collection entitled *So Very English* (ed Marsha Rowe, 1991), 'stories and poems about Englishness', almost all of the writers are non-English. But, in 1998, A S Byatt deliberately chose stories by English writers only (excluding Welsh, Scottish and Irish authors) for her selection of *The Oxford Book of English Short Stories*, thereby acknowledging that 'English' English writers are identifiably different. In her introduction Byatt admits that:

> There is a reluctance to think about Englishness. The English are what other English-speakers define themselves against. They are seen as imperialist, insular, nostalgic for merrie England, class-ridden, complacent. There is even a hinted feeling that to think about Englishness might lead to racism or xenophobia. It is not quite nice to think about being English.

Anglo-Saxon attitudes

At the risk of being 'not quite nice', I am using the word 'English' to describe a nation and a culture which possesses a peculiar quality of Englishness, an 'Anglo-Saxon attitude' to life which will be encountered in England only, and in the specifically English works of English fiction. English writers use English differently. As a general rule, they are less likely to be imaginative and innovative in their use of the language. Significantly, James Joyce and Samuel Beckett were both Irish. More recently the Scottish writer Irvine Welsh has given us the linguistic challenge of the drug culture of the young underclass of Scotland in *Trainspotting* (1993). English writers, having absorbed Englishness naturally, use their fiction to reflect on and to respond to the world around them. They rely on a set of social and linguistic signifiers that their English readers understand and can decode immediately and intuitively. George Orwell said that England resembled a family, 'a rather scruffy Victorian family', one that had 'its private language and its common memories' (*The Lion and the Unicorn*, 1941). Later I shall look more closely at 'its private language' and 'its common memories'. For now, I will observe only that England is still like a family; a family that is both united and divided by its very Englishness. Many writers, English and 'foreign', have attempted to define this quality of Englishness, and I can only outline here what seem to me (as 'one of the family') to be its most distinguishing features.

It may be as well to mention now an important but often infuriating aspect of the English, and that is their ability to hold completely contrasting opinions at the same time. Sometimes it's called (kindly) compromise, sometimes (justifiably) hypocrisy. For example, the English are very proud of being English and, at the same time, deeply ashamed of it too. The greatest critics of the English tend to be the English themselves; the greatest monsters of Englishness have been created by the observing eye and unerring hand of an English writer. A saving grace of the English is their ability to mock themselves and their faults. But they laugh at themselves with affection, and feel an extraordinary pride at being so awful. Their acknowledgement of their own faults generously allows foreigners to mock too. The Hungarian George Mikes spent thirty years wryly observing and writing about the English and their Englishness, beginning in 1946 with *How to be an Alien*. Mikes claimed to be astonished by the response to his satire: 'I expected the English to be up in arms against me but they patted me on the back.' In fact, his satires have been reprinted again and again, to be enjoyed by new generations of English readers. More recently, the American writer Bill Bryson has seen his bemused observations on this country, *Notes From a Small Island* (1995), in England's list of top best-selling paperbacks for two years running.

Of course, this English ability to laugh at themselves has not always been seen as an endearing quality, not even by the English. In his essay 'Notes on the English Character' (*Abinger Harvest*, 1936), E M Forster condemns the Englishman's attitude towards criticism:

> He is not annoyed by criticism.... It never occurs to him that the fellow may be accurate as well as jealous, and that he might do well to take the criticism to heart and profit by it. It never strikes him – except as a form of words – that he is capable of improvement; his self-complacency is abysmal. Other nations, both Oriental and European, have an uneasy feeling that they are not quite perfect. In consequence they resent criticism. It hurts them; and their snappy answers often mask a determination to improve themselves. Not so the Englishman. He has no uneasy feeling. Let the critics bark. And the 'tolerant humorous attitude' with which he confronts them is not really tolerant, because it is insensitive....

More recently the eponymous hero of John Fowles' novel *Daniel Martin* (1977) considers 'the heart of Englishness':

> ... being unhappier at being unhappy than doing something constructive about it. We boast of our genius for compromise, which is really a refusal to choose; and that in turn contains a large part of cowardice, apathy, selfish laziness.... That is what permits in England our extraordinary tolerance of national decay, of muddling through; our socialising conservatism and our conservative socialism.

English fiction writers continue to describe the awfulness of England and the English. Their attitudes range from ironic acceptance to savage satire. There is some truth in Mikes' observation:

> You can be as rude about the English as you wish, they positively like it. In any case you cannot be as rude about them as they are about themselves. (*How to be Decadent*, 1977)

Or, to put it another way, the English agree that there is nothing worse than being a narrow-minded, hypocritical, xenophobic Englishman – apart, of course, from being a foreigner!

Englishness is a quality that is hard to define, yet it seems to have survived for over 500 years. It seems even to have survived the 'global networking' of the twentieth century. Indeed, there is something particularly English about the muddle and compromise that went into the production of the Millennium Dome.

'Not English'

In 1977, Mikes concluded that, although there had been a few surface changes to England since 1945, 'the world still consists of two clearly divided groups:

the English and the foreigners' (*How to be Decadent*). Writing in about 1500, the Venetian Ambassador to the court of Henry VII had observed:

> ... the English are great lovers of themselves, and of anything belonging to them; they think that there are no other men than themselves, and no other world but England; and whenever they see a handsome foreigner, they say that 'he looks like an Englishman'. (Andrea Trevisano, *A Relation, or rather a True Account of the Island of England* ...)

In 1856, when Nathaniel Hawthorne was the American Consul in England, he was introduced to an English clergyman who had read and admired *The Scarlet Letter*:

> He inquired whether I had spent much time in America, appearing to think that I must have had an English breeding, if not birth, to be so much like other people. This English narrowness is very queer, and is just as much a characteristic of gentlemen of education and culture, as of clowns. (*Our Old Home*, 1863)

'The insularity of the English,' observed Orwell grimly, 'their refusal to take foreigners seriously, is a folly that has to be paid for very heavily from time to time.' When the very English and middle-class Charles Dickens created Mr Podsnap in *Our Mutual Friend* (1865), he created a monstrous character who is quintessentially and recognisably a middle-class Englishman:

> Mr Podsnap's world was not a very large world morally; no, nor even geo-graphically: seeing that although his business was sustained upon commerce with other countries, he considered other countries ... a mistake, and of their manners and customs would conclusively observe, 'Not English!'.

Jim Dixon of Kingsley Amis' *Lucky Jim* (1954) is a similar English grotesque who could only have been created by an Englishman. Famously xenophobic and anti–intellectual, he spends most of the novel raging against an equally ludicrous adversary, the pompous and pretentious pseudo-intellectual Professor Welch. Jim's fury covers a wide range of topics, but includes the fact that Professor Welch 'without being French himself' had given his sons French names. Jim is delighted to learn that one of the sons, the 'indefatigably Gallic' Michel, has 'made himself ill by stuffing himself with filthy foreign food'. Mrs Welch is also an object of Jim's derision for being, as Professor Welch describes her, 'a Western European first and an Englishwoman second'. Although Jim Dixon belongs to a very specific period in English history, an angry young man of the 1950s Angry Decade (see below), the English prejudice against foreigners (especially the French) remains a constant feature in the English soul.

Suspicion of the French goes back many centuries, and has much to do with our fear of invasion (the one historical date that every English person knows is 1066!). But there is also the typically English mix compounded of both fear and envy which views France as the land of sexual freedom – wickedness, sin and immorality; in short, forbidden pleasures. It is to France that many English writers dispatch their characters in order for them to be enlightened or ruined or both. It is part of the adolescent rebellion against their English suburban background that inspires Chris and Toni to adopt French art and culture in Julian Barnes' *Metroland* (1980). When Chris goes to Paris in 1968, he spends his time discovering sex with a French girl, totally unaware of the social and political upheavals going on around him. In a very English way, Chris comes home to settle down in a suburban English home with an English wife and family. His friend Toni remains true to his adolescent ideals, but then, an English reader might well have predicted that, for early in the novel Chris, the narrator, enviously observes, 'Toni far outclassed me in rootlessness. His parents were Polish Jews....' Chris consoles himself with the fact that he comes from a small family who don't have much to do with one other: 'Despite the handicaps of being English and non-Jewish, I tried to do my bit in a Home Counties sort of way.' (For 'Home Counties' see below.)

In Fowles' short story 'The Cloud' (*The Ebony Tower*, 1974), the English visitors in France discuss what one of them describes as 'the curious middle-classishness of English relations with France', France being 'a good place to forget all the disadvantages of living in a deeply puritanical country'. In Byatt's novel, *Babel Tower* (1996), the prosecuting counsel challenges the French professor who has given evidence on behalf of an allegedly obscene book. Having heard her evidence, he observes:

> These preoccupations are very *French* preoccupations, are they not? Your country has always given more latitude to sexual freedom?

Warming to his theme, he continues, in true Podsnap style:

> English people have had to go to France and buy books thought unsuitable for English readers, to see the Folies Bérgère, and so on. Some people think it is a good thing to have these latitudes. Some believe that our greater care for our own public morals, our greater concern for restraint ... has something to be said for it.

D J Taylor notes that:

> With minor exceptions the attitude to foreign countries, their customs, landscape and representatives, is deeply insular – an ingrained suspicion that

frequently borders on outright hostility. (*After the War: The Novel and England since 1945*, 1993)

The narrator in Alice Thomas Ellis' *The Skeleton in the Cupboard* (1988) observes that her son seems perturbed when his fiancée, Margaret, admitted liking the people in Egypt: 'I think it was because it was unusual for the English to express a fondness for any foreigners at all....' It is true that most English no longer fear 'abroad'. Mikes' observation that the English travel to the continent and 'drink tea with milk in Paris, eat roast beef with Yorkshire pudding in Monte Carlo, keep to one another's company everywhere and are proud of how cosmopolitan they have become' (*How to be Inimitable*, 1960) still has an awful element of truth. But the English now also travel abroad and not only eat 'filthy foreign food', they return to England laden with foreign foods, wines, fads and fashions. In this, they are not breaking with English tradition at all. It is the same spirit that an English audience would have recognised in the 1590s when Portia in *The Merchant of Venice* comments on the visiting Englishman:

How oddly he is suited! I think he bought his doublet in Italy, his round hose in France, his bonnet in Germany, and his behaviour everywhere. (Act I, sc 2)

This is the same spirit that inspired the eighteenth-century gentlemen to go on their Grand Tours of Europe, returning triumphantly with vases from Italy, fashions from France and marbles from Greece.

But entry to the European Union and the building of a tunnel to France under the English Channel have so far done little to make Europeans of us, much less Francophiles. Barnes addresses this subject in his essay 'Froggy! Froggy! Froggy!' in *Letters From London* (1995). Barnes, a Francophile himself, longs for the day when we can overcome our 'complicated and self-destructive feelings about the French'. Making fun of the French and their funny French accent has been an English pastime for generations, stretching from Shakespeare's Dr Caius of *The Merry Wives of Windsor* to Peter Sellers' Inspector Clouseau in the *Pink Panther* movies.

To imitate the French speaking English with a French accent is one thing; to speak French at all, regardless of accent, is quite another. There is more than a grain of truth in Mikes' assertion that 'A true-born Englishman does not know any language.... Indeed, inability to speak foreign languages seems to be the major, if not the only, intellectual achievement of the average Englishman' (*How to be Inimitable*). Portia could not communicate with the visiting Englishman because 'he hath neither Latin, French, nor Italian'. Shakespeare confirmed Henry V's heroic status by having him admit he found it easier to conquer France than to speak French. Mr Podsnap and his fellow-English address a visiting Frenchman 'as if he were a child who was hard of hearing'. Mikes concludes, 'The knowledge of foreign languages is very un-English. A little French is permissible, but only with an atrocious accent' (*How to be an Alien*).

When the English travel to Europe they are always tremendously impressed to discover that even very small French children speak French, young Italians speak Italian and so on. Thus they conclude, since they themselves speak little or no French and no other language at all, foreigners must be very clever. Mikes recalled an English lady saying to him: 'You foreigners are so clever.' At first, he had assumed this to be an extravagant compliment. He learned subsequently that 'These few words expressed the lady's contempt and slight disgust for foreigners.' For only later did he understand that 'In England it is bad manners to be clever....'

'Too clever by half'

The real trouble with the French, as far as the English are concerned, is that they are far too clever. They have a fine appreciation of the arts and discuss abstract philosophy with enormous enthusiasm. In France, intellectuals are revered. 'The English are not intellectual', said Orwell. 'They have a horror of abstract thought, they feel no need for any philosophy or systematic world view.' And if you are clever, you are expected to keep rather quiet about it ... especially if you are a woman. In Kate Atkinson's *Behind the Scenes at the Museum* (1995), a novel that weaves its way skilfully to and fro through the history of an English family in the twentieth century, the heroine, Ruby, says, 'People are always eyeing me doubtfully and saying to Bunty [her mother], "She's very advanced for her age, isn't she?" "Too clever for her own good, that one," Bunty confirms.' In Byatt's *Babel Tower*, Frederica recalls that: 'Girls at school disliked her for being clever and she accepted this, as her due, both as a compliment and as a punishment.' When people asked Clara's mother, in Margaret Drabble's *Jerusalem the Golden* (1967), 'where her daughter got her brains from, she would sniff and shrug her shoulders, as though disclaiming a vice or a disease, "Well, she certainly didn't get them from me...."' This is a typically English disclaimer as, in fact, Clara's mother 'had done well at school'.

In 1998, the award-winning author Jeanette Winterson described one of her own books as 'brilliant'. The English were outraged at this English author's un-English arrogance. Newspaper protests did not debate the merits of self-alleged brilliance or otherwise, but focused on the fact that she had praised her own work in public. In a radio interview Winterson pointed out, quite reasonably, that there would be no point in trying to get her novels published at all if she didn't think they were any good. But for the English she had confirmed their worst fears about 'clever' women.

In fairness, the English of both sexes learn from an early age not to be clever: 'Don't get clever with me, sonny', 'you're sharp, mind you don't cut yourself!' and 'Stop showing off!' Eustace in Susan Hill's *Air and Angels* (1991) wins a scholarship to Cambridge University:

> When the letter of acceptance and congratulations had come from the Senior Tutor of the College, his father had held it at arm's length.
> 'Cleverness,' he had said, 'cleverness is all very fine. And what about the rest of it?'

'The English – so suspicious of cleverness', observes Rowe in her introduction to *So Very English*. Even in academic circles, it isn't considered 'quite the thing'. In Angus Wilson's novel *Anglo-Saxon Attitudes* (1956), the English historian Sir Edgar grimly observes a German colleague as he correctly identifies the provenance of a small ivory box in Sir Edgar's possession:

> 'Walrus ivory, I suppose. Perhaps Norwegian, no? Of the late ninth century, I may suggest. Perhaps from the Hebrides Islands?' He turned his tall, distinguished figure towards Sir Edgar, and his clear blue eyes smiled in anticipation of applause. Sir Edgar's heavy grey eyebrows drew together in distaste. The fellow's a mountebank, he thought.... But the Professor ... was quickly aware of the response he evoked.... 'Oh, my God!' he cried. 'I am showing off. That will never do in England.'

In his 1987 diary, the playwright Alan Bennett recorded that he and a friend were chatting in the street when they were shoved aside by a man wheeling a basket of shopping:

> 'Out of the way, you so-called intellectuals,' he snarls, 'blocking the fucking way.' It's curious that it's the intellectual that annoys, though it must never be admitted to be the genuine article but always 'pseudo' or 'so-called'. It is, of course, only in England that 'intellectual' is an insult anyway. (*Writing Home*, 1994)

A visiting American professor of my acquaintance who was in the process of recruiting British faculty for his London Programme despairingly observed that English academics don't know how to 'present themselves'. Instead of a glossy package, he complained, they offer two or three scruffy pages smudgily photocopied, covered with hand-written corrections, apparently put together on several different typewriters and omitting all mention of their Gold Medal for Excellence or Nobel Prize or whatever, on the grounds that 'they didn't like to mention it'.

'I didn't say anything'

The English fear of 'showing off' involves hiding any emotion of pride in one's achievements. And this fits with the general English desire to hide *all* their emotions. In Fowles' *Daniel Martin*, the hero laments 'feeling caught in that dreadful English middle-class trap of never showing or saying what you really feel'. Later in the novel he talks about the impossibility of making a film which will capture the English psyche: 'any true picture of the English must express what the camera cannot capture – the continual evasion of the inner self, the continual actual reality of saying one thing and thinking another'. The novel can, of course, tell the reader what a character is actually thinking, but it comes as no surprise to the English reader that the character very rarely, if ever, actually gives voice to those thoughts. In Virginia Woolf's *Mrs Dalloway* (1925), Richard Dalloway walks across London determined to tell his wife that he loves her: 'Which one never does say, he thought. Partly one's lazy; partly one's shy.' Repeating to himself his determination to 'tell Clarissa that he loved her, in so many words', he buys her a bouquet of roses and, arriving home, presents his gift:

> He was holding out flowers – roses, red and white roses. (But he could not bring himself to say he loved her; not in so many words.)

> But how lovely, she said, taking his flowers. She understood; she understood without his speaking ...

It is fortunate for the continuance of the race that the English are very good at reading the subtext and de-coding such unspoken declarations, but it is very baffling to outsiders. Here is the fifteenth-century Italian ambassador again:

> I have never noticed anyone, either at court or amongst the lower orders to be in love; whence one must necessarily conclude, either that the English are the most discreet lovers in the world, or that they are incapable of love.

And the Hungarian, Mikes:

> If a continental youth wants to declare his love to a girl, he kneels down, tells her that she is the sweetest, the most charming and ravishing person in the world ... and that he would be unable to live one more minute without her.... In England the boy pats his adored one on the back and says softly: 'I don't object to you, you know.'

In Winterson's *Written on the Body* (1992), the narrator recalls an early meeting with Louise. As the sexual attraction sparks between them across the table,

She touched me and I yelped.
'Did I scratch you?' she said, all concern and remorse.
'No, you electrocuted me.'
She got up and put on the coffee. The English are very good at those gestures.

To the narrator's delighted surprise, Louise speaks:

'Are we going to have an affair?' she said.
She's not English, she's Australian.

It is not lovers alone who find it difficult to convey emotion; English families suffer from the same reticence. When the hero of Martin Amis' *The Rachel Papers* (1973) tells his father that he has won a place at Oxford University:

My father appeared to be genuinely delighted. He came up and cuffed me on the shoulder. It was the first time we had touched for years. It made me blush.

Forster's novels explore this theme of the English inability to express love, usually by juxtaposing correct middle-class English people with foreigners (Italians or Indians). In his essay 'Notes on the English Character', Forster concludes that:

… it is not that the Englishman can't feel – it is that he is afraid to feel. He has been taught … that feeling is bad form. He must not express great joy or sorrow.… He must bottle up his emotions.…

Ellis' narrator in *The Skeleton in the Cupboard* is shocked by an emotional outburst from her neighbour, 'normally so perfect an example of the English lady', reflecting later that: 'that one display of emotion had been as shocking and strange as if she'd suddenly taken all her clothes off'.

This takes us back to Richard Dalloway's feeling of shyness. The English are very shy. They do not like to expose themselves – either in the taking off of their clothes or the exposing of their feelings. (Fear of someone invading their 'island' perhaps?) One must maintain one's dignity at all costs. Over a hundred years ago a visiting Frenchman, Hippolyte Taine, noted that 'The English custom of reserve leads to a kind of stoicism. There is no confiding, no letting go, even with one's nearest and dearest' (*Taine's Notes on England*, tr E Hyams, 1957).

In Byatt's novel *Still Life* (1985), Stephanie undergoes the horrors of giving birth in an English hospital. In the ante-natal clinic she calls out to a Mrs Owen and points to the blood that is trickling down Mrs Owen's leg:

She bent to peer down. She stammered.

'Oh, how embarrassing. Oh dear. I kept trying to ask them, was a bit of bleeding all right, and the pains, but there wasn't the opportunity....'

Almost at once she collapses and has a miscarriage. A little later Stephanie sobs to the doctor who is examining her:

'The English. Are so damned. Polite. For hours and hours we stand – with no girdles – in cold draughty places. That woman. That Mrs Owen. Lost her baby – I know – because. Because no one would let her tell them. Because I wouldn't. Because nobody here ...'

The doctor reprimands her for becoming hysterical:

'She would almost certainly have lost it anyway.' It sounded as though he was conceding a point.

When Stephanie is about to give birth she hears someone nearby 'screaming regularly and on a rising pitch'. And 'Stephanie heard herself thinking that it would be helpful, but not English, not good manners, to make a noise like that.' It is all part of what Stephanie has earlier described as 'the infinite English capacity for underplaying dramas, ignoring situations, pretending things were normal'.

Towards the end of the novel, Stephanie is killed in a tragic accident. The terrible shock and numbness of grief is vividly portrayed. Only Stephanie's small son becomes hysterical and angry. Stephanie's father joins his bereaved son-in-law at the funeral and observes: 'In the Middle East they put ashes on their heads, they tear their clothes, they scream and weep. We walk reasonably along together.' Stephanie's husband later thinks: 'So quickly, so quickly the English stop speaking of grief.' As with love, the English feel grief, but don't like to mention it. The three surviving friends who attend Marcia's funeral in Barbara Pym's *Quartet in Autumn* (1977) discuss frying pans on their way to the crematorium. Then:

'I brought Phyllis here,' said Edwin, in a matter-of-fact way. 'It's the nearest crematorium for where I live.'
    'Oh yes, of course.' Letty was momentarily embarrassed but Edwin did not seem to be affected by the memory of his dead wife, only going on to say that they had had a service at the church first which had been very well attended.

As the coffin is consigned to the flames, Norman suddenly thinks of a humorous couplet, but 'He didn't know whether to laugh, which you could hardly do here, or cry, which you couldn't do either and it was a long time since he had shed tears.'

The sudden death of Princess Diana in 1997 caused a totally uncharacteristic outpouring of grief that was much commented on in the newspapers at the time. The whole country seemed to be weeping and this was considered to be very un-English. The English have, in fact, experienced occasional outbursts of public grief (the deaths of the Duke of Wellington and of Charles Dickens, for example). But it is perhaps worth noting that, on the day of the funeral itself, what was remarkable was the silence of so many thousands who watched the cortège. In fact, the horses pulling the gun-carriage, and trained to ignore shouts and cries, were momentarily spooked by the solemn quietness of the multitudes.

Not only are love and grief kept bottled up inside the English breast – so too are anger and rage. In Beryl Bainbridge's novel *The Bottle Factory Outing* (1974), the very English Brenda is attacked by her estranged husband's mad mother. The gun used in the attack turns out to be a starting pistol, and anyway she misses. In bed that night, Brenda, who has refused to press charges against her mother-in-law, Mrs Haddon, wears 'a small gratified smile':

> She [Brenda] understood perfectly why Mrs Haddon had wanted to do her damage. Inside her own brain she had on numerous occasions perpetrated acts of brutality against friends and enemies alike.

Brenda is typically English in many other ways: 'she didn't like foreigners', 'was easily embarrassed', and 'would have died rather than let the other occupants of the house know she used the toilet'. Desperately afraid of calling attention to herself, making a fuss or becoming involved, she personifies English reticence perfectly.

It is this shyness which makes it difficult for visitors to strike up a conversation, much less a friendship, with the natives. English people don't like to introduce themselves in case they are considered too forward or interfering. When they do talk, they talk quietly, and cast disapproving looks at 'noisy foreigners'. In the mid-1800s, a French visitor noticed that 'the English talk very quietly. I happened to find myself for a while in Italian company and was absolutely deafened, for I had become used to the moderate tones of English voices' (quoted in *Taine's Notes on England*).

It is a wall of English reticence that Morris Zapp encounters in David Lodge's *Changing Places* (1975). Zapp is an American professor, newly arrived in England's fictional University of Rummidge on an academic exchange visit. As this is his first visit to England, he has already found much to baffle and enrage him. Now he sits alone in his office at the university pondering on his isolation:

> ... he had vaguely supposed the faculty would introduce themselves, show him around, offer the usual hospitality and advice.... From behind his desk he heard them passing in the corridor, greeting each other, laughing and

opening and shutting their doors. But when he ventured into the corridor himself they seemed to avoid him, bolting into their offices just as he emerged from his own, or else they looked straight through him as if he were the man who serviced the central heating. Just when he had decided that he would have to take the initiative by ambushing his British colleagues as they passed his door at coffee-time and dragging them into his office, they began to acknowledge his presence in a way which suggested long but not deep familiarity, tossing him a perfunctory smile as they passed, or nodding their heads, without breaking step or their own conversations.

Returning to England, Fowles' Daniel Martin re-encounters his fellow English in the silence of a train journey: 'No other caste in the world,' he reflects, 'are so certain that public decency and good breeding is silence', thus giving them a 'tribal homogeneity'. He is more than usually disturbed by 'that absolutely normal English silence … a silence like a scream', as he realises that such silences had ruined his marriage: 'We had used our silences like sabres, in the end.' It is the playwright Harold Pinter who has perhaps best captured the use that the English can make of silence to convey menace and unspoken threats of violence. But time and again in English fiction, mild-mannered English men and women endure humiliation and cruelty, thinking the most violent thoughts, but never saying them aloud. In silence they will plot their revenge, address imaginary vituperative speeches to their tormentors but actually say nothing. It is a defining moment in Kingsley Amis' *Lucky Jim* when instead of just inventing improbable insults against his rival Bertrand Welch he not only hits him, but voices the insults as well:

The bloody old towser-faced boot-faced totem-pole on a crap reservation, Dixon thought. 'You bloody old towser-faced boot-faced totem-pole on a crap reservation,' he said.

It is at this point that the mature student Michie enters and restores English decorum:

'Good afternoon, Mr Dixon,' he said, then added politely 'Good afternoon' to the still-prostrate Bertrand, who at this stimulus struggled to his feet. 'I seem to have come at an inconvenient time.'
'Not at all,' Dixon said smoothly. 'Mr Welch is just going.'

More usually, however, cries of despair and rage remain unspoken:

I thought – battling against the urge to shriek 'Say something, you tiresome little lump' – that I had better discuss the weather.

'It's nice here in the summer,' I remarked. (Ellis, *The Skeleton in the Cupboard*)

I hate you, Frederica's head says, I hate you, I hate you, I should never have come here, I cannot *live* here, I have been a fool, a fool, a fool. She holds tight to her letter under the table and chews a little bread, thoughtfully ... (Byatt, *Babel Tower*)

... I don't count, I'll just do as his messenger-boy, and I want to hit him, I want to smash his poxy four-eyed face. But I say, 'I'll go and get her.' (Graham Swift, *Last Orders*, 1996)

All this is, perhaps, part of the famous 'stiff upper lip', and this, Forster explains in his 'Notes on the English Character', is what gives the English their reputation for bravery:

When a disaster comes, the English instinct is to do what can be done first, and to postpone the feelings as long as possible. Hence they are splendid at emergencies. No doubt they are brave – no one will deny that – but bravery is partly an affair of the nerves, and the English nervous system is well equipped for meeting a physical emergency. It acts promptly and feels slowly.... And when the action is over, then the Englishman can feel.

The perfect Englishman – and perfect butler – Stevens, the narrator in *The Remains of the Day*, observes:

Continentals are unable to be butlers because they are as a breed incapable of the emotional restraint which only the English race is capable of. Continentals – and by and large the Celts, as you will no doubt agree – are as a rule unable to control themselves in moments of strong emotion.... We English have an important advantage over foreigners in this respect and it is for this reason that when you think of a great butler, he is bound, almost by definition, to be an Englishman.

(Indeed, the greatest English butler of them all is, of course, P G Wodehouse's ever-impassive Jeeves.) Stevens' reference to 'the Celts' is a useful reminder that the English are Anglo-Saxons. Garnet Bowen, in Kingsley Amis' *I Like It Here* (1958), warns a visiting American of the violence of the Welsh Nationalist Party with threats of border raids and shootings. The American tells him he is being 'fantastic'. 'That's not the way they settle things in England.' 'This isn't England,' argues Bowen. 'The Welsh are Celts – like the Irish.'

Because Ishiguro's *The Remains of the Day* is told from Stevens' point of view, and, because he maintains perfectly his English emotional self-denial throughout, it is an excellent exercise in decoding the English. The end of Stevens' journey, the grand climax, is his meeting with Miss Kenton (now Mrs Benn). The reader realises (although Stevens apparently does not) that they have been in love with each other for many years. Since she left the house where they had both worked, they have corresponded regularly. It is twenty years since they last saw each other and now, in a superb and precisely observed scene of pure Englishness, they meet again:

> 'Ah, Mr Stevens. How nice to see you again.'
> 'Mrs Benn, how lovely.'

The light in the room was extremely gloomy on account of the rain, and so we moved two armchairs up close to the bay window. And that was how Miss Kenton and I talked for the next two hours or so, there in the pool of grey light while the rain continued to fall steadily on the square outside.

Stevens reflects that 'the Miss Kenton I saw before me looked surprisingly similar to the person who had inhabited my memory over these years. That is to say, it was, on the whole, extremely pleasing to see her again.' The combination of the grey light and the rain, emotional restraint and understatement, makes this a perfectly judged and beautifully expressed English encounter.

Understatement and irony

It was Ralph Waldo Emerson who observed that 'an Englishman understates, avoids the superlative, checks himself in compliments'. This reticence presents a general difficulty to those trying to understand the English, but it is a difficulty compounded by their constant use of irony. 'I began to brood on the complexity of writing a novel about English life', says the narrator of Anthony Powell's *The Acceptance World* (1955): 'Intricacies of social life make English habits unyielding to simplification, while understatement and irony – in which all classes of this island converse – upset the normal emphasis of reported speech.'

Given that the English have difficulty in saying what they feel, it is all the more disconcerting to discover that when they do say something they might well mean the exact opposite of what they say! When speaking to the English, it is essential to learn the art of listening in order to pick out the fine discriminations of emphasis which signal that the speaker is being ironic. So if an Englishman says something is 'bloody marvellous', he might mean it really is marvellous or, alternatively, that it isn't marvellous at all. Having a lifetime of experience, the English are constantly using irony, listening for irony, and always expecting it. It does not occur to the English to make their irony obvious, no more than most Americans would expect to have to listen out for it. Many Anglo-American misunderstandings have resulted from this basic failure of communication.

Because so much irony depends on slight variations in spoken tones, conveying irony in fiction is, as Powell suggests, a difficult task (although Jane Austen managed it extremely well). It may be comforting to know that the English themselves are not always certain about irony. In Peter Ackroyd's *Chatterton* (1987), Cumberland, the owner of an art gallery, encounters a man who observes of the paintings on display, 'Hot stuff.' 'Cumberland did not detect any irony in his tone, but he could not absolutely discount it.' There is another example in Will Self's story 'Dave Too', where the narrator is also unsure when the waiter says 'Double espresso?' 'Has he forgotten,' he asks himself, 'that it was I who placed the order, from this very seat, not three minutes ago? I scrutinise his face for traces of irony.' But, the narrator concludes, the waiter 'doesn't have the contrast control necessary to express irony – he's only looking *at* me' (*Tough, Tough Toys for Tough, Tough Boys*, 1998).

'Its private language'

> 'So?' Bunty says, weighting the one little syllable with a heavy mixed cargo of disdain, indifference and wilful misunderstanding, not to mention twenty years of marital antipathy. Even a Mandarin-speaking Chinaman would be floored by the subtleties of Bunty's intonation. (Atkinson, *Behind the Scenes at the Museum*)

The English are, on the whole, good listeners. I think that is why they enjoy puns so much. They are entertained by different words sounding alike. It's a device much used in advertising, and is the stock in trade of bawdy humour, where intonation of a double-entendre will give rise to shrieks of laughter.

The English listen very carefully to each other. Apart from noticing stress and intonation for signs of irony, they will also be 'placing' someone, i.e. determining that person's class, education and place of origin and making fine judgements which accord with their own class, education and place of origin. This is done so naturally and automatically that the English are scarcely conscious that they are doing it. A writer of English fiction, however, when creating an English character, will be very aware of specific nuances. The details of a character's way of speaking will be given just as clear a description as are their physical features, age, dress, and emotional condition. Often the character's accent and use of language will be *more* significant than physical details, for it is, above all, the accent that will signify a character's social standing in the complex hierarchy of the English class system. The English reader's response will be manipulated and guided by the author's knowledge of the 'private language' of the English. This semiotic minefield becomes more hazardous when we have to consider the author's view of the narrator's view, or worse, the author's view of the narrator's view of a character's accent. Here are just a few random examples taken from a range of modern English fiction:

> It was only in his use of 'that' for 'it' and in an occasional glottal stop that Frank's East Anglian origin could be detected. (Wilson, *Anglo-Saxon Attitudes*)

> ... probably a North countryman, with flat, assertive vowels in his speech ... (Angela Carter, *The Magic Toyshop*, 1967)

> Veale's lust for the plural was a shrill result only of his posh emphasis on the terminal *t* (a decade ago, no doubt, he would have said *car-po'* and *runabar'* ...). Hence also, presumably, his fondness for the husky initial *h*. (Martin Amis, *Success* 1978)

> Nobody knew where she came from, although she claimed it was Hampstead. She said *Hempstid* the way royalty might.... Her accent was odd, very out of place in Arden with its nicely buffed-up northern vowels. Eliza sounded stranded somewhere between a very expensive boarding-school and a brothel (or to put it another way, upper class). (Atkinson, *Human Croquet*, 1997)

Although England is a small country, it has a vast number of local accents and dialects. Naturally, a writer will attempt to reproduce the flavour of the local speech to give the story its necessary sense of authenticity. This is not complicated or unusual. It is worth noting, however, that a northern accent, especially a Yorkshire one, implies more than a geographical location. Yorkshire 'folk' are considered to be bluff, plain-speaking and honest. This stereotype owes something to both fact and fiction. The plain-speaking, honest and working-class writers who came to prominence in the 1950s and 1960s were northerners like Alan Sillitoe, John Braine, David Storey. They reproduced the world that they knew and fixed it forever in the English reader's conscious-ness. The hero, Joe Lampton, of Braine's *Room at the Top* (1957) encounters the wealthy mill owner, Brown:

> 'Ah've met you at t'Town Hall, lad,' Brown said.... He looked as sure of himself as Jack, but in a different way; the Yorkshire accent, which I suspected him of overdoing a bit, was one of the marks of that self-assurance.

It is often useful to exaggerate a Yorkshire accent in order to convey honesty, and the Oxford-educated Yorkshire politician Harold Wilson was to use it in his television broadcasts in the 1960s to great effect. By Oxford-educated, I mean that he had been a student at Oxford University. If characters in a novel 'met at Oxford', or 'had known each other since their Cambridge days', then they have been students at the Universities of Oxford or Cambridge. I can think of no other English universities that can be referred to by the names of their cities alone. These descriptors will invoke either a class (upper or upper-middle) or a high intelligence (middle or lower class), depending on the context. The usual pattern in English fiction is to have lower or lower-middle-class characters win scholarships to Oxford or Cambridge and find themselves surrounded by rich but dim upper-class characters who have been to good public schools (for 'public school', see below). The 'poor scholar' John Kemp in Philip Larkin's *Jill* (1946) arrives at Oxford University to find his roommate, Chris Warner, already installed. John feels 'a twinge of distrust'. 'There was a swagger in his bearing....'

'We're just having tea: there's rather a crowd inside, I'm afraid I've sort of taken possession.' He began filling the kettle from the tap. 'Come from Town?'

'From Huddlesford,' said John, not knowing that Town meant London.

Kemp is right to feel distrust. He spends the rest of the novel lending Warner money and writing essays for him. Feckless Warner is, of course, upper class.

The whole topic of the English class system and its various linguistic indicators has been the subject of several books, so I will merely sketch a few general observations. First of all, England is still a class-conscious society. Some English people will tell you that class doesn't matter anymore and that no one cares about class. But they will also be able to tell you to a hair's breadth which class they come from, making such fine distinctions as 'upper-lower-middle class' or 'upper-upper-middle class'. The twentieth century produced an increase in the 'under class' (i.e. working class who no longer have either work or hope) and in the 'chattering class' (i.e. educated middle class, and the ones most likely to tell you that class doesn't matter). It is certainly true that being working or lower class is no longer a handicap in some fields (notably in the media and the arts). Indeed, during the 1960s it became fashionable to be working class. Typical of the period is Tony, the 'fake' in Byatt's *Babel Tower*. Tony is the son of a distinguished man of letters but has adopted 'a whole repertoire of working-class tastes and mannerisms, and an assiduously cultivated accent, part-Birmingham, part-Cockney'. It may no longer be true that 'When one Englishman opens his mouth, another Englishman despises him' (George Bernard Shaw, *Pygmalion*, 1914), but there is always an element of judgement implied in one Englishman's description of another Englishman's voice. And class is still conveyed by accent and vocabulary.

The American reader must keep firmly in mind the fact that in England wealth alone cannot convey class. A self-made millionaire who has worked his way up from the gutter will still be essentially lower class. He will still have the accent and the lack of good taste that reveals him as hopelessly 'common'. In *The Collector* (1963) the middle-class author, Fowles, has created a lower-class character called Frederick, a clerk, and a collector. At the beginning of the novel, Frederick wins a fortune on the football pools. (Winning the Pools has been replaced in British dreams by Winning the Lottery. Either way, it may change your life, but not your class.) With his new-found wealth Frederic goes to a grand hotel with his Auntie Annie and his cousin Mabel, and here he first discovers the limitations of wealth:

> ... of course they were respectful on the surface, but that was all, they really despised us for having all that money and not knowing what to do with it.... It was no good throwing money around. As soon as we spoke or did something we gave the game away. You could see them saying, don't kid us, we know what you are, why don't you go back where you came from?

They have a similar experience when they dine at a grand restaurant (or, as lower-class Frederick puts it, 'supper at a posh restaurant'):

> It was good food, we ate it but I didn't hardly taste it because of the way people looked at us and the way the slimy foreign waiters and everybody treated us, and how everything in the room seemed to look down at us because we weren't brought up their way. I read the other day an article about class going – I could tell them things about that.

On his journey south the English butler, Stevens, in *The Remains of the Day* is forced to stop in a village where he gets involved in a discussion about what makes a 'gentleman'. To his embarrassment he is taken by the locals to be a real gentleman, and compared favourably to a Mr Lindsay who 'was no gentleman. He may have had a lot of money, but he was never a gentleman.' Another of the party agrees: 'You could tell just watching him he was no gentleman. All right, he had a fine house and good suits, but somehow you just knew.'

What makes a real gentleman (or real lady) is, above all, having the right voice. It is possible to change your accent, and many lower- or lower-middle-class people spend years practising until they can pass themselves off as being of a higher class:

> He played rugger and put on weight and changed his accent to camouflage his lower-middle-class origins and impress his father-in-law. Taking as his model a bluff, old-fashioned medical tutor, he used quaint phrases like 'doncha know', and 'shouldn't wonder'. He was self-conscious at first, sometimes winking when he caught George's eye to show he knew it was only a joke, this absurd game of social mobility, but quite soon it became second nature and he could say 'old boy', or 'the wireless', without twitching an eyelid. (Nina Bawden, *George Beneath a Paper Moon*, 1974)

For it is a question of vocabulary as much as accent. In Martin Amis' *The Rachel Papers*, the narrator Charles goes to stay with his sister and her socially inferior husband, Norman. He spends the journey 'quietly rehearsing lower-middle-class accents for the benefit of my brother-in-law'. To clarify the social gulf between his family and Norman, Charles recalls their first meeting:

> My father paced the hearth. When Norman gave voice to such idioms as 'settee', 'pardon?' and at one point 'toilet', my father could be seen to wince as a man who is in pain will wince. He was a bit thrown by the opulence of Norman's car and accoutrements – but he wasn't a man to be gulled by the mere tokens of privilege.

But to acquire both accent and vocabulary, not to mention a certain manner, a 'dignity' (according to Stevens in *The Remains of the Day*), 'a formula, a secret, I don't know what' (muses the heroine of Jeanette Winterson's *Oranges are Not the Only Fruit*, 1985), you have to have been to a public school, preferably a 'good' public school. There's a significant difference between a 'good' public school and a 'minor' public school as far as English fiction writers are concerned. And in England, 'public' school means 'private', fee-paying and usually boarding school. The class-conscious Frederick of Fowles' *The Collector* says grimly, 'London's all arranged for the people who can act like public schoolboys, and you don't get anywhere if you don't have the manner born and the right la-di-da voice.' When he starts looking for a house to buy, he describes the estate agent as 'the public schoolboy type, full of silly remarks that are meant to be funny, as if it was below him to sell anything'. On a boat journey to France, the state-school-educated, middle-class Clara collides with a young man who helps her to her feet and apologises. As he leaves her, 'she said to herself, there goes a public school boy. She was not familiar with the type, but she recognised it when she saw it as she would have recognised the Eiffel Tower' (Drabble, *Jerusalem the Golden*).

In English fiction it is a common shorthand device to describe a character simply as 'very public school'. In Byatt's *Babel Tower*, Hugh writes to Stephanie: 'Perhaps I will try to describe Parrott. He's curly, and plump, and not very tall, and public school.' When Stephanie later meets Parrott she notes that, indeed, 'his voice has a public school drawl'. Essentially this 'drawl' or 'la-di-da' voice involves rounding and slightly elongating the vowels. A 'public school voice' is usually given to male characters only, probably because almost all public schools are male-only institutions.

Its female equivalent is usually described as 'Home Counties', sometimes abbreviated simply to 'county'. Geographically speaking, the home counties are Berkshire, Surrey, Kent, Sussex, all counties outside of and south of London (though not at all to be confused with South London). In fiction though, 'home counties' is used, not as a geographical descriptor, but as a class signifier, usually taken to mean an upper- or upper-middle-class female. She too will have round vowels, or what Joe Lampton in Braine's *Room at the Top* describes as 'the plum-in-the-mouth of the Home Counties'. And again, Home Counties will convey an attitude, a 'dignity', a 'stiff upper lip' control, as well as a particular voice. Letty, in Pym's *Quartet in Autumn,* is described as 'fluffy and faded, a Home Counties type, still making an effort with her clothes'. Fowles' Daniel Martin recalls meeting English actresses of the 1950s ('before London working class came into their own') and describes them as:

> vacuous young starlets from the Home Counties (or who at least aped that background) ... whose only notion of a Cockney accent was to replace an impeccable middle-class *a* by an impeccable middle-class *i.*

Really, if you are lower or lower-middle class and suddenly come into wealth, you cannot change your own class, but you can change your children's class by sending them off to a good public school. In Martin Amis' *Success* (a novel which depends very much on a good understanding of the English class system), the upwardly mobile Stanley Veale (whose room is 'full of pink chairs and motley scatter-cushions') can make valiant attempts to improve his own accent by 'his posh emphasis', but his elder son who attends a public school, speaks 'in comparatively courtly accents'. His younger son still speaks in 'unreclaimed Cockney' and Veale himself occasionally lets his accent slip saying 'Yur' (instead of Yes) and 'Nah' (instead of No). To speak with a cockney accent is to be hopelessly lower class. During the war many cockney families were bombed out of central London and moved to the South of London; those in the East of London (the docks area, and very heavily bombed by the Germans) moved further East and out to Essex. In recent years the Essex (or Estuary) voice, along with the South London voice, has taken over as the signifier indicating lower- or lower-middle-class status. In Carter's *The Magic Toyshop*, the newly orphaned Home Counties family are forced to move to South London. The eldest child Melanie frets about her younger sister Victoria: 'Would she grow up into a street urchin ... with a London accent grating on a nicely-brought-up ear?' Meeting her cousin she notes that 'his flat, South London voice seemed coarse and ugly' and 'once again, she hoped Victoria would not pick the accent up'.

Here is a good point to state the obvious, but significant, fact that London is, in so many ways, quite a separate entity from England. Lessing recalls her London friend Rose's observation: 'I wouldn't say I was English so much, as a Londoner, see? It's different.' London certainly is different, full of slightly shifting boundaries that separate enclaves of wealth and poverty, classes and nationalities. English writers will assume that their readers know which set of values goes with which areas. London districts may change their fashionability, and thus their affordability, on a regular basis, but assuming you are just a reader and not an estate agent, here are a few basic guidelines.

Swift's *Last Orders* opens with the heading 'Bermondsey'. Bermondsey is an area in the east of London, the 'East End'. And the East End is lower class. The opening line of *Last Orders* is 'It ain't like your regular sort of day ...' The heading and the accent together put us firmly in the world of lower-class Londoners. EastEnders (now famously the title of an enormously popular television soap opera) will go 'up West', to the West End for 'a posh night out'. Also lower-class is South London, which is, as Dora observes at the beginning of Carter's *Wise Children* (1991), 'the wrong side of the tracks'. That is to say it is the wrong side of the River Thames. Even here, as Dora admits, 'you can't trust things to stay the same', and the affluent have started to move into the South. ('You'd never believe the price of a house round here, these days.') But it is the authentic South London voice of Dora that takes us on an extraordinary journey as she and her twin sister Nora sing and dance their way through the twentieth century. In the final chapter they cross 'over the river to the other side', to a party in Regent's Park.

Regent's Park abuts on to the West End, and both areas suggest wealth. One of the main arteries between Regent's Park and the West End is Harley Street, a street of expensive private doctors and clinics ('seeing a man in Harley Street', or just 'going to Harley Street' means that someone is wealthy enough to be consulting a private doctor). In Drabble's *The Radiant Way* (1987), Liz lives in Harley Street and 'still, after all these years, found satisfaction in giving her address'. All her social fears have been 'banished by the invocation of a street name'. Other 'rich' areas of London include Hampstead in the north and Kensington in the west:

'They're marvellous.' His pronunciation of the word was like a mixture of a small boy's and a Kensington hostess'. (Angus Wilson, *Anglo-Saxon Attitudes*)

A 'Kensington hostess' is a 'county' woman, with the upper-class drawl. Nearby are Knightsbridge and Sloane Square, both famously the haunt of the braying upper class, or the rich would-be upper/upper-middle-class female. Home Counties women who have flats in and around Sloane Square and who shop at Harrods and Harvey Nichols are known as 'Sloane Rangers', or 'Sloaneys'. In Self's nightmare world where everyone has turned into chimpanzees, *Great Apes* (1997), the sounds are still familiar and recognisable: 'Sloaney mothers lolloped along the paths ... vocalising to one another with the extended grunts of their class.'

Bloomsbury is considered to be 'intellectual'. Indelibly linked with Woolf and the rest of the Bloomsbury Group who lived and worked in this area of London in the early decades of the twentieth century, it is still 'academic' territory, embracing the British Museum, several University of London buildings and numerous bookshops. The heroine of Anita Brookner's *Hotel du Lac* (1984), the emotionally repressed lady novelist, is described as looking 'remarkably

Bloomsburian'. Bloomsbury is not rich, but like its neighbour Fitzrovia is vaguely 'artistic'.

The real money-making area of London is the City, not to be confused with the city, of course. To be 'something in the City' is to be something to do with banking, insurance and the stock market, all focused in one small central area of London, the 'Square Mile' known as the City of London. During the 1980s the City was invaded by clever young men from Essex who wheeled and dealed and made small fortunes, and led to another brief period (like the 1960s) when it became almost fashionable to have a lower-class accent, and newspapers solemnly printed guides to the new 'Estuary English'. The young men may have been clever, but the Essex girls were considered famously stupid, leading to numerous 'Essex girls' jokes.

Cosmopolitan Ladbroke Grove and Notting Hill Gate have been made famous by the novels of Martin Amis; London present and past explored in the novels of Peter Ackroyd. 'There's something strange about London ... some kind of magic or something,' says Spenser Spender in Ackroyd's first novel, *The Great Fire of London* (1982). London continues to be the magic beacon seductively luring the provincial Englishman and woman, all latter day Pips with their great expectations.

Over a century ago in Dickens' *Great Expectations* (1860), the beautiful 'lady' Estella sneered at Pip, the blacksmith's boy, for being 'common'. ('He calls the knaves, Jacks,' she exclaims in disdain.) Nowadays to be 'common' means much more than using the wrong words or even having an 'ugly' accent. Rich people will be considered 'common' if they lack the subtle qualities of taste and discernment deemed essential by the English. To refer to someone as 'common' is the greatest insult an English character can bestow on another. In J B Priestley's *Out of Town* (1968), Isabel observes a very wealthy widow from America and notes that she is wearing 'a pastel mutation mink that must have cost thousands and thousands, looked smart but was too determinedly blonde and by any decent English standard looked rather common'. The eccentric lady novelist Harriet in Ackroyd's *Chatterton* queries a statement made by her Oxford-educated secretary:

> 'And who are *they* exactly dear?' Harriet always pounced upon the pronoun, which in this usage she regularly denounced as being 'as common as muck'. Having thoroughly embarrassed her secretary she 'relented', and, put on her cockney landlady voice, which had been her standard 'funny' turn since the Fifties. 'You really tike the biscuit and neow mistike!'

Pretending to be common when you are not really common is considered highly amusing to the English. Just as amusing is the sound of common people pretending to be 'posh', which can be done for the purposes of satire, or simply camaraderie, as in this gentle example, also from Ackroyd's *Chatterton*:

'Oh, I say. Bloody marvellous.' Both men had come from poor London families, and on occasions Charles amused Philip with his extravagant parodies of an 'upper class' accent.

But actually to *be* common is, in the words of Bennett, 'the ultimate condemnation'. Recalling his mother's fine sociological distinctions, Bennett remembers her 'catalogue of disapproval that ranged through (fake) leopard-skin coats, dyed (blonde) hair to slacks, cocktail cabinets and statuettes'. For her, as for so many of the English, places can be common too:

> Blackpool was common (people enjoying themselves), Morecambe less so (not enjoying themselves as much) and Grange or Lytham not common at all (enjoyment not really on the agenda). (Introduction to *Talking Heads*, 1988)

When the prostitute Brenda in Pat Barker's *Blow Your House Down* (1984) is first arrested by the police and charged with being (in the legal phrase) a 'common prostitute' she is outraged:

> It was terrible, it was really humiliating, and it changed you completely. You felt as if you'd had the words 'common prostitute' stamped right through you, like 'Blackpool' through a stick of rock. It was the 'common' that hurt. 'Prostitute', well, you couldn't very well deny it; but she wasn't common. They had no right to say that.

Incidentally a 'stick of rock' is a long stick of candy, a traditional souvenir of a seaside resort, which has the name of that resort printed all the way down the middle of its inside in pink candy lettering. The printed candy stick of Brighton, the south coast seaside resort, was made famous by Graham Greene in his novel *Brighton Rock* (1938). Like 'naughty' English postcards, sticks of rock are very 'common' souvenirs!

As with the English class system, the difference between English English and American English has been the subject of several books, so I will conclude this section on 'private language' with what might be termed *very* private language, giving just a few definitions of words which are frequently used by the English and which are regularly misunderstood, or not understood at all, by American readers and visitors:

fanny – in England this means female genitalia, so be careful how you use this word. Americans often refer to a 'fanny packet' which naturally causes much misunderstanding (we call it a 'bum-bag'). What we call 'bum', Americans call 'fanny'. What Americans call 'bum', we call 'tramp'. What Americans call 'tramp', we call 'slut'.

loo – a very public private word, and a very useful word. All classes in all areas of England use the word 'loo'. It means lavatory. You will not necessarily be understood if you ask for the 'bathroom' as many English will think (or pretend to think, if they are being ironical) that you want to take a bath. The English favour baths over showers, by the way. Demands for 'the little boy's room', 'the little girl's room', 'powder room' or 'comfort station' will be met by blank incomprehension, except in the grandest London hotels where they are used to that sort of thing.

randy – to be 'randy' is to be in a state of sexual desire and excitement. The American equivalent is 'horny'. The poet Philip Larkin chose his words carefully in his poem 'Church Going' where he considers the decline of Christian faith in England, and imagines that, in the end, churches will be visited only by 'Some ruin-bibber, randy for antique,/Or Christmas-addict....' Americans named Randy should be particularly careful when introducing themselves to the English with the words, 'Hi, I'm Randy.'

wank – to wank is to masturbate – literally and metaphorically. To call someone a 'wanker' is a common, all-purpose insult. In Julian Barnes' *Metroland*, Chris' adolescent obsession with art and French culture causes his Uncle Albert to describe him as 'an intellectual wanker', a very formidable English insult!

'It's bound to rain'

This is not a reference to English weather, though it is a useful rule to remember. England does not have a reliable climate, but it does have a lot of weather. Morris Zapp, the visiting American professor of Lodge's *Changing Places,* listens in bewilderment to the weather forecasts in England, 'predicting every possible combination of weather for the next twenty-four hours without actually committing itself to anything specific, not even the existing temperature'. At first he assumes this is satire, but it isn't. 'When two Englishmen meet,' said Dr Samuel Johnson in 1787, 'their first talk is of the weather.' The weather is, as Mikes observed, 'the most important topic in the land … an ever interesting, even thrilling topic' (*How to be an Alien*). English weather is not famous for its extremes (more of a compromise, like the English character), but for its sheer variety. It can be dry and warm, cold and wet, mild, windy, and any combination thereof, all in the same day. It can be warm and sunny in December and cold and snowing in April. Thus, weather has long functioned as a significant factor in the English writer's armoury, and can be used to invoke a particular mood or emotion, whatever the season.

Variety is also a significant factor in the English landscape. As with the people and their accents, despite the smallness of the country, there is an extraordinary range of geographical differences. Each small area of England has its distinctive features and colours and an English writer will take pains to capture the essence of their particular landscape. You will gain a far greater appreciation of the poetry of Wordsworth if you visit the Lake District, or of the novels of the Brontës if you venture on to the wild Yorkshire moors. It is a tradition that has survived into the twentieth century. In Swift's *Waterland* (1983), for example, the Fens become a living character, breathing and informing the narrative:

> Realism; fatalism; phlegm. To live in the Fens is to receive strong doses of reality. The great, flat monotony of reality; the wide, empty space of reality ... a flat, rain-swept, water-logged land.

The weather colours an English landscape whenever characters are on the move, making decisions, or confronting a new experience. But even if the sun is shining now, the English know that 'it's bound to rain', and that, moreover, 'it never rains but it pours'. It is the constant awareness of this certain knowledge that best sums up the English attitude to life in general, the national acceptance that life is hopelessly flawed. The English know that there's no point in getting too enthusiastic about anyone or anything as 'it'll only end in tears' and 'there'll be tears before bed-time'. Happiness is only, in the words of Thomas Hardy, 'the occasional episode in a general drama of pain' (*The Mayor of Casterbridge*, 1886).

This is perhaps the most significant contrast to American expectations of life, and there is some truth in the old adage that an American sees a glass as half-full, but an English person sees it as half-empty. It is Jenny in Fowles' *Daniel Martin* who observes that Americans 'simply don't understand this awful English attachment to defeat and loss and self-negation'. American visitors may find this attitude most apparent in English shops, booking offices and restaurants: that 'I'd like to help you but I can't, and anyway there's no point' attitude to which the English themselves are accustomed. Or, as Garnett Bowen of Kingsley Amis' *I Like It Here* describes it, it is 'the land of sorry-sir (sorry sir bar's closed, sorry sir no change, sorry sir too late for lunch, sorry sir residents only sir)'. A typically English exchange takes place in Elizabeth Jane Howard's *Odd Girl Out* (1972):

> 'We don't *repair* lamps, madam, I'm afraid. Oh no – we've never done that.'
> 'Well, could you recommend someone to me who could?'
> 'It's hard to say, madam. We don't like recommending people....'
> His face, Anne thought, was unctuous with trying not to seem too unhelpful....
> 'Well thank you,' she said. For nothing, she thought.
> 'Thank *you*, madam.'

It was Orwell who observed this 'English attachment to defeat' when he noted that 'the most popular battle poems in English literature are poems of disasters and retreats. The most stirring battle poem in English is about a brigade of cavalry which charged in the wrong direction.' He concludes his catalogue with the telling observation that the most popular display of military manoeuvres is the Beating of Retreat. The English have a natural sympathy with the underdog, and are particularly fond of 'losers'. 'Eddie the Eagle' became a national hero because he kept failing at the Winter Olympics. It is difficult to convey the English reader's sense of triumph when Smith deliberately loses the race in Sillitoe's *The Loneliness of the Long-Distance Runner* (1958).

The realistic Brenda in Bainbridge's *The Bottle Factory Outing* 'felt it was unwise to see things as other than they were'. Throughout the novel she utters decidedly English pronouncements like, 'It's never been any different', 'Everything breaks … All sorts of things break down these days …', and, of course, 'It was bound to rain'. It does. Brenda is typical of a host of characters who appear in English fiction, and in English life. The English respond to the world around them like Letty in Pym's *Quartet in Autumn*, 'holding neatly and firmly on to life, coping as best she could with whatever it had to offer, little though that might be'; or like Jim Dixon in Kingsley Amis' *Lucky Jim*, deciding that

> The one indispensable answer to an environment bristling with people and things one thought were bad was to go on finding out new ways in which one could think they were bad.

'Its common memories'

Despite the English contempt for being clever, as a race we have an extraordinary fund of knowledge about our own history and literature. Perhaps it's just because we have so much of it. The English are certainly aware of the many layers of history that lie beneath their feet and all around them. Like England's own history, the English interest in history goes back a long way. Shakespeare's history plays were enormously popular: his *Henry VI* was his first box office success. And although there were dramatists at work all over Europe during Shakespeare's day, there are no European equivalents to the English history or 'chronicle' play.

Historical fiction is still incredibly popular with the average English reader. The fictions of Jean Plaidy and Georgette Heyer have topped the lists of 'books most borrowed from public libraries' for years. More recently, the stories of Catherine Cookson have not only been bestsellers, but have become ratings-winning television series. Historical dramas are always popular television fodder (*Upstairs, Downstairs* for example), and it is, perhaps, through television that the average English person can conjure up a reasonably accurate vision of the differences between, say, Elizabethan and Victorian England. At any rate, an

English writer can mention a style or a time period and rely on the English reader's general working knowledge of that period without further explanation.

In modern English fiction references to 'the war' mean the Second World War and even the youngest generation will think of bombs falling all over England (so many places still bear the scars, or terse references to 'destroyed by enemy action'), bomb-sites, air raid shelters, rationing and blackouts. Again, popular English television series help to 'educate' the English about their history. One thinks of such enduringly popular comedy series as *Dad's Army*, still repeated regularly, and a perfect study of the English at war, heroic in their hopelessness, muddling through and stolidly maintaining class boundaries even in the midst of a united front. Another popular comedy series, *Blackadder*, takes a similar set of class-divided English 'losers' through a panorama of English history from medieval to modern times. The *Blackadder* series ended with a typically English mixture of humour and heart-breaking poignancy, as the last episode, set in the Great War (i.e. the First World War), sees the team setting off for 'the last push' and therefore, as every English viewer realises, to their certain death. The line between tragedy and comedy in English life and in English humour is a desperately fine line indeed.

Not only do they know their history, but the English also know their literature. Again, this probably owes much to television. Glossy television versions of Austen's or Dickens' novels regularly top the ratings, and publishers issue reprints featuring a still from the television version to boost their sales. Thus do modern classics reach the English 'couch potato' as the nation has tuned in to lengthy and lavishly produced television series such as John Galsworthy's *The Forsyte Saga*, Evelyn Waugh's *Brideshead Revisited* and Paul Scott's *The Jewel in the Crown*.

From reading English detective fiction, you might suppose that the average English detective needs little more than a good working knowledge of the English classics (especially minor Jacobean dramatists) to be able to solve a murder. Unlike his gun-toting, testicle-stomping American counterpart, the English detective follows a paper chase of literary clues, quoting Milton, Tennyson or, of course, Shakespeare, to his bemused junior officer. (In English fiction, police constables are lower class.) Again, television plays its part in promoting the fiction industry. Colin Dexter's novels became bestsellers after his poetry-quoting, opera-loving Inspector Morse established himself through television as a national institution.

For some modern English novelists, the weight of the great and the good behind them can be inhibiting as well as inspiring. Some plunge in to try and write 'a modern *Pilgrim's Progress*', or 'a *Tom Jones* for our times'; others attempt to be a modern Austen, Dickens or George Eliot. And many are rewarded by critics who praise their 'Austen-like irony', or their 'truly Dickensian vision of modern England'. Shakespeare's comedies are invoked, as in Iris Murdoch's *A Severed Head* (1978) or Carter's *Wise Children*. More self-consciously still, many

English novels will be constructed round a network of literary allusions, quotations, references and collages of parody, both literary and historical. Examples that spring immediately to mind are Fowles' *The French Lieutenant's Woman* (1969), Ackroyd's *Hawksmoor* (1985), and Byatt's *Possession* (1990), all of which have been bestsellers, and *Possession* a Booker Prize Winner.

This literary cannibalism extends to introducing real contemporary writers into the web of fictional writers' lives: the fictional author Kenneth Toomey, hero of Anthony Burgess' *Earthly Powers* (1980), recalls his meetings with the real authors Henry James and James Joyce, amongst others; in Byatt's *Babel Tower*, we are told that the real Anthony Burgess, amongst others, will be 'sounded out' on the literary merit of a fictional book called *Babbletower*. It's all a bit confusing, and begins to feel like you have blundered in to a private party. Too many English writers perhaps suffer from the problem experienced by Philip (significantly, a librarian) who, in Ackroyd's *Chatterton* had to give up writing his novel for it

> seemed to him to be filled with images and phrases from the work of other writers whom he admired. It had become a patchwork of other voices and other styles, and it was the overwhelming difficulty of recognising his own voice among them that had led him to abandon the project.

And it helps if you know that the eighteenth-century Thomas Chatterton himself was famously a mimic of earlier literary styles.

The self-referential quality of much English fiction is, perhaps, merely another aspect of Englishness that has been with us so long ('The English are great lovers of themselves'). After all, Shakespeare also used the devices of literary reference, allusion and parody. In 1970, Bergonzi pondered on what he considered to be the decline of the English novel, ascribing it to the circumstances of England's recent history:

> ... throughout the twentieth century the English have had to make a long and painful process of adjustment from being the rulers of the most powerful Empire in the world to being a moderately important power of the middle rank.... There are times when to be English is, it seems, to be destined for endless humiliations. In these circumstances I do not think it surprising that many English writers, and some of the most talented among them, have exhibited the classic neurotic symptoms of withdrawal and disengagement, looking within themselves, or back to a more secure period in their own lives or the history of their culture. (*The Situation of the Novel*)

It seems to me that the English have been looking back for a very long time. And as for looking within, it was William Hazlitt who said, 'There is no romance like the romance of real life' (*The Spirit of the Age*, 1825).

Social realism

Social realism (or, 'the romance of real life') has always been the most favoured subject of English fiction. And the English novel has a long tradition (indeed, a great tradition) of concerning itself with contemporary events and attitudes. These attitudes have always been primarily middle-class attitudes. The novel is *the* middle-class art form (all other art forms like music or painting being considered suspiciously 'clever'), and the vast majority of English authors and readers are irredeemably middle class.

The primacy of the realistic novel owes much to the puritan origins of the middle class and to the puritan distrust of fiction. To write fictions, that is 'to tell stories', was to tell lies, and lying was sinful and wicked. In the true spirit of English compromise, a way was found round this by telling lies so skilfully that the reader felt 'it must be true'. Or if not exactly true, then based on truth and, what's more, conveying a worthy moral truth, like a parable. It is a tradition that goes back to Daniel Defoe, who arguably started it all with his documentary fictions like *Robinson Crusoe* (1719), *A Journal of the Plague Year* (1722) and *Moll Flanders* (1722). Even the 'sensation novels' of the Victorians paid lip service to this myth of truth, and in the Preface to *Bleak House*, Dickens solemnly assured his readers that death by spontaneous combustion was a verifiable, scientific fact.

My reference to 'puritan' should not be thought to have anything essentially to do with religion, by the way. The English spirit seems always to have been more secular than religious. The difference between the English medieval Mystery plays with their bawdy humour and secular settings compared to their spiritual and serious European counterparts, the Miracle plays, is instructive. It was Forster who noted that 'In Germany the Reformation was due to the passionate conviction of Luther. In England it was due to a palace intrigue.'

The Englishman's faith has more commonly been to do with social signifiers than with spiritual convictions, and just as hedged in with class indicators. The higher the church, the higher the class. The Church of England, with the sovereign as its head, was long described as 'the Tory Party at prayer'. That the position of clergymen should have been in the hands of rich families (as in Austen), or politicians (as in Anthony Trollope), seems quite extraordinary to anyone who is not English. That secular priorities should take precedence over spiritual ones may seem irreligious enough, but that class should enter the equation of Christian worship would appear to be decidedly un-Christian. But so it is. Going to chapel (or 'low church', to use the English expression) suggests lower or lower-middle class, but going to church (Church of England and 'high church') signifies upper-middle or upper class. These distinctions are necessary to understand in order to appreciate numerous subtle references in nineteenth- and early twentieth-century English fiction. In D H Lawrence's story 'Daughters of the Vicar' (1914), the reader is expected to know that a vicar is a Church of

England clergyman and therefore of a higher class than the chapel-going miner, for example. And Barbara Pym's *Excellent Women* (1952) makes even finer distinctions between low-high church and high-high church. ('I could imagine my mother, her lips pursed, shaking her head and breathing in a frightened whisper, *Incense.*')

In contemporary fiction, however, as in contemporary England, church-going forms little part of the landscape. 'No one goes to church nowadays,' laments Norman in Pym's *Quartet in Autumn*. Indeed, Norman's habit of regular church-going is exhibited as a sign of his eccentricity. Much more typical, and recognisable, is Harriet Scrope's observation in Ackroyd's *Chatterton*, 'Whenever I see someone reading the Bible, I assume they're mad, don't you?'

In Victorian novels religion was 'in', and sex was 'out'. In modern English fiction, religion is 'out' and sex is 'in'. Now, however, the truth-telling puritan impulse demands to know the brand names of food and clothes and condoms.

Thus the English novel has always been upholstered with detailed inventories of dress and furniture and possessions (with what James called 'solidity of specification'), designed to give a solid realism to fiction. In his study of the English novel, *After the War*, D J Taylor notes that 'English novelists generally rely on externals – accent, dress, real or imagined status'; and Byatt refers to the very English concern with 'the thinginess of things' (Introduction to *The Oxford Book of English Short Stories*). Given the residual puritan distrust of lying, even the most extravagant and playful of English fantasies (like those of Carter, for instance), or the most depressing visions of grim dystopias (like those of Orwell, Martin Amis or Self) are conceived in a recognisable world of fixtures and fittings. The English preference for facing facts ('it's bound to rain') continues to influence the content of English fiction. There's little place in the English soul for fantasy and escapism. Similarly, the most popular television soap operas, such as *Coronation Street* and *EastEnders*, revolve around ordinary 'realistic' people leading ordinary lives, all coping as best they can with unemployment, illness and death.

To read modern English fiction, then, is to learn much about modern English society, and reading modern social history is to learn much about English fiction. Reading novels set in the late 1940s and 1950s will need an awareness of bomb-sites, ration books and National Service. A knowledge of the Welfare State, the building of new universities, the betrayal of post-war hopes and the Suez crisis, will help you to understand novels set in the late 1950s and early 1960s (and note the difference between when novels are set and when they are written). The 1950s are now generally described as the Angry Decade: a period which saw the rise of 'working-class fiction' with working-class heroes rising up through a working-class environment (Sillitoe, Braine, Storey, for example). Or, there are the lower-middle-class heroes educated 'above their station' (as in the fiction of Kingsley Amis and John Wain). Novels set in the 1960s assume a good working knowledge of Harold Wilson (the pipe-smoking Yorkshireman) and the Labour government, the 'swinging sixties', strikes, student revolutions and the contraceptive pill. Novels of the 1970s and 1980s plunge towards the gloom of a world dominated by Conservatives, money and Margaret Thatcher.

In the great novels of social realism, characters have always moved in a solid and identifiable world of manners and objects. Austen was a realist creating a world of houses and rooms and gardens that she knew, objects that were valued and familiar to her. The later 'social purpose' novels of Dickens, Elizabeth Gaskell, and many others created bleaker worlds by accumulating and incorporating contemporary research material into their fictions. Time moves on, and what was once contemporary becomes historical. To read a nineteenth-century novel now is to read nineteenth-century social history. And so it goes on: the real world of twentieth-century England is told by the fictions of twentieth-century English writers. For it is through fiction that the English can best reveal the truth about themselves, their world and, above all, about their Englishness.

Twentieth-century works cited

Place of publication is London.

Ackroyd, Peter, *Chatterton*, Hamish Hamilton Ltd, 1987.
— *The Great Fire of London*, Hamish Hamilton Ltd, 1982.
— *Hawksmoor*, Hamish Hamilton Ltd, 1985.
Amis, Kingsley, *I Like It Here*, Gollancz, 1958.
— *Lucky Jim*, Gollancz, 1954.
Amis, Martin, *The Rachel Papers*, Jonathan Cape, 1973.
— *Success*, Jonathan Cape, 1978.
Atkinson, Kate, *Behind the Scenes at the Museum*, Doubleday, 1995.
— *Human Croquet*, Doubleday, 1997.
Bainbridge, Beryl, *The Bottle Factory Outing*, Gerald Duckworth and Co, Ltd, 1974.
Barker, Pat, *Blow Your House Down*, Virago Press, 1984.
Barnes, Julian, *Letters from London*, Picador, 1995.
— *Metroland*, Jonathan Cape Ltd, 1980.
Bawden, Nina, *George Beneath a Paper Moon*, Allen Lane, 1974.
Bennett, Alan, *Talking Heads*, BBC Books, 1988.
— *Writing Home*, Faber and Faber Ltd, 1994.
Bergonzi, Bernard, *The Situation of the Novel*, Macmillan and Co, Ltd, 1970.
Braine, John, *Room at the Top*, Eyre and Spottiswoode, 1957.
Brookner, Anita, *Hotel du Lac*, Jonathan Cape, 1984.

Bryson, Bill, *Notes From a Small Island*, Doubleday, 1995.

Burgess, Anthony, *Earthly Powers*, Hutchinson and Co Ltd, 1980.

Byatt, A S, *Babel Tower*, Chatto and Windus Ltd, 1996.

— *Possession*, Chatto and Windus Ltd, 1990.

— *Still Life*, Chatto and Windus Ltd, 1985.

— (ed) *The Oxford Book of English Short Stories*, Oxford University Press, 1998.

Carter, Angela, *The Magic Toyshop*, William Heinemann Ltd, 1967.

— *Wise Children*, Chatto and Windus Ltd, 1991.

Drabble, Margaret, *Jerusalem the Golden*, Weidenfeld and Nicolson, 1967.

— *The Radiant Way*, Weidenfeld and Nicolson, 1987.

Ellis, Alice Thomas, *The Skeleton in the Cupboard*, Gerald Duckworth and Co, 1988.

Forster, E M, *Abinger Harvest*, Edward Arnold, 1936.

Fowles, John, *The Collector*, Jonathan Cape Ltd, 1963.

— *Daniel Martin*, Jonathan Cape Ltd, 1977.

— *The Ebony Tower*, Jonathan Cape Ltd, 1974.

— *The French Lieutenant's Woman*, Jonathan Cape Ltd, 1969.

Greene, Graham, *Brighton Rock*, William Heinemann Ltd, 1938.

Hill, Susan, *Air and Angels*, Sinclair-Stevenson Ltd, 1991.

Howard, Elizabeth Jane, *Odd Girl Out*, Jonathan Cape Ltd, 1972.

Hyams, E (tr), *Taine's Notes on England*, Thames and Hudson, 1957.

Ishiguro, Kazuo, *The Remains of the Day*, Faber and Faber Ltd, 1989.

Larkin, Philip, *Jill*, The Fortune Press, 1946.

— 'Church Going', *The Less Deceived*, The Marvell Press, 1955.

Lawrence, D H, 'Daughters of the Vicar', *The Prussian Officer*, Duckworth, 1914.

Lessing, Doris, *In Pursuit of the English*, MacGibbon and Kee Ltd, 1960.

Lodge, David, *Changing Places*, Martin Secker and Warburg, 1975.

Mikes, George, *How to be an Alien*, Andre Deutsch, 1946.

— *How to be Decadent*, Andre Deutsch, 1977.

— *How to be Inimitable*, Andre Deutsch, 1960.

— (Published in one volume, *How to be a Brit*, Andre Deutsch, 1984).

Murdoch, Iris, *A Severed Head*, Chatto and Windus Ltd, 1961.

Orwell, George, 'The Lion and the Unicorn', *The Collected Essays, Journalism and Letters of George Orwell, Volume 2, My Country Right or Left, 1940–43*, Martin Secker and Warburg, 1968.

Powell, Anthony, *The Acceptance World*, William Heinemann Ltd, 1955.

Priestley, J B, *Out of Town*, William Heinemann Ltd, 1968.

Pym, Barbara, *Excellent Women*, Jonathan Cape Ltd, 1952.

— *Quartet in Autumn*, Macmillan London Ltd, 1977.

Rowe, Marsha (ed), *So Very English*, Serpent's Tail, 1991.

Self, Will, *Great Apes*, Bloomsbury, 1997.

— *Tough, Tough Toys for Tough, Tough Boys*, Bloomsbury, 1998.

Sillitoe, Alan, *The Loneliness of the Long-Distance Runner,* W H Allen and Co, Ltd, 1958.

Swift, Graham, *Last Orders,* Picador, 1996.

— *Waterland,* William Heinemann Ltd, 1983.

Taylor, D J, *After the War,* Chatto and Windus, 1993.

Welsh, Irvine, *Trainspotting,* Secker and Warburg, 1993.

Wilson, Angus, *Anglo-Saxon Attitudes,* Secker and Warburg, 1956.

Winterson, Jeanette, *Oranges Are Not the Only Fruit,* Pandora Press, 1985.

— *Written on the Body,* Jonathan Cape Ltd, 1992.

Woolf, Virginia, *Mrs Dalloway,* Hogarth Press, 1925.

2
The United Kingdom's Minority Nations

Michael Doorley

The United Kingdom is a multinational state made up of four separate territories: England, Scotland, Wales and Northern Ireland. In population terms alone, England is by far the dominant power in the United Kingdom. With a population of 49 million, it far outnumbers the five million who live in Scotland, the 2.7 million in Wales, and the 1.5 million people who live in Northern Ireland.

The English, Welsh, and Scots are British citizens yet all have a distinct national identity. The question of national identity in Northern Ireland is more complicated as the province contains two separate communities who cling to rival national allegiances. The minority nationalist community identifies its nationality with the entire island of Ireland and regards itself as Irish rather than British. Meanwhile, Unionists, who take pride in their Britishness, regard Northern Ireland or 'Ulster' as a distinct political community that has nothing in common with the remainder of the island.

Since Tudor times the history of the British Isles has witnessed the gradual extension of a more centralised English state over its Celtic neighbours. Wales, still with its own language and culture, was politically united with England in 1536. In 1603, Scotland was united with England in a union of crowns. Under the Act of Union of 1707, the remaining Scottish parliament was dissolved. Henceforth, Scottish representatives attended the Westminster parliament, which has since legislated on Scottish issues. A similar Act of Union brought Ireland under formal Westminster control in 1801 although England had exerted varying degrees of control over Ireland since the Anglo-Norman invasions of the twelfth century.

The first weakening of the bonds that bound the United Kingdom together occurred in 1921 with the departure of twenty-six southern Irish counties to form the Irish Free State. This took place in the context of reactions to the Easter rebellion of 1916 and a subsequent war of independence. At first, Ireland remained within the Commonwealth but, in 1949, the Irish severed all remaining constitutional bonds with the United Kingdom by forming the Republic of Ireland. However, since 1921, six counties in the northern province of Ulster continued to remain part of the United Kingdom. An elected Assembly based at Stormont near Belfast governed the internal affairs of Northern Ireland until 1972. Following the outbreak of the Northern Irish 'troubles', the British government dissolved this Assembly. Northern Ireland was then governed directly from the United Kingdom under a system known as 'Direct Rule'.

Unlike the United States, the United Kingdom has no entrenched division of power upheld by a written constitution. Subordinate assemblies such as the Scottish parliament of the seventeenth century and the Stormont assembly were each dissolved by acts of parliament. More recently, following referendums held in the autumn of 1997 and elections in May 1999, a parliament was set up in Scotland and an assembly was established for Wales. A majority of the electorate in Northern Ireland also agreed to a power-sharing assembly although because of disagreements between the main political parties, an executive for this body only briefly and uncertainly held office up to June 2000. Yet, even before these dramatic changes to the constitutional map of Britain, Scotland, Wales and Northern Ireland enjoyed a limited degree of administrative devolution in the form of a territorial office headed by a cabinet minister. The Scottish Office was established in 1885, the Welsh Office in 1964 and the Northern Ireland Office in 1972, following the abolition of the Stormont Assembly. Such concessions were never extended to the English regions. Yorkshire is denied any institutional or legislative privileges, yet its population of 4.6 million far exceeds that of Wales. The establishment of separate regional administrations for Scotland, Wales and Northern Ireland, over the course of centuries, signals London's recognition that the UK is made up of several national identities.

In the immediate aftermath of World War Two, the position of Scotland, Wales and Northern Ireland within the United Kingdom seemed unassailable. Even Northern Ireland with deep sectarian divisions between its majority Protestant and minority Catholic communities had fought loyally on Britain's side. However, since the 1970s all three countries have witnessed resurgent nationalist movements that have sought to redefine their constitutional relationship with their more powerful neighbour. In the case of Northern Ireland, this gave rise to a bloody civil conflict that has resulted in over 3,000 deaths. The emergence of these movements must be seen in the context of the cultural, political and economic changes that have taken place in the United Kingdom as a whole.

Scotland

While majority opinion in Scotland still retains an overarching British identity, Scots display a fierce attachment to their own culture. Such displays of cultural patriotism are particularly visible in the sporting arena, especially at rugby and soccer football matches. The imagery of the highland tradition, as expounded in the novels of Sir Walter Scott (1771–1832), has also done much to shape Scotland's sense of itself as a nation. This imagery of claymores, kilts, sporrans, bagpipes, and separate tartans, which supposedly represents the ancient lineage of the individual clans, was once peculiar to those who lived in the Highlands of Scotland. These superficial and heavily romanticised symbols of Highland identity are used by both Highland and Lowland Scots to differentiate themselves from the 'Sassenach' (English) who live across the border.

Of course, there are more fundamental cultural differences between Scotland and England. Scottish cultural identity is partly based on shared memories of Scotland's history as an independent country before the union of 1707. Indeed some institutional aspects of Scotland's history as an independent nation have survived the union. Since 1707, Scotland has possessed a separate legal and educational system from that of England. It also has an important national press that helps maintain a separate sense of Scottishness. Scots too have a greater sense of pride in their community. With ninety-seven per cent participation in comprehensive state-run schools, there is a greater trust in state intervention than is the case in England. Scottish traditional music, which has a close affinity with that of Ireland, has also undergone a revival in recent decades and has become increasingly popular among Scots of all social classes.

Scotland today appears united in its attachment to its own unique identity. However, differences remain between the populated and industrialised Lowlands and the more thinly populated Highland region. While Scotland has a national Presbyterian Church it also contains a significant Catholic minority, mainly of Irish or Highland descent. Catholics have experienced discrimination in the past and sectarian divisions have coloured local politics in the industrial cities of the Lowlands. In recent decades, such religious animosities appear to have waned although support for football teams in Glasgow still tends to reflect the sectarian divide in the city. Catholics support Glasgow Celtic while Protestants support Rangers. Football matches between both teams are sometimes the scenes of violent clashes between rival bands of supporters.

Although the Scots have prided themselves on their distinctive cultural traditions, there has been no tradition of rebellion against British rule as was the case in Ireland. It is important to stress that union with England did not come about because of conquest and annexation but because of free negotiation and voluntary treaty. Powerful Scottish interests felt that union with England would serve Scotland's economic needs. With the abolition of its parliament in 1707 and the defeat of the Highland Clans in 1745, Scotland settled down to become an enthusiastic junior partner in the British Empire. Scottish soldiers, businessmen and administrators participated in British imperial adventures abroad. The Scottish Lowlands became fully incorporated into Britain's industrial revolution. Central Scotland in particular became a noted centre of heavy industry and shipbuilding while Edinburgh became an important commercial and legal centre. Of course, not all of Scotland benefited from union with England. The Scottish Highlands were left behind in this wave of industrial expansion and witnessed dramatic depopulation throughout the late eighteenth and nineteenth centuries.

In the nineteenth century, Scotland was traditionally a stronghold of the Liberal Party. However, with the demise of the Liberals after the First World War, the Conservative Party built up their strength in the rural areas and especially among the Protestant working class. From the 1920s until the 1960s, Conservative support was normally equal to Labour's and often greater. By 1955, the Conservatives had fifty per cent of the Scottish vote.

In the same period, the Labour Party attracted strong support in the more urbanised central belt of Scotland. These urban areas were characterised by a strong trade union movement and social radicalism born out of poverty and social deprivation. This has sometimes produced radical leftist movements in times of economic turmoil. In 1919 over 100,000 demonstrators brandishing red flags staged protests in Glasgow in a reaction to mass unemployment that followed the First World War. Further protests spread to the entire Clydeside region. An anxious British government worried about the possibility of a Communist revolt despatched troops to 'Red Clydeside' to quell the disturbances and the Communist leaders were arrested. After their release, many of these activists dominated the founding of Britain's small Communist Party. More fundamentally, Scottish radicalism has influenced the Labour Party in Scotland, which has traditionally remained more left-wing than its counterpart in England.

The decline of the British Empire and Britain's post-war economic malaise had a profound impact on Scotland. Scotland's heavy industry, notably shipbuilding and steel-making, went into decline. Unemployment rates became higher than the average for Great Britain while the economic situation of rural communities and small farmers became another source of discontent. These developments had an impact on the political complexion of Scotland. From the 1960s, the Conservative Party went into decline while the Labour Party strengthened its hold. Imperial decline and the economic downturn also contributed to a revival of nationalist sentiment in the 1970s. The SNP, the Scottish National Party, which advocated complete independence for Scotland, had been founded in 1934, but its share of the vote had only stood at 1.3 per cent in 1945. However, in the early 1970s its share of the vote jumped to thirty per cent. The SNP was helped by the discovery of oil in the North Sea. It was now easier for advocates of Scottish nationalism to preach political and economic sovereignty. The SNP exploited Scottish fears that the profits from this resource, like the oil itself, would flow out of Scotland.

In 1978, a Labour government, dependent on the support of Scottish nationalists in parliament, put forward proposals for Scottish Home Rule. Under these proposals Scotland would have had considerable powers over its own internal affairs but defence and foreign policy would still rest with the Westminster parliament. A referendum was held in March 1979. For the proposal to succeed, it had to be approved by forty per cent of those entitled to vote. In fact, while fifty-two per cent of those who voted said 'Yes' they only made up thirty-three per cent of the electorate. Taking this as a sign that most Scots were not yet ready for Home Rule, the government, which had always been lukewarm on the project, took no action.

Any further moves on Scottish Home Rule were forestalled by the Conservative victory of Margaret Thatcher in 1979. The Conservatives were vehemently opposed to any tampering with the integrity of the United Kingdom. But while Thatcher's government was clearly popular in the south of England, this was not the case in Scotland. Her brand of new right Conservatism with its emphasis on free markets and individualism offended the more community-minded Scots. Her economic policies led to the privatisation of many industries, notably coal and steel, and caused further job losses in industries that had already witnessed widespread redundancies. Other policies, such as the imposition of the poll tax on all adults in Scotland in 1989, in order to finance local government, caused outrage. Scots were particularly annoyed at having such a tax imposed on them one year before a similar unpopular poll tax was introduced in England. Such policies did much to popularise the idea of Home Rule for Scotland.

Throughout the 1980s, it was the Labour Party rather than the SNP that capitalised on this hostility to Conservatism. Labour recognised the growing support for Home Rule by adopting this measure in its party political programme. A Scottish Constitutional Convention was also set up in 1989 with the backing of both Labour and Liberal Democratic parties as well as trade union and church leaders. Ironically the SNP did not participate in the workings of the Constitutional Convention and viewed demands for Home Rule as a distraction from the real goal of full independence. This absolutist line may have alienated many Scots and support for the SNP went into decline in the 1980s

The Scottish Constitutional Convention was important in building a coalition for change and developing a consensus in favour of Home Rule. The Convention presented its findings in November 1990. It proposed a Scottish parliament with tax-raising powers and a bill of rights. Not surprisingly, the Conservatives opposed such proposals. But Conservatism was a declining force in Scotland. In the 1992 election, despite a Conservative victory at Westminster, the Conservative Party won only a quarter of Scottish votes. Almost seventy-five per cent of Scottish voters voted for parties in favour of some form of Scottish self-government.

Under the leadership of Alex Salmond, the SNP again enjoyed a revival in the early 1990s. Salmond sought to make the SNP more attractive to the Scottish middle class. Plans to nationalise oil, gas, and rail were dropped. The SNP also became more positive on Europe, arguing that an independent Scotland could take full advantage of European development grants like other small countries in the European Union (EU), such as Ireland and Greece. Indeed the economic prosperity of the Irish Republic in the 1990s has been continually used by Salmond to demonstrate what a small Celtic country can achieve if given control over its own resources. Although the SNP advocates Keynesian economic intervention in the economy, this would be linked to Irish-style tax exemptions to lure investment. The SNP also tapped into Scotland's cultural revival of the 1980s and 1990s. Mel Gibson's *Braveheart*, which glorified the fourteenth-century Scottish leader who fought the English, was cleverly exploited by the SNP to arouse a heightened sense of nationalism. Endorsements by celebrities such as Sean Connery also received widespread media attention. Salmond also took a more pragmatic line on a Scottish Home Rule parliament. While still seeking independence as the ultimate aim, he saw the proposed Scottish parliament as a step towards this goal. In the 1997 general election, the SNP won twenty-two per cent of Scottish votes cast although because of Britain's 'first-past-the-post' system this only resulted in six of the seventy-one seats. As if to illustrate Tory decline, the Conservatives failed to hold any of their seats.

Following the Labour victory, a referendum on a 129-member Scottish Home Rule parliament with tax-raising powers was held. On this occasion, there was no doubting the result. In this double referendum, 74.3 per cent of the electorate voted in favour of a parliament while sixty-three per cent voted in favour of tax-raising powers. The Labour Party, the SNP, and the Liberal Democrats campaigned vigorously in favour of a 'Yes' vote to both proposals. The Conservatives had campaigned against it, arguing that Scottish Home Rule would culminate in a movement towards independence and therefore the break-up of the United Kingdom. Conservatives and some English Labour critics of Scottish Home Rule also pointed to some anomalies that would arise with the setting up of a Scottish parliament. They questioned why Scottish members of parliament in the House of Commons should have the right to vote on English legislation governing issues that in Scotland would have been devolved to a Scottish parliament. This so-called West Lothian question, named after the constituency of the Labour MP who first raised it, remains unresolved.

In late 1998, opinion polls suggested that the SNP would take a majority of seats in the new Scottish parliament. The suddenness of the SNP rise puzzled the Labour leadership. In part this rise may have been due to Scottish dissatisfaction with the 'New Labour' Party under Tony Blair. His centrist policies with their emphasis on tight control of public spending and free market economics led the SNP leader, Alex Salmond, to denounce New Labour as merely another Tory Party. Certainly, New Labour's pride in 'Cool Britannia', with its emphasis on style over substance, appeared to have little appeal in Scotland. A widening gulf between the more traditional Scottish Labour Party and New Labour also became apparent.

In the run-up to the elections for the new Scottish parliament in May 1999, opinion polls suggested a fall in support for the SNP. An SNP campaign pledge to raise taxes in return for better public services may have caused second thoughts among many of its supporters. Alex Salmond's opposition to British involvement in a popular war to oust the Serbs from Kosovo may also have damaged SNP support. The Scottish Labour Party also ran a successful campaign fronted by its popular leader, the late Donald Dewar. Labour continually stressed the costs to Scotland of full independence ranging from a new welfare and revenue service to a separate defence force. This negative campaigning may well have had the desired effect as the Labour Party gained the most seats in the new parliament winning fifty-six out of 129.

In an election with proportional representation, the SNP secured a respectable thirty-seven seats in the new parliament putting them in second place to Labour. This result accurately reflected their thirty per cent share of the vote. Both the Liberal Democrats and the Conservatives gained seventeen seats each. The failure of Labour to gain an overall majority over the other parties led to a Labour and Liberal Democratic coalition in the new Scottish parliament, heightening the role of the SNP as official opposition.

The outcome of the election indicated that majority opinion in Scotland was not yet ready for independence. Whether this will change in the future is an open question. Much will depend on the performance of the Labour and Liberal Democratic Scottish government. Perhaps an interesting result of the election was the success of traditional 'Old Labour' candidates who had accused Blair's New Labour government of control freak tendencies. Such tensions are bound to increase and are likely to be exploited by the SNP. Indeed, the policies pursued by the new Scottish parliament have not always been welcome in London. By early summer 2000, significant divergences had emerged, notably over the administration of fees for higher education.

Wales

Wales is more culturally diverse than Scotland with a less developed sense of nationhood. The Welsh have found it difficult to imagine Wales within an institutional framework in a way that comes naturally to the Scots. The Welsh press is not as influential as its Scottish counterpart in moulding a national identity and its legal and educational system is indistinguishable from that of England.

While Welsh identity is relatively weak in terms of national institutions, it is strong in terms of cultural markers such as language. Indeed Wales has been the most successful of the Celtic nations at retaining its own language. The Welsh language is a core curriculum subject in state schools. In 1982 a Welsh language television channel, S4C, was launched which now attracts up to thirty per cent of Welsh viewers for its more popular programmes. About eight per cent of the population still speak Welsh as their first language and these are concentrated in the north and west of the country. However, this figure compares unfavourably with the mid-nineteenth century when over fifty per cent of the people of Wales spoke Welsh. This decline in Welsh language usage can in part be attributed to the industrialisation of Wales and the gradual integration of Wales into the English economy. By 1911, the Welsh-speaking Welsh were a minority in Wales.

It is important to stress that the majority of non-Welsh speakers also consider themselves Welsh. However, with the decline of the language, attempts have been made to create a definition of Welsh nationality that would be common to all the people of Wales. These national characteristics are largely associated with the coal-mining communities of South Wales and would include political radicalism, communal solidarity, a love of singing, enthusiasm for rugby and a lack of obsession with class divisions.

This stereotypical view of Welsh identity may have some basis in historical fact. Some of these Welsh values can be traced to the peculiar religious tradition of Wales. In contrast to England, Wales has remained a bastion for nonconformist religions such as Methodism. In the mid-nineteenth century, it was estimated that there were three nonconformists for every member of the Anglican church, which was then the official state church of Wales. Indeed much of political debate in Wales in the late nineteenth century focused on efforts by Welsh Liberals to disestablish the Anglican Church in Wales. Ironically, it was a British government led by a Welshman, David Lloyd George, which finally carried out this task. In 1920, Anglicanism ceased to be the official religion of Wales.

To heighten further differences with England, much of Wales was won over to an evangelical brand of Protestantism in the late nineteenth century. Movements such as the Calvinistic Methodist Forward Movement (1891) and the Home Mission of the Independents and the Baptists (1895) became especially popular in the coal-mining districts of Wales, which still remain famous for their amateur choirs. While religious observance has declined in recent decades, the legacy of these evangelical movements has permeated its political culture. Community consensus is prized over individualism and the history of both liberalism and socialism in Wales has a strong evangelical flavour.

While there certainly exists a common sense of Welsh identity, the Welsh tend to identify most strongly with their valley, town or village rather than with a sense of Wales as a whole. To complicate matters even further, there is a strong cultural divide between North Wales and South Wales. In part, this can be attributed to uneven economic development. In the mid-nineteenth century South Wales developed coal and steel industries while North Wales remained more rural and agricultural. In areas where large-scale industrialisation took place, the use of Welsh declined. This trend was exacerbated by an influx of immigrants from both Ireland and England in the late nineteenth century. Consequently, a cultural divide emerged between a more Welsh-speaking North and West and a mainly English-speaking South.

The development of Welsh nationalism has been closely associated with the need to protect Welsh linguistic culture. The Welsh Nationalist Party, Plaid Cymru, was founded in 1925 as a pressure group to protect the language, poetry, and music of Wales. The party's principal aim was the achievement of a Welsh-speaking independent Wales and the Welsh language was the only medium of party activity. In its early years the party attracted only a handful of supporters but the establishment of the party was itself a declaration of the distinctiveness of Wales.

The establishment of a Welsh Office by the British government in 1964 strengthened the concept of the territorial unity of Wales. This may partly explain the increased support for Plaid Cymru, which won its first parliamentary seat in 1967 and went on to win two further seats in 1974. In 1979, a minority Labour government dependent on the support of these Welsh and Scottish nationalists held a referendum on a proposed Welsh Assembly. In the event, the referendum obtained even less support than its counterpart for Scotland. 58.3 per cent of the electorate voted in the referendum; 243,048 in favour and 956,330 against. The proposal was defeated decisively.

The reasons for the failure of the referendum are complex. Nationalists complained that the referendum had been held at a time of economic chaos, widespread strikes causing the disruption of public services. Certainly, credibility in the government was at an all-time low. Perhaps more fundamentally, the Welsh electorate was not yet ready for even a limited measure of self-government.

The Conservative government that took power in 1979 had no interest in any form of Welsh devolution. However, Conservative economic policies would have a far-reaching impact on Welsh society. Its national policy of closing uneconomic coal-mines hit South Wales particularly hard. Despite large-scale strikes in 1984 and unprecedented union solidarity, the government refused to withdraw its plans. By the end of the decade, there were only seven pits and 4,000 miners in the whole of South Wales. Over 100,000 miners had worked the South Wales coalfields in 1947. A remarkable period in Welsh history had ended.

To compensate for the loss of mining jobs in the 1980s, the British government pursued interventionist policies aimed at job creation. Such policies ran counter to the dominant Thatcherite free market ideology that shaped government policy in the rest of Britain and the driving force behind these policies lay with the Welsh Office under the energetic Secretary of State for Wales, Peter Walker. A valleys initiative was launched aimed at reconstructing the economy of South Wales after the run-down of the coal and steel industries. Financial incentives were also offered to European and Asian companies to invest in Wales. During Walker's three years as Secretary of State, Wales, with only five per cent of the population of the UK, received over twenty-two per cent of British inward investment. Yet despite job creation by many foreign manufacturing firms, from Japan and South Korea in particular, the Welsh economy remained characterised by high unemployment and low pay.

Based on election results in the 1980s, some political commentators have identified three political regions in Wales: 'British Wales', comprising the eastern constituencies and the southern coastal areas where Conservatism was strong; 'Welsh Wales', the southern coalfields where Labour support was concentrated; and Welsh-speaking Wales – Gwynedd and most of Dyfed – a region where the Conservative Party, Labour, the Liberal Democrats and Plaid Cymru were struggling for supremacy. Despite staunch support by Plaid Cymru for the miners, the Labour Party garnered the Welsh protest vote against the Conservative government throughout the 1980s and 1990s, especially in the more populous Welsh Wales. In the 1997 election, Labour won thirty-four out of forty seats in Wales, while Plaid Cymru only won four. The Conservatives failed to win any seats, even in British Wales.

It was the Labour victory in 1997, and not any political breakthrough by Plaid Cymru, that again put the prospect of constitutional change for Wales on the political agenda. Constitutional change for Wales must therefore be seen in the context of Labour's policy of dismantling the over-centralised British state. In September 1997, the Labour government held a referendum in Wales on Welsh devolution. Voters were asked to decide on the setting up of a sixty-member Assembly or Welsh Senedd. It was proposed that this Assembly would take over from the Welsh secretary responsibility for such areas as economic development, agriculture, housing, and education. Westminster would still retain responsibility for foreign affairs, defence and taxation.

Under these proposals, the Welsh Assembly would not have tax-raising powers or the same level of autonomy as Scotland. This in part reflected the reality of Welsh nationalist demands. Even so, the proposals generated stiff opposition. The Conservative leader and former Welsh Secretary, William Hague, described the proposed Welsh Assembly as an expensive talking shop. Up to six Labour MPs declared that they would vote 'No'. The Assembly was denounced as adding an unnecessary layer of bureaucracy to the administration of Wales.

Such criticism of the proposed Assembly may have had a telling effect on the Welsh electorate. The electoral turnout for the referendum was low, particularly in the more Anglicised towns close to the English border. The metropolitan areas of the south also registered a majority against the referendum. Cardiff voted 'No' by fifty-five per cent. Clearly many voters in English-speaking areas feared that in any future Welsh system of self-government English speakers would be discriminated against. In the rural Welsh-speaking areas turnout was higher and was just sufficient to carry the referendum by a slim majority of 50.3 per cent in favour to 49.7 per cent against. A mere 6,721 votes decided the constitutional position of Wales within the UK.

While the majority in favour of the assembly was low, the referendum was nevertheless carried. Inevitably, comparisons were drawn with the result in 1979. Why was the referendum successful on this occasion? Clearly, the popularity of Tony Blair's Labour government in 1997, which put its full weight behind the referendum, was an important factor. Memories of eighteen years of Conservative government, whose economic policies had caused so much devastation to the mining and steel industries, may also have played a role in persuading a slim majority of Welsh voters that a greater degree of Welsh control over their economic and political affairs was in the best interests of Wales.

In May 1999, elections were held to the new assembly. An electoral turnout of only forty per cent reflected a considerable degree of apathy. Labour at twenty-eight seats was the largest party but had failed to obtain an overall majority, despite which it proceeded to form a single-party executive. The Conservatives obtained nine seats while the Liberal Democrats won six. However Plaid Cymru performed far better than anticipated, gaining seventeen out of sixty seats in the new assembly. Under the proportional representation system, Plaid obtained about thirty per cent of the seats for its thirty per cent vote share. It even managed to break out of its traditional stronghold in Welsh-speaking Wales to win seats in the staunch Labour constituencies of the Rhondda Valley and Islwyn.

Commentators are at a loss to explain the sudden surge in support for Plaid Cymru. Labour activists pointed to the low turnout and complained that Labour voters simply failed to turn out to vote, perhaps viewing the new assembly as largely irrelevant to their daily lives. Other commentators have argued that many voted for Plaid Cymru because of Labour's failure to deliver on public services. Certainly badly-run Labour councils, such as in the Rhondda Valley, hurt Labour and may have been a source of voter apathy. Welsh Nationalists may also have gained ground from arguments within Labour. Some Labour activists were opposed to setting up a Welsh Assembly in the first place. The resignation of the former Welsh Secretary Ron Davies some months prior to the election following a sex scandal in London also caused much controversy. The appointment of Alun Michael as his successor, first as Welsh Secretary and then as leader of the Assembly executive, caused bitter recriminations within Welsh Labour. Michael was seen as a Blairite candidate imposed by London over the heads of Labour activists who would have preferred the more independently-minded Rhodri Morgan.

On 1st July 1999, the functions of the Welsh Office were transferred to the Welsh Assembly. Unlike the Scottish parliament, the Assembly does not have tax-raising powers or the ability to pass primary legislation. Nevertheless, its creation symbolically recognises Wales as a country separate from England.

Though it failed to win the affections of the Welsh people in its first year, this separateness was emphasised in spring 2000 when Michael – facing certain defeat in a no-confidence vote – was replaced by Morgan.

Northern Ireland

The Irish question has bedevilled British politics for centuries. At first, the partition of Ireland in 1921 seemed to provide a painful if workable solution to this age-old question. The twenty-six southern counties with a ninety-five per cent Catholic majority became an independent Irish Free State. Meanwhile Northern Ireland with its majority Protestant population remained within the United Kingdom though with its own local Assembly based at Stormont.

The Protestant population of Northern Ireland has very different historical and cultural traditions from its Catholic neighbours, demonstrating a fierce attachment to their British identity. Many are descendants of Scottish and English settlers who came to Ireland during the seventeenth century in order to maintain English power in Ireland. Living in the midst of a Catholic and Gaelic society, a siege mentality has coloured their attitudes towards its Catholic neighbours which has long outlived the religious turmoil of the Reformation. Memories of the Protestant victory of William of Orange at the Battle of the Boyne in 1690 and the sacrifices made in defence of Britain in both World Wars are deeply embedded in their cultural traditions. Historically they have objected to all plans for Irish self-government; hence their identification with 'Unionism'.

However, from the beginning the new Northern Ireland state was built on very shaky foundations. It contained within its borders a substantial Catholic minority that comprised more than thirty per cent of the population. Many of these Catholics did not accept the legitimacy of the new Northern Ireland administration. They felt cut off from their co-religionists in the South and felt that their Irish identity was not recognised by the Protestant-dominated Stormont parliament.

In turn, the Unionist authorities remained suspicious of such a sizeable and potentially "disloyal" Catholic minority within its gates. The Catholic minority faced discrimination in housing, employment, and social services. Catholics were twice as likely to be unemployed as Protestants. Political gerrymandering in local government ensured Unionist control of local authorities even where Catholics were in the majority. The police force in Northern Ireland, the Royal Ulster Constabulary (RUC), was overwhelmingly Protestant.

Politics in Northern Ireland thus became divided on religious and ethnic lines. The vast majority of Protestants voted for the Unionist Party, which dominated the Stormont Assembly. Most Catholics voted for the Nationalist Party. However, the in-built Unionist majority in the Stormont parliament meant that no change in the constitutional status of Northern Ireland was possible. A small minority of nationalists supported the Irish Republican Army

(IRA), which wished to reunite Ireland by means of an armed struggle. However, after short abortive campaigns in the 1930s and 1950s, the IRA seemed on the point of extinction by the early 1960s.

In the 1960s the real threat to the Northern Irish state came not from the IRA but from a broadly based civil rights movement that drew its support from the bulk of the Catholic population and a significant section of the Protestant intelligentsia. The civil rights movement, with tactics modelled on the campaigns of Martin Luther King in the United States, focused on winning civil rights for Catholics and not on a united Ireland. However, this provoked hostility from the Unionist-dominated Stormont parliament, who believed that the civil rights agitation was really a cover for a nationalist rebellion. In the disturbances that followed, Stormont appealed to London for support. Fearing a pogrom, the British government sent troops to cordon off the Catholic areas. Initially, British troops were welcomed by the Catholic minority, who saw them as protectors against the mainly Protestant police force. However, heavy-handed tactics by the army, which was seeking to impose order soon led to the alienation of sections of the Catholic population. A newly reorganised IRA emerged, committed to achieving a united Ireland by means of terrorist attacks involving bombings and shootings both in Northern Ireland and the British mainland.

It is important to stress that most Catholics still supported constitutional nationalism and were appalled at the violence of the IRA. This brand of nationalism was given a powerful voice by the formation the Social Democratic and Labour Party (SDLP) in 1970. Yet the IRA continued to maintain a core of support in the more socially deprived Catholic areas of Northern Ireland. The IRA campaign also had an effect on the Unionist community. Equally ruthless Protestant or so-called Loyalist paramilitary organisations, notably the Ulster Volunteer Force (UVF) and the Ulster Defence Association (UDA), emerged in the early 1970s. Innocent Catholics were killed in sectarian attacks, often in retaliation for attacks by the IRA. Because of such violence by both sides, politics in Northern Ireland had become even more polarised.

Efforts by the British government to deal with the Northern Ireland 'troubles' by security measures alone have sometimes served to make matters worse. The introduction of internment without trial in the early 1970s and the 'Bloody Sunday' shootings of unarmed civil rights protesters by British troops in Derry in 1972 were exploited by IRA propagandists and only served to harden their support, especially among the Irish in the USA.

Successive British governments have attempted various political initiatives to deal with the Northern Ireland problem. The Unionist-dominated Stormont was dissolved in 1972 and Direct Rule from Westminster was introduced. In 1973, the British government concluded an agreement with the Irish government, the SDLP and moderate Unionists at Sunningdale in England. As a result of the Sunningdale Agreement, as it came to be known, a power-sharing executive involving both moderate Nationalist and Unionist parties was set up. There was also provision for a Council of Ireland that would involve co-operation between the new Assembly and the Dublin government. This was too much for hard-line Unionists. Following a huge strike by Protestant workers that brought the province to a standstill, the power-sharing executive collapsed in 1974. Direct Rule was reimposed from London and the British government went back to its drawing board.

By the early 1980s, following military stalemate, the IRA began to recognise the merits of building a more mass-based political movement through its political wing, Sinn Fein. In the words of IRA leader Danny Morrison, a united Ireland could be achieved by means of 'a ballot box in one hand and an armalite in the other'! Events were to play into Morrison's hands. After the deaths of IRA hunger-strikers who were intent on winning political status as political prisoners, this support base was widened. Sinn Fein began to win about one-third of the nationalist vote, the remaining nationalists still voting for the SDLP.

In 1985, the British government sought to marginalise the IRA and the increasingly powerful Sinn Fein through an Anglo-Irish agreement. Under this agreement, the British government recognised the legitimate role of the southern Irish government in defending the interests of Nationalists in Northern Ireland. The Dublin government in turn openly recognised that there could be no constitutional change in Northern Ireland without the consent of the majority. The agreement provided for regular meetings between British and Irish ministers and even a permanent staff of British and Irish civil servants based at Stormont to help iron out any Anglo-Irish disputes.

In one sense, the agreement was a success. Nationalist support for the moderate SDLP had been consolidated and there was greater co-operation between Dublin and London on security matters. Nevertheless, violence continued since Sinn Fein and the IRA opposed the deal as a partitionist settlement. The agreement also caused uproar among the Unionist parties who refused to countenance any role by Dublin in Northern Ireland affairs.

By the late 1980s, the leader of the SDLP, John Hume, had become convinced that to achieve real and lasting peace a political settlement, which would include all of the political parties, would be necessary. Hume began talks with the leader of Sinn Fein, Gerry Adams, in an effort to encourage the IRA to enter a talks process. Meanwhile both the British and Irish governments contributed to this new strategy through the Downing Street Declaration of December 1993. It was hoped that if the British and Irish governments brought together their positions in a single statement or 'Joint Declaration', it might encourage the IRA to end its campaign and permit Sinn Fein to enter a talks process. It also represented an attempt to win the support of the Unionist parties and the Loyalist paramilitaries for an all-inclusive settlement.

As a result of the Declaration, the British government declared that it had no strategic or economic interest in remaining in Northern Ireland. However, no change could come about without the wishes of the majority in the province.

It also spoke of 'encouraging and facilitating an agreement, based on the rights and identities of both traditions ... which may take the form of agreed structures for the island as a whole'. The Irish government in turn again embraced the concept of majority consent in Northern Ireland and also promised to amend Articles 2 and 3 of its constitution, which laid claim to the territory of the North. On 31st August 1994, the IRA declared a ceasefire. This was followed by a similar ceasefire declaration from the Loyalist paramilitaries.

To consolidate the peace process further, the British government published in February 1995 a so-called 'Framework Document', which, as its name suggests, added a proposed institutional framework to the principles outlined in the earlier declaration. This institutional framework envisaged a Northern Ireland parliament that would still be linked to Westminster. More controversially, it also provided for All-Ireland or so-called North-South bodies which would have executive and harmonising functions. The scope of these bodies would have to be agreed by the parties but proposed areas of co-operation would include education, health, agriculture, and tourism.

Agreement on the Framework Document was overshadowed by an intense debate over the decommissioning of terrorist weapons. The Unionist parties and the British government refused to admit Sinn Fein into a talks process as long as Sinn Fein retained its weapons. Sinn Fein argued in turn that for the IRA to give up its weapons would be tantamount to surrender. Frustrated by the long delay in gaining admission to talks, the IRA broke its ceasefire in February 1996 with a bomb at Canary Wharf in the heart of London's Docklands. It seemed that the peace process, so carefully crafted by both governments, was about to break down completely.

The election of Tony Blair's Labour government in May 1997 gave a new impetus to the peace process. Shortly after the election, the issue of decommissioning was shelved for the moment. The IRA renewed its ceasefire and Sinn Fein was finally admitted to the talks process. Not all Unionists welcomed these developments but the largest Unionist Party, the Ulster Unionist Party (UUP), led by David Trimble, remained in the talks. Chairing the talks process was a former US senator, George Mitchell. Mitchell's appointment illustrated the growing role of the Clinton administration in Washington in the peace process.

To the surprise of most commentators, the diverse range of parties, which included not only moderate Nationalist and Unionists but also Sinn Fein and representatives of the Loyalist paramilitaries, finally reached agreement on Good Friday, 10th April 1998. The last-minute intervention of President Clinton was considered crucial in persuading Adams of Sinn Fein and Trimble of the Ulster Unionists to sign up to the deal.

The so-called Good Friday Agreement was a comprehensive peace plan based on the earlier Joint Declaration and Framework Document. The main points of the deal involved the setting up of a Northern Assembly with 108 seats. The

Assembly would elect a twelve-strong executive committee of ministers. It also envisaged a North-South Ministerial Council to deal with areas of common concern to both Dublin and Belfast such as tourism, education, and agriculture. As a concession to Unionists, an intergovernmental Council or Council of the Isles would also be set up with members drawn from the Irish parliament (Dail), the Northern Ireland Assembly, the House of Commons, and the new assemblies in Cardiff and Edinburgh.

In an unprecedented development, the Agreement was put to the people of Northern Ireland and the Republic of Ireland simultaneously by means of a referendum in each jurisdiction in May 1998. The principle of self-determination for the whole of Ireland, outlined in the Framework Document, was thus upheld. In the Republic over ninety per cent of the electorate endorsed the Agreement by agreeing to amend Articles 2 and 3 of the Irish constitution, which laid claim to Northern Ireland. The majority in Northern Ireland in favour of the agreement was somewhat smaller but still convincing: seventy-two per cent voting 'Yes' and twenty-eight per cent voting 'No'. A closer examination of the results indicated that over ninety per cent of Nationalist voters supported the agreement. However, Unionist opinion seemed more evenly divided with only a slim majority in favour. Clearly many Unionists distrusted the role of the southern government in Northern Ireland affairs. There was also concern about Sinn Fein ministers in government, the early release of IRA prisoners and the continued refusal of the IRA to decommission its weapons.

In elections to the Assembly, which followed in June 1998, these concerns among Unionists were reflected in the still significant vote for those Unionist parties who opposed the agreement, notably Ian Paisley's Democratic Unionist Party (DUP). Paisley's party still advocates religious apartheid as the natural order of things in Northern Ireland and is totally unmoved by any talk of reconciliation, fresh starts and new horizons. The DUP still seems to attract much of the Protestant working class and small farmers and represents about eighteen per cent of the Northern Ireland electorate. Yet the intellectuals, the senior businessmen, churchmen, and academics within the Protestant community seem to be overwhelmingly in favour of the agreement and have helped to swing many wavering Protestant voters into the 'Yes' camp. These 'Yes' voters, when combined with the vast majority of nationalists, represent over seventy per cent of the electorate.

On 1st July 1998, the Assembly met for the first time. Trimble, representing the main Unionist Party, was elected First Minister, while Seamus Mallon of the SDLP became Deputy First Minister. However, almost immediately, divisions emerged over the distribution of cabinet seats for the new executive that would govern Northern Ireland. Sinn Fein's eighteen per cent of the vote entitled it to two seats in the new executive. However, Trimble opposed the setting up of an executive that would include Sinn Fein Ministers until a credible start had been made to IRA weapons decommissioning. Sinn Fein in turn sought to distance itself from the IRA arguing that it is a separate organisation. Sinn Fein also claimed that it was wrong to link the entire peace process to the issue of decommissioning. They argued that under the terms of the Good Friday agreement, IRA decommissioning did not have to take place until after the setting up of the executive and before a deadline of May 2000.

The failure to resolve this impasse over decommissioning led to continual delay over the establishment of an executive despite a number of 'deadlines' imposed by a frustrated British government. In July 1999, a marathon session of talks between all the pro-agreement parties and the British and Irish governments failed to make a deal, even after a Sinn Fein promise to use their best efforts to persuade the IRA to decommission. After considerable pressure from the British, Irish and American governments, Trimble would not accept this promise as a basis for moving forward. This surprised many commentators and angered both the national governments. Mallon resigned his commission, charging that the Unionists 'had bled the process dry in search for concessions'. Yet while Trimble himself might have accepted the deal, his party was divided on the issue. Indeed, if he had entered government without a start being made to IRA decommissioning, he might have faced desertions from his own party. This would have allowed the anti-agreement parties the numerical strength to disrupt the business of the assembly.

The Northern Ireland peace process remained stalled over this issue until late in 1999. The IRA was adamant that it would not decommission in the present 'context' though it hinted that this could change if the executive was up and running. The message emanating from the Unionist camp remained the same: 'No Guns, No Government'. However, Trimble also sought to demonstrate his good intent. In a conciliatory message to Sinn Fein he stated: 'We know this can't work without you, but you must also know it cannot work without decommissioning.' Ironically his refusal to bend to British and American pressure may have strengthened his position within Unionism which had been evenly divided. For in the end a form of words was found which allowed the power-sharing executive (including its Sinn Fein members) to take office, even though renewed disagreements about decommissioning led to its suspension by the British government for several months of 2000.

Conclusion

The late 1990s witnessed dramatic changes in the constitutional position of Scotland, Wales and Northern Ireland. Both Scotland and Wales achieved a significant measure of local autonomy, but the future of Northern Ireland remains uncertain. Clearly, Tony Blair's Labour government sees this programme of decentralising powers to regional assemblies as a means of preserving the United Kingdom rather than driving it apart. It is argued that each assembly will represent the distinctive cultural traditions of the peoples of each country. Economic development will be encouraged by local administrations better able to understand the potential of their respective regions. Perhaps the greatest gain will be in the political realm. The regional parliaments may come to command the loyalty and participation of local people who will no longer feel alienated from a distant and unfeeling administration in London. Blair believes that this recognition of national identity will strengthen rather than weaken the United Kingdom.

Nevertheless, a question mark still hangs over the continued participation of all three in the United Kingdom. While the SNP failed to gain a majority of Scottish parliament seats in 1999, it has become a significant force. The British government may be unable to resist demands for an even greater degree of autonomy either from a revitalised SNP of a disgruntled 'Old Labour'-dominated Scottish parliament. Commentators are divided as to whether a fully independent Scotland could survive. Organisations opposing full independence, including the three main British parties, argue that it would be worse off as it would lose the economic benefits of belonging to the UK. This argument appears to have won the day with a majority of Scottish voters.

Not surprisingly, this view is opposed by the SNP, which argues that Scotland would prosper because wealth would remain in Scotland rather than going south. At present, tax revenues from oil production – about £2 billion per year – go directly to London. The SNP argues that with independence, this money could be better spent in Scotland. As well as oil, Scotland has a thriving whisky industry and has developed an important electronics industry in 'Silicon Glen' of west central Scotland. Edinburgh is also an important financial centre. It seems likely that an independent Scotland could survive, particularly in the context of an increasingly powerful European Union of which Scotland would be an integral part. Most Scottish voters are not yet prepared to take this step, but much depends on the performance of the parliament in its first term.

Given the nature of Welsh nationalism it appears that the Welsh assembly will be the culmination of nationalist demands. Plaid Cymru's surprising thirty per cent vote may represent a seismic shift in political allegiances in Labour strongholds or merely a protest against London control. A silent majority of sixty per cent of the Welsh electorate stayed away from the polls. This poor turnout signals not only opposition to independence but little enthusiasm for limited self-government.

Welsh nationalists seem more interested in protecting Welsh language and culture than in pursuing full independence. Issues that concern the Welsh language dominate nationalist rhetoric in Wales. Already schools give their instruction in Welsh as well as English or only in Welsh. The Welsh language station, S4C, is heavily subsidised. Most road signs and street names are also written in both Welsh and English. A Welsh assembly can provide continuing protection for Welsh culture while at the same time its limited powers will reassure majority opinion in Wales that the link with Westminster will be maintained.

As ever, the case of Northern Ireland after the Good Friday Agreement remains more complicated. Yet despite the failure of the parties to sustain an executive, much has changed during the quarter century since the failure of Sunningdale. The Agreement enjoys majority support among the electors. Sinn Fein and the IRA, as well as the Loyalist paramilitaries, have signed up.

In 1974, the violence was at its height. The IRA was committed to a British withdrawal. Meanwhile, much of the Unionist community opposed power-sharing and any truck with the Irish Republic. The contrasts with Northern Ireland in the summer of 2000 could not be more stark. The paramilitary ceasefires remain. Even the tense Orange marching season of 1999 passed off relatively peacefully. The IRA has accepted the principle of Unionist consent and appears committed to a political strategy through its political wing Sinn Fein. Sinn Fein, with a Northern Ireland core vote of eighteen per cent, has also begun to make inroads into politics in the Republic, doing well in local elections in June 1999. An IRA return to violence would wreck this political strategy. Meanwhile an opinion poll conducted by the *Belfast News Letter* in July 1999 indicated that eighty-four per cent of Ulster Unionists were in favour of power sharing: even fifty-eight per cent of Ian Paisley's Democratic Unionist Party supported the principle. Interestingly, the issue of decommissioning rather than cross-border bodies has provoked Unionist outrage. Most Unionists, although vehemently opposed to a united Ireland, now appear to accept that some degree of economic co-operation with the thriving economy in the south would be in the best interests of Northern Ireland. If the decommissioning issue can be resolved, the secure establishment of an executive will surely follow.

What then about the future of Northern Ireland? Given the increasing prosperity of the Republic and the growing economic ties binding north and south it seems likely that links will grow stronger in the years ahead irrespective of the fate of the agreement. The role of the European Union and the United States in strengthening these ties should not be underestimated. But, if a united Ireland should eventually emerge, it will be only as a very long-term consequence. Indeed Blair has attempted to reassure Unionists by declaring that such a development would not occur in his lifetime.

The United Kingdom looks set for further constitutional change in the years ahead: the growing confidence of nationalist movements in the 'Celtic Fringe' may well reflect the terrible insecurity of the English nation at this time in its history. The gradual loss of empire, relative economic decline, and a Royal Family beset by scandals have done much to undermine a common sense of English identity. This has naturally helped to weaken the cultural bonds between the English and the nations on their frontiers. As one commentator has put it: 'We are witnessing the end of the United Kingdom as a nation state whose government exercises total sovereign power within its borders.' Britain's growing integration into a possible federal Europe will only serve to exacerbate this process. Subordinate parliaments in Edinburgh, Cardiff and Belfast may well prefer to deal directly with Brussels rather than with an increasingly irrelevant English-dominated parliament in London.

Further reading

Davies, J, *A History of Wales*, Penguin, London, 1994.
Mallie, E and D McKittrick, *The Fight For Peace*, Heinemann, London, 1996.
Marr, A, *The Battle of Scotland*, Penguin, London, 1992.

3
Modernisation versus Managed Decline: Britain after 1945

Peter Grosvenor

A framework for understanding Britain's post-war history

If there is one distinctive British national talent, it is for stability achieved through the twin devices of continuity and compromise. The history of Britain is characterised, for the most part, by reform and gradual change, and by the relative absence of major social and political upheavals. For this reason, the ancient, medieval and modern rest alongside each other in everything from architecture to the institutions of government.

This genius for managed change has served the country well, enabling it to avoid the societal collapses and political revolutions that have punctuated the modern histories of many of Britain's global rivals. Yet, since World War Two, the British have come to realise that their prized constancy has often been purchased at the price of necessary innovation. Nineteenth-century Britain was the powerhouse of the Industrial Revolution and the growth of free trade, but by the start of the twentieth century the country had obviously lost ground to emerging competitors. For much of the period since World War Two, the British seem to have abandoned managed change in favour of managed decline.

Over the same period the country has at times sought, with varying degrees of success, to counter this decline by abandoning those aspects of traditional practice that are judged to be impediments to effective and efficient functioning in the present. These attempts at modernisation can be found in the economy, in social attitudes and in the political system.

The Attlee years: the high tide of British socialism (1945–51)

The Second World War has pride of place in British historical consciousness. It was, in Winston Churchill's words, their 'finest hour', during which the people made collective sacrifices in the face of national danger and adversity. At no point since has the country experienced such social cohesion and unity of purpose. Yet beneath the nostalgia for the wartime solidarities lies a realisation that the war did immense damage to the economic infrastructure and brought the age of empire to an end. Recognition of this underlying reality shaped the political priorities of the mid-to-late 1940s.

In July 1945, even before hostilities with Japan had ended, Churchill was rejected by the British electorate and Clement Attlee's Labour Party was propelled into power in a landslide victory. Churchill's brilliant wartime leadership is now legendary, and his defeat requires some explanation. Firstly, the Conservatives, though not Churchill himself, were still blamed for the policy of appeasement and were also associated in the minds of the voters with the economic hardships of the 1930s. Secondly, Labour leaders had assumed national prominence and political respectability through their roles in the wartime coalition government. Thirdly, to maintain civilian morale, the wartime coalition had promised a number of sweeping social reforms, and Labour was judged to be the party most likely to deliver on those promises. Fourthly, the collectivist nature of the successful war effort served to legitimise much of Labour's ideological programme. This last factor was probably reinforced by the positive representation of Britain's Soviet allies in wartime propaganda, which gave additional respectability to left-wing political ideas.

Labour's programme

In its six years in office, the Attlee government created the mixed economy and welfare state that were to form the basis of consensus politics in Britain for one-third of a century.

Central to Labour's economic policy was a programme of nationalisation. In 1946, the Bank of England was brought into public ownership, and by 1948 the state had also taken over the coal industry, the railways, road haulage, the docks, electricity and gas. Iron and steel followed. For the party's ideological left, nationalisation was a litmus test of the government's socialist credibility; for the more pragmatic elements in the government, it was a necessary measure to rescue strategically vital industries that had been damaged during the course of the war. The pragmatists, led by Attlee himself, were the majority in the cabinet. Only the nationalisation of the profitable steel industry could plausibly be interpreted as an assault on the 'commanding heights' of British capitalism. Consequently, the industry took on symbolic significance. Over the next three decades it was to be returned to the private sector by the Conservatives, renationalised by Labour and finally privatised again by Prime Minister Margaret Thatcher in the 1980s.

In the area of social policy, the government set about implementing the key recommendations of the 1942 Beveridge Report, which had promised a 'cradle to grave' welfare state based on national schemes of unemployment insurance, sickness benefits and pensions. Essentially this meant that the state would take on all or part of the responsibility for individuals' well-being in youth, sickness and age. In 1948 Aneurin Bevan, a self-educated former coal-miner from South Wales and now charismatic Minister for Health, introduced the National Health Service (NHS), a comprehensive system of socialised medicine, which provided healthcare free at the point of demand.

The Attlee government implemented its radical programme in the most difficult of circumstances at home and abroad. British industry had been subject to heavy wartime bombardment. Gold and dollar reserves had been seriously depleted. Export markets had been disrupted and, in some cases, permanently lost. In addition, following the surrender of Japan, the Americans had abruptly terminated Lend-Lease whereby Britain had paid for war supplies by ceding territories to the USA. The replacement loan, negotiated by the economist John Maynard Keynes, was made conditional upon the convertibility of sterling, a specification that severely circumscribed the British ability to intervene in the economy. The replacement of the Pax Britannica by the Pax Americana was vividly illustrated during the Greek Civil War (1946–49) when, under the Truman Doctrine, the United States took over from Britain the lead responsibility for containing Soviet influence in the eastern Mediterranean. The end of empire – welcomed by many Labour politicians – was confirmed by Britain's ignominious retreat from Palestine in February 1947 and by the granting of independence to India in August of the same year. By the end of the reign of King George VI in 1952, the British had begun to think in terms not of the empire but of the Commonwealth, the voluntary association of nations that had replaced it.

The legacy of 1945

Praise for what the Attlee government achieved in these difficult circumstances has by no means been confined to socialist circles. It rescued strategically vital industries; created a welfare state that successfully attacked the worst social injustices of the pre-war period; established a system of socialised medicine that still ranks as one of the country's most prized institutions; initiated the long process through which colonised peoples achieved self-government; and integrated millions of demobilised troops into the civilian workforce.

Yet this is not the full story. Britain's first majority socialist government had rehabilitated a war-damaged country, but the causes of the country's relative economic decline and social stasis – antecedent to the war – remained unaddressed. The problems of British competitiveness were disguised by nationalisation and by the temporary debility of Germany and Japan. The antiquated structure of the British state also remained intact except for two reforms: the government abolished university seats in parliament (an anomaly which had effectively given graduates two votes) and it reduced from two years to one the power of the House of Lords to delay legislation.

In the 1950 general election, Labour was returned with only the slimmest of majorities. This was because of strong resentment that wartime austerity measures had been prolonged so far into peacetime. Five years after the war had ended wartime damage was still evident everywhere, shortages were endemic and rationing of essential foodstuffs still prevailed. The Conservatives had rebuilt their party and again become a formidable electoral force. There was also a concerted campaign by business interests against any further nationalisations. At the same time, the Berlin crisis of 1948–49 and the onset of the Korean War in 1950 greatly increased concern over a potential Soviet threat and served to discredit socialist ideas in general.

The Korean conflict also occasioned a damaging split in the government. In order to finance the British contribution to the war against North Korea, the Labour Chancellor of the Exchequer, Hugh Gaitskell, reluctantly imposed NHS prescription charges on false teeth and spectacles. To Bevan, this was a violation of the central principle on which the NHS had been created, and he and Harold Wilson resigned from the Cabinet. After narrowly losing a second general election in October 1951, Labour fell from office and Sir Winston Churchill, knighted for his wartime services, returned as prime minister.

The new Elizabethan age

The early 1950s presented the British with the appearance of a fresh and extremely propitious start. In 1952, Britain reaffirmed its intention to retain a place at the 'top table' in world affairs with the detonation of its first atomic bomb. The televised coronation of Elizabeth II in June 1953 prompted the heralding of a 'New Elizabethan Age', and the national sense of confidence and renewal was reinforced by a spate of internationally recognised British achievements. On the day of the Coronation, a team of Commonwealth mountaineers led by Sir John Hunt, became the first to reach the summit of Mount Everest. Later that year, Churchill received the Nobel Prize for Literature. Then, in 1954, the British athlete Roger Bannister became the first man to run the four-minute mile. In 1956, Calder Hall, the world's first nuclear power station, became operational, reviving nineteenth-century notions of British scientific leadership.

All this took place in the context of a general expansion in the world economy that created what the economist J K Galbraith called 'the affluent society'. In 1959, Prime Minister Harold Macmillan captured the new national mood. The phrase 'you've never had it so good', inaccurately attributed to him, nevertheless expressed the new experiences of the majority. A spectacular proliferation of consumer goods induced major social changes. The most important of these was the creation of a new individualism, as previously public and collective activities became private: television brought entertainment into the home and cinemas around the country began to close; domestic washing machines began to replace the commercial laundry; an increase in car ownership reduced the usage of buses and trains; and in the field of housing the proportion of owner-occupiers increased relative to tenants.

Critics of this period date from the 1950s the dissolution of communities and the rise of materialistic and consumerist attitudes. By contrast, others view the decade as a period of new-found freedoms, greater personal autonomy, increased personal comforts, and a decline in traditional and anachronistic class identities. What is certain is that the new affluence worked to the great political advantage of the Conservative Party, which remained in power from 1951 to 1964.

The formation of consensus

From the early 1950s, the leaderships of the two major parties appeared to converge ideologically. The similarities between the policies of the Conservative Chancellor of the Exchequer, R A Butler, and Gaitskell, his opposite number, gave rise to the term 'Butskellism'. In 1945, Churchill had warned that Labour's manifesto could only be implemented by a Gestapo. Yet, on their return to power, the Conservatives retained most of Labour's reforms and adopted Keynesian demand management as the basis of economic policy.

In many respects, this was not surprising. Before returning to the Conservative fold in the early 1920s, Churchill himself had served in the reforming Liberal administrations that had governed Britain before and during the First World War. His successors as Prime Minister, Anthony Eden (1955–57), Harold Macmillan (1957–63) and Sir Alec Douglas-Home, formerly Lord Home (1963–64), were patrician or 'One Nation' Tories of the nineteenth-century Disraelian variety. Their experience in the trenches in World War One and (in the case of the first two) their ideological debt to Churchill, inclined them to heal rather than deepen social divisions. The result was a substantial agreement between the Conservative and Labour parties on the mixed economy, the welfare state, progressive taxation, and, later on, corporatist economic management through a forum of government, employers and unions.

There was dissent from the consensus within both parties. A minority of Conservatives argued that 'One Nation' Toryism bore too close a resemblance to socialism, giving too much power to the state and undermining private enterprise. Labour, meanwhile, suffered deep ideological splits. Gaitskell, after he became party leader in 1955, contended that the major injustices of capitalism had been substantially eradicated by the Attlee governments. In *The Future of Socialism* (1956) Labour's Tony Crosland argued that capitalism had solved the problems of wealth creation: only those of redistribution remained. Consequently, class struggle was at an end, and nationalisation was no longer relevant. On the left, Bevan's supporters replied that the socialist project remained incomplete, and they called for the nationalisation of the 'commanding heights' of the economy in order to break the remnants of capitalist power. The two factions clashed in 1959 over Gaitskell's ultimately unsuccessful attempt to remove from the Labour Party's constitution its Clause IV commitment to public ownership. In one manifestation or another, this split between 'traditionalist' Bevanite democratic socialists and 'modernising' Gaitskellite social democrats was to hamstring the Labour Party into the late 1980s.

The search for a global role

For the most part, the Conservatives in the 1950s were divided not by ideology but by the uncertainty of Britain's post-colonial identity, as the British Empire continued to unravel. Britain's changing position in world affairs was soon put to the test in a crisis in the Middle East. In 1956, following nationalisation of the Suez Canal by Colonel Nasser, leader of the Egyptian government, Prime Minister Anthony Eden committed British troops to an Anglo-French-Israeli invasion of Egypt. Under threat of American economic sanctions, the operation was terminated, leaving both the canal nationalisation and Colonel Nasser in place. Eden resigned (ostensibly due to ill-health), and an acrimonious debate began within the Conservative Party over the managed decline of the British Empire. Like Labour's domestic policy differences, this too persisted through subsequent decades.

Macmillan, Eden's successor, was then confronted with the dilemma over relations with Europe that has run through British politics ever since. In 1957, the European Economic Community (EEC) was created, without the participation of the British: even after Suez, the country was not yet ready to redefine itself as a European regional power. The early 1960s vividly illustrated the country's foreign policy dilemma. In 1960, Britain had initiated the European Free Trade Association (EFTA) which, in contrast to the EEC, had no supranationalist political potential. Yet, in the following year, the government submitted Britain's first application to join the EEC. However, any notions that Britain had finally learned the lessons of Suez, and had become reconciled to a European future, were dispelled in 1962, when Macmillan negotiated the purchase of the Polaris nuclear weapons system from the Kennedy administration in Washington. Shortly afterwards, convinced that Britain would be a 'Trojan horse' for American influence in Europe, President Charles de Gaulle of France vetoed its application to join the EEC. Four years later he gave a second British application the same treatment.

Social changes

Affluence and the legacy of empire, the two dominant themes of the 1950s, together accounted for Britain's transformation into a multicultural society. Immigrants from Asia, Africa and the Caribbean were invited to Britain to make up the labour shortage caused by the economic boom. Arriving by invitation to fulfil a national need, the immigrants expected to be welcomed. They found that they were expected to take the jobs no one else wanted. At the same time, their rapid arrival in large numbers inevitably changed the character of the communities in which they settled. The result was white resentment that expressed itself in verbal racial abuse and formal acts of discrimination, with landlords refusing to rent property to black and Asian people and publicans refusing to serve people on racial grounds. In the summer of 1958, racial tension erupted into violence for the first time when whites physically attacked immigrants in Notting Hill, west London. There were other disturbances in Leeds and elsewhere. Against this background of rising tension, in 1961 parliament passed the Commonwealth Immigrants Act, which limited immigration by a quota system.

While the Conservatives were credited with much of the unprecedented rise in living standards between 1951 and 1964, they seemed increasingly unable to keep pace with the profound and rapid changes going on in British society. Not only did the new affluence stimulate a new individualism and consumerism, it also led to a questioning of many traditional values, particularly those relating to gender roles and sexual morality. A landmark event in this process of attitudinal change was the unsuccessful prosecution of Penguin Books in 1960 for the publication of D H Lawrence's *Lady Chatterley's Lover*. Around the same time, theatre and the cinema began to broach subjects previously considered taboo, such as racial prejudice, homosexuality and single parenthood.

The new affluence also gave unprecedented financial independence to youth. Young people became a significant economic market in their own right and, by the beginning of the 1960s, their new purchasing power was producing remarkable changes in the music and fashion industries. The Beatles rocketed, first to national and then to global fame, from their home town of Liverpool, and were soon followed by other innovative bands such as the Rolling Stones and The Who.

By this time, the Conservatives had come to be seen as representatives of an out-of-date and stuffy British Establishment of yesteryear. Much of this image was attributable to the aristocratic lifestyle and demeanour of the leaders, which made them easy prey for the first generation of television satirists on shows like *That Was the Week That Was*. The collision of the old Establishment and the new social mores was dramatically illustrated by a scandal of 1963, in which John Profumo, the Minister for War (as the Secretary for Defence was then known), was forced to resign after having misled the House of Commons about his relationship with prostitute Christine Keeler. Keeler had shared her favours with a Soviet Embassy attaché. This, coming after a lengthy series of spy scandals involving members of the British Establishment, further destabilised the Conservatives.

In the 1964 general election, Harold Wilson, who had succeeded Gaitskell as the leader of a now more united Labour Party, emulated the youthful appeal of the recently assassinated John Kennedy and associated Labour with the new youth culture. Wilson brilliantly positioned himself as a 'moderniser' promising national renewal. He was helped in this by the Conservatives, who had picked the hereditary peer Lord Home as Macmillan's successor the previous year. Despite Wilson's personal appeal, however, Labour came to power with a slim and vulnerable majority.

The 1960s: economic frustration and social reform

The incoming government sought to express the spirit of the times with an agenda of economic and social modernisation. Wilson had promised to renew the country's economic base 'in the white heat of the scientific revolution'. In reality, his economic agenda was frustrated by persistent inflation, an unfavourable balance of trade and government budget deficits. His Labour government responded with unsuccessful wage and price freezes, which brought it into conflict with its trade union base. Industrial disputes multiplied.

At first, the government believed in economic planning. A Department of Economic Affairs (DEA) was created for this purpose but proved ineffectual as it clashed repeatedly with the Treasury. Its ambitions for growth faltered as the economy remained sluggish and it was wound up in 1967. In 1969, concerned at the number of unofficial, or 'wildcat', strikes, Employment Secretary Barbara Castle produced *In Place of Strife*, legislative proposals to modernise industrial relations structures. Castle's initiative was defeated by union protest and by opposition from within the Cabinet. As a result, Labour was made to look divided, ineffectual and too closely allied to the unions.

Economic modernisation had proved a mirage but the government was more successful with social reform. In 1965, following a number of controversial executions, Britain finally abolished the death penalty. In 1967, private acts of homosexuality between consenting males over the age of twenty-one were legalised. The Labour majority in the Commons supported Liberal MP David Steel's bill to legalise abortion. In the same year, the government also liberalised the law on family planning, allowing local authorities to provide contraceptives and give advice on birth control. 1968 saw the abolition of theatre censorship. And, in 1969, divorce was made possible on the grounds of an irretrievable breakdown in the marriage.

In the late 1960s, thousands of Asians (ethnic Indians resident in East Africa) sought and were granted asylum in Britain in order to escape a brutal and racist campaign of 'Africanisation' in Kenya. Labour was perceived as favouring immigration, but public opinion was by now bitterly opposed, and the race issue was to be a major electoral factor in key marginal seats. In April 1968, the leading Conservative politician Enoch Powell made an incendiary speech in which he seemed to foresee the River Thames, like the Tiber, 'foaming with much blood' unless Britain halted, or even reversed, the process of non-white immigration. Powell was instantly sacked from the Shadow Cabinet by the Conservative Leader of the Opposition, Edward Heath. Nevertheless, against this background of rising racial tension, the Wilson government strengthened immigration controls in 1965 and again in 1968.

To some, the 1960s was an era of energy and progress, during which social bigotry and prejudice were successfully challenged by emancipatory social movements, led by students and youth, the result of which was a more tolerant and humane society. To others the 1960s inaugurated the 'permissive society', in which traditional values, public morality and the family were undermined by an irresponsibly libertine exhortation to 'do your own thing'. Disagreements over the 1960s continue to play a prominent part in the British national debate, on issues as diverse as welfare reform and architecture.

The consensus begins to crumble

The Conservatives came to power under Edward Heath in the general election of June 1970. The Heath years mark the twilight of the post-war consensus but also the dawning of a new age in British politics, as the country finally joined the EEC. Heath had long been positively committed to the European ideal and had been part of the negotiating team during Britain's first application to join. While many Conservatives saw Europe only as a pragmatic solution to the problems of the British economy, and others remained opposed, for Heath it was an opportunity to recast Britain in a new and more realistic role in the international community. In the absence of a French veto, Britain formally became a member of the EEC on 1st January 1973.

But Heath's success on the European front was not matched at home. He was plagued by domestic crises stemming from three sources: the diminishing returns on Britain's ageing coalfields; an antiquated and adversarial system of industrial relations; and the oil crisis occasioned by the Yom Kippur War in the Middle East in October 1973. These three factors were to become explosively interrelated and were eventually to bring his government down.

By the 1970s, Britain had been exploiting its coal resources for considerably longer than its major competitors. The more accessible coal having long been mined, the deeper coal reserves were becoming more expensive to extract. This accounted for a wave of pit closures under the Wilson government. By the early 1970s, the industry was in visible decline and the miners, traditionally the best-paid British workers, were falling in the industrial pay league. The result was a significant increase in militancy on the part of the National Union of Mineworkers (NUM). In the autumn of 1973, against the background of an energy crisis arising from the Arab-Israeli War, the NUM struck for a major pay increase. In response, the government eventually declared a state of emergency, and the country experienced its worst period of austerity since the war, with power-cuts and a three-day working week in industry. Confronted with a proposed escalation of strike action by the miners, Heath called an election in February 1974. The issue, he dramatically claimed, was 'Who is to govern Britain?'.

Though they polled more votes than Labour, the Conservatives lost ground and won fewer seats. They unsuccessfully sought a coalition agreement from Jeremy Thorpe's Liberals. When this failed, Wilson returned at the head of Britain's first minority government since 1929. This new Labour administration resolved the immediate crisis but was in a weak position to contend with its formidable challenges: a fall in industrial output; rising inflation; growing support for the nationalist parties in Wales and Scotland; increasing disturbances in Northern Ireland; and unresolved questions over Britain's membership in the EEC. That October, Wilson called a second general election, in which his government was returned but only with a highly vulnerable majority of three seats. Wilson himself remained at the helm until his surprise (and still largely mysterious) resignation in March 1976. Under his successor, James Callaghan, the government's majority was gradually eroded as a result of by-election defeats. From March 1977 it could survive only on the basis of a pact with the Liberal Party.

The corporatist experiment

The period 1974–79 represents the low point in the Labour Party's experience of office. Though the country was to enjoy lighter moments, such as the street party celebrations that marked the Queen's Silver Jubilee in 1977, on the whole the mid-to-late 1970s were characterised by economic crisis, bitter industrial conflict, violent racial tension, Northern Irish terrorism and renewed ideological polarisation in politics.

Initially, Labour's economic policy was a continuation – indeed a development – of its 1960s' interventionism and corporatism. A National Enterprise Board (NEB) was created to co-ordinate national industrial policy, and the government and the Trades Union Congress (TUC) concluded the 'Social Contract', by which the unions would exercise voluntary pay restraint in return for improvements in non-wage benefits, such as pensions and social services. By 1976, however, confronted by the persistence of 'stagflation' – the tendency of unemployment and inflation to rise simultaneously – the government abandoned Keynesian demand management. This historic shift was symbolised by Callaghan, waggishly described as the most conservative prime minister since Lord Salisbury!

The 'monetarist' theory that inflation could only be controlled by restrictions on the growth of the money supply became the basis of policy, and for the remainder of its term of office, the government sought to tackle inflation with expenditure cuts and public sector pay restraint. The result was a spate of strikes by public service workers in the early months of 1979, to which Callaghan himself gave the ostensibly Shakespearean label of 'the winter of discontent'. Images of these strikes, with uncollected refuse in the streets and, most grimly of all, the dead going unburied, were to haunt Labour for a decade and a half. Worse yet, the government also appeared divided at the highest levels over two key issues: the renegotiated terms for Britain's continued membership of the EEC (which were reaffirmed by popular referendum), and the creation of Scottish and Welsh parliaments (which were controversially voted down).

Dire recollections of these times have obscured from view some of Labour's successes. Once again, as in the 1960s, these tended to be in the area of social reform. The 1975 Sex Discrimination Act made it unlawful for employers to discriminate on the basis of gender. The following year, against the background of violent clashes between the anti–immigrant National Front and demonstrators organised in the Anti-Nazi League, the government also introduced a comprehensive Race Relations Act. Labour successfully delivered many aspects of the 'Social Contract', the most important provision being the introduction of the State Earnings-Related Pension Scheme (SERPS) for workers without occupational pensions. Nonetheless, the mid-to-late 1970s were bitter and miserable times for Britain, and an exhausted, divided and demoralised Labour Party limped into opposition, where it was to stay for eighteen years.

'Thatcherism'

In May 1979, Margaret Thatcher became Britain's first woman prime minister. A grocer's daughter who had read chemistry at Oxford and worked as a research scientist before qualifying at the English bar and entering parliament, she had successfully challenged Heath for the leadership of the Conservative Party in 1975. To Mrs Thatcher and her supporters on the party's right wing, the Tory establishment, with its inherently collectivist instincts, was an accomplice in the failings of the post-war economic and social settlement. The Thatcherites' alternative was a fusion of classical liberalism's emphasis on individual freedom, economic enterprise and minimal government, with traditional conservatism's belief in strong law and order and defence policies. During the eleven years of her premiership, Mrs Thatcher presided over changes in the country's economy and political culture that can only be termed revolutionary.

Once in power, the Conservatives rigorously pursued their ideological goals. They dismantled protectionism and industrial subsidies, aiming to invigorate the British economy by exposing it to international competition. They cut personal and corporate taxation and returned to the private sector key nationalised industries, such as the major public utilities (gas, electricity, telecommunications, and water), and the politically symbolic coal and steel industries. Working from monetarist theory, like its Labour predecessor, the government instituted major cuts in public spending and suppressed inflation with a regime of high interest rates. The resultant massive unemployment undermined the government's opponents in the trade union movement. The weakened unions were also the targets of a legislative programme designed to further constrain their power. 'Secondary' picketing (of workplaces not party to an original dispute) was made illegal, and pre-strike ballots, along with ballots for union executive posts and unions' political funds (used mostly to bankroll the Labour Party), became compulsory.

The government's confrontation with the unions reached a climax in the miners' strike of 1984–85. The militant miners' leader Arthur Scargill called the strike in protest against a government pit closure programme. Nottinghamshire miners, working in more profitable pits not earmarked for closure, refused to join the strike and, protesting against Scargill's autocratic leadership of the NUM, broke away to form a separate union. The year-long dispute was a bitter one: Mrs Thatcher denounced the miners as 'the enemy within'; there were pitched battles between police and pickets; and soup kitchens returned to mining communities for the first time since the 1930s. The comprehensive defeat of the miners signalled Britain's impending transition to a post-industrial service economy and marked the end of industrial militancy as a force in British politics. It also revealed radical Thatcherism's break with the national penchant for continuity and compromise: the decline of the British coal industry was forced, rather than managed, change.

The Conservatives' radical economic project had set in motion a social revolution that remains Thatcherism's most enduring legacy. The sale of shares in privatised industries and of local authority housing, along with the proliferation of private pensions and health insurance schemes, seemed to herald the arrival of a culture of American-style popular capitalism, which had previously failed to take root in Britain. 'Essex Man' emerged as the symbol of those upwardly mobile skilled workers who, previously loyal to Labour, began in the mid-1980s to transfer their political allegiance to the Conservatives.

At the same time, those parts of the UK traditionally dependent upon heavy industry went into sharp decline. In the de-industrialised inner cities, including London, youth unemployment increased crime rates and exacerbated racial antagonisms, resulting in riots in 1981 and again in 1985. Renewed social polarisation led some critics of the Thatcher governments to accuse them of creating a society two-thirds affluent and one-third excluded.

A further social consequence of Thatcherite economic philosophy was a decline in social deference. Though the Conservatives were historically the party of traditional élites and established institutions, the Thatcher government's economic radicalism brought them into conflict with major bastions of conservative opinion. Opposition in the House of Lords to aspects of government policy was often simply faced down. Oxford University denied the prime minister an honorary degree in protest against her education cuts. Senior Anglican clergy inveighed against government's alleged indifference to inner-city poverty, but their remarks were brusquely discounted by ministers, even construed as 'Marxism'. One of Mrs Thatcher's leading lieutenants, Norman Tebbitt, even went so far as to rebuff the Prince of Wales for his opinions on youth unemployment, dismissing him as 'a forty-year-old man who had never had a job'! In subjecting all institutions and practices to tests of utility, efficiency and profitability, the Thatcherites did more to undermine the social standing of the British establishment than the political left had achieved in the previous half century. Radicalism had arrived but from the right rather than from the left.

Thatcherism on the world stage

Mrs Thatcher frequently laid claim, with some justice, to having pioneered an international free market revolution that would eventually convert even her ideological opponents. She was a close political soul-mate of US President Ronald Reagan, and during her term of office the Anglo-American 'special relationship' was renewed. Britain became a stalwart ally of the United States in the revived Cold War of the early 1980s, and Mrs Thatcher agreed to the stationing of American Cruise and Pershing missiles in Britain. To the Soviets she was the 'iron lady', a sobriquet she accepted with pride.

Within the European Community (EC, as it was known from 1986), the Conservatives secured a reduction in Britain's disproportionate budgetary contribution and enthusiastically supported moves to complete the internal free market. At the same time, Mrs Thatcher adopted a Gaullist resistance to political integration, insisting that the Community should remain an international forum and a free trade area, and not develop towards a 'superstate'. She was unpopular with EC heads of government and known to the French as 'Madame Non'.

Yet much of her reputation as a strong leader derives from her handling of the crisis in the South Atlantic. In April 1982, the military junta in Argentina invaded the Falkland Islands, and a British taskforce was dispatched to recover the territory. The ensuing war enjoyed massive public support, though there was some controversy over the sinking of the *General Belgrano* – an Argentinian battle cruiser that was actually sailing away from the Falklands – and also over the jingoistic war coverage offered by tabloids such as *The Sun*. The islands were recaptured that June, but at the cost of 225 British and 750 Argentinian lives.

Chaos on the left

Mrs Thatcher's re-election in 1983, with a vastly increased majority, was made possible not only by the Falklands victory but by the implosion of the British left. Led by Michael Foot in Opposition, the Labour Party had immersed itself in a bitter ideological civil war. There was a spectacular resurgence of the party's socialist left, under the leadership of the radical parliamentarian Tony Benn. In response, leading figures on Labour's right wing broke away to form a new force, the Social Democratic Party (SDP). The SDP entered into an electoral pact with the Liberals, and for the first time since the war there seemed to be a realistic prospect of a permanent third force in British politics. Together the parties claimed more than a quarter of the popular vote in 1983 but thereafter failed to make a breakthrough. Meanwhile, a deeply divided Labour Party committed itself equivocally to further nationalisations, withdrawal from the European Community, and unilateral nuclear disarmament. One senior Labour politician described the party's 1983 election manifesto as 'the longest suicide note in history'.

Foot was succeeded as leader by the Welsh socialist Neil Kinnock, who set about modernising Labour's image and taking the party closer to the political centre. Left-wing infiltrationists were expelled, and electorally unpopular policies on Europe, nuclear weapons and nationalisation were progressively jettisoned. Labour consequently made steady electoral progress in the 1987 and 1992 elections, but still failed to oust the Conservatives. Under Kinnock, Labour eclipsed the SDP, though only by adopting most of their policy platform. In 1988, the SDP entered into an initially awkward merger with their Liberal allies, and eventually the Liberal Democrats emerged under the leadership of Paddy Ashdown.

The Conservatives in decline (1990–97)

The unravelling of the Conservative Party began shortly after Mrs Thatcher's third successive electoral triumph in 1987. That October, a major stock market crash brought to an end the mid-1980s boom and undermined public confidence in the magic of the market. Furthermore, by the late 1980s, an electorate that had rewarded the tax-cutting policies of the Conservatives began to express concern at their neglect of the social services, especially health and education.

During her first administration, Mrs Thatcher had gradually replaced patrician Tory members of her cabinet with her supporters from the radical right. Over time, concern grew within the Conservative Party that the prime minister and her most senior colleagues were out of touch with mainstream opinion. The government's determined implementation of the community charge only strengthened this view. The community charge was a flat-rate local government tax levied on a per capita basis, and it replaced a property tax known as the rating system or 'rates'. Widely referred to as the 'poll tax', the new levy was regressive, deeply unpopular and led to a riot in central London in March 1990. At the same time, Britain was increasingly isolated in a European Community that was progressing towards greater economic and political integration. At home and abroad, Mrs Thatcher's abrasive leadership style had become an electoral issue. Taken in tandem, these factors created a political crisis that culminated in her downfall.

In November 1990, Sir Geoffrey Howe, formerly a staunch Thatcher loyalist, resigned as Foreign Secretary and, in a remarkable speech to the House of Commons, denounced what he claimed was the authoritarian leadership style of the prime minister. Later in the same month, Michael Heseltine, a Tory moderate, mounted a challenge for the party leadership, and Mrs Thatcher withdrew her candidature after a disappointing performance in the first round of voting. The Chancellor of the Exchequer, John Major, entered the contest in the second round and emerged as the surprise winner.

John Major was relatively unknown and, in stark contrast to his predecessor, lacked personal charisma. However, he defied the predictions of pollsters by leading the Conservatives to a fourth consecutive election victory in 1992. His handling of the Gulf War the previous year had earned him respect and credibility, and the voters were as yet unconvinced either by Kinnock's reformed Labour Party or indeed by Kinnock himself.

But the remaining five years of Major's premiership were strained and challenging. His declared aims were the creation of a 'classless society' and a 'country at ease with itself', but he presided over a nation in the grip of a malaise. In politics, British institutions appeared to be decaying. Adultery and divorce stripped the royals of their mystique and helped to bring the monarchy under financial scrutiny. There were several high-profile corruption scandals, including one where MPs accepted cash payments for asking parliamentary questions on behalf of business interests. The judicial system had been damaged in recent years by a series of miscarriages of justice, particularly in cases relating to Northern Ireland. Public concern was also growing over journalistic ethics and tabloid invasions of privacy. In the economic sphere, the government's standing in the opinion polls never recovered from the currency crisis of September 1992, when sterling fell out of the European Community's Exchange Rate Mechanism (ERM), an attempt to maintain a system of fixed exchange rates.

The government's efforts to regain public confidence were severely undermined by deep and public rifts within the Conservative Party over relations with Europe. Despite the opt-outs and safeguards negotiated by Major at the 1991 Maastricht conference on European integration, the 'Euro-sceptic' wing of the party, which included members of the cabinet, continued to view what was now the European Union (EU) as a threat to British sovereignty and to the free enterprise achievements of the Thatcher years. Indeed the government as a whole refused to join most EU countries in implementing the *Social Chapter* and projected common currency agreed at Maastricht. To the voters, the government appeared to be a spent and divided force. After eighteen years of Conservative rule, the country was at last ready to elect a Labour government – but one radically different from any Labour government in the past.

New Labour, New Britain?

On 1st May 1997, the Conservatives went into electoral meltdown and Tony Blair's Labour Party was elected with an unprecedented parliamentary majority of 179. This Labour victory was the result of Conservative exhaustion and fifteen years of concerted Labour rapprochement with the electorate after the fiasco of 1983. In 1992, John Smith, an experienced and highly respected Scottish barrister, had become Labour leader. Upon Smith's untimely death in 1994, the leadership passed to Blair, a zealous party reformer who aimed to reinvent Labour in recognition of the permanent realities of the 'Thatcher Revolution'. The Clause IV commitment to public ownership was this time removed from the Labour constitution, and the party leadership distanced itself from the trade unions. Inspired by President Clinton and the New Democrats in the US, 'New Labour' declared itself in favour of the enterprise culture and the extension of its benefits to those who had been left behind in the 1980s. It also set itself the task of modernising the British state apparatus and ending what it perceived as Britain's isolation in Europe.

Once elected, the Blair government moved with speed and resolution on its political priorities. In a surprise move, the new Chancellor of the Exchequer, Gordon Brown, gave the Bank of England independent control over interest rates. In combination with an election pledge to stick to Conservative spending limits for the first two years, this confirmed the government's post-socialist financial orthodoxy. The government's left-wing supporters were kept on board with a statutory minimum wage, the promise of legislation enforcing union recognition and a radical package of constitutional decentralisation. Referenda in Scotland and Wales produced positive votes for national assemblies in those countries (indeed in Scotland's case a parliament). Building on solid work by John Major, the Blair government also secured a promising Ulster peace agreement and held peaceful elections for a revived Northern Ireland assembly. Further anticipated constitutional reforms include the removal of hereditary peers' voting rights in the House of Lords, electoral reform and the incorporation of the European Convention on Human Rights into British law.

In Europe, habitual British recalcitrance was tempered by a more conciliatory tone, and the government indicated support in principle for British participation in a single currency. At the same time, Blair made clear his reservations about the European (interventionist) model of political economy and pressed for greater labour market flexibility within the EU. Britain's unwavering support for controversial aspects of US foreign policy, especially in the Middle East, caused tensions with some of Britain's EU partners.

Culturally, Blair's 'Cool Britannia' project was devised as an attempt to modernise the country's image by emphasising its strengths in popular entertainment and fashion, while downplaying its worthier but more staid associations with pageantry and high culture. To this end, Blair and his colleagues have openly courted the support of pop stars, film, television and sports personalities. The prime minister even encouraged the monarchy to relaunch itself in the wake of the Royal Family's apparent failure to comprehend the outpouring of national grief which followed the death of Princess Diana in September 1997.

Conclusion

Britain is an instinctively traditionalist country that, especially since the Second World War, has been exposed to the de-traditionalising forces of a rapidly changing world, particularly in the inter-related areas of technological change and global economic competition. The post-war social democratic consensus, which endured until the mid-1970s, was remarkably successful in maintaining living standards and social cohesion as the country entered its post-imperial era of relative decline. But the consensus years failed to address, and often reaffirmed, important rigidities and anachronisms in the British cultural disposition: class antagonism and social immobility; an imperial mindset in foreign affairs; an industrial and technological complacency inherited from the Industrial Revolution; and an archaic and overly centralised state apparatus.

The 'Thatcher Revolution' was a radical and purposeful assault on some of these problems. Protectionism and industrial subsidies were ended, and the British economy became leaner and fitter. In its promotion of meritocracy, Thatcherism also subverted traditional élites and created a culture of ambition and enterprise. But all this was achieved at the cost of painful social dislocations and divisions, to which the Thatcherites often responded with an authoritarianism that worsened Britain's democratic deficit. As the century drew to a close, Britain, like other economically advanced polities around the world, was trying to square economic innovation with social stability. It was also reforming its antiquated constitution. However, Britain is still not yet reconciled to a European identity, and its position as a permanent member of the UN Security Council, together with its close alliance with the US, continue to distract the country's attention away from present challenges and towards its imperial past. Nonetheless, even if Britain has still some way to go in its task of modernisation it seems, over the final two decades of the last century, to have cast off its acceptance of managed decline.

Further reading

Childs, David, *Britain Since 1939: Progress and Decline*, Macmillan, London, 1995.

Thomson, David, *England in the Twentieth Century, 1914–63*, Penguin, Harmondsworth, 1965.

4
Social Trends in Britain Today
Karen Kleeh-Tolley

Introduction

An examination of any society shows us a common characteristic: an unequal distribution of rewards. These rewards may be economic and material, political, social and cultural, or psychological. From a sociological perspective, what is interesting about the unequal distribution of rewards in any society is its non-random nature. Members of certain social groups seem to be persistently privileged or disadvantaged. Such patterns of social inequality suggest that there are systematic social forces shaping the allocation of societal rewards. The presence of patterns of social inequality gives rise to a number of questions about how rewards come to be distributed in a society.

The first, and most obvious, question is *who gets what*? That is, how are different social groups, and the individuals who comprise those groups, arranged in a societal reward hierarchy? The second question concerns the *consequences* of a particular distribution of rewards for individuals, social groups, and larger society. In other words, in what ways does an unequal distribution of rewards affect both the 'quantity' and 'quality' of life for members of a society, and what does this mean for the well-being of the society as a whole? A third question is *why are societal rewards arranged as they are*? In particular, what role do societal arrangements, such as social institutions, play in the distribution of rewards within a society? And, finally, *how much mobility exists within the reward hierarchy*?

In exploring these questions as they relate to contemporary British society, class, gender, race, and ethnicity are of particular importance because these are major dimensions of social inequality. Class position, gender, and racial and ethnic identity affect how people live their lives: their access to goods and services, their leisure pursuits and lifestyles, their health and life-expectancy, their housing, and their educational and employment opportunities and outcomes. Class position, gender, and racial and ethnic identities even influence aspirations, self-identity, feelings of self-worth, and the ways in which individuals and social groups are perceived and valued by other members of society.

Dimensions and consequences of inequality in Britain today

Overall, Britain leads Europe, the USA, Australia, Japan, and Canada in rising inequality (Spybey, 1997). In fact, the British economy has declined more than nearly any other economically comparable nation. When we examine the first two questions raised at the beginning of this chapter, we begin to see how privilege and disadvantage are arranged in Britain today and what consequences this arrangement has. An unequal distribution of societal rewards, resources, and opportunities affects the life-chances of every member of society. It means that some members of society have every opportunity to realise their full potential, while others struggle just to subsist.

Class: income, wealth, and life-chances

Social classes are groups of people that share similar economic positions in terms of income and wealth. While we may like to believe that class position is no longer a relevant factor in the lives of people, in reality class is important because income and wealth are the means by which people purchase their life-chances. When the *Titanic* sank in 1912, fifteen hundred lives were lost. However, social class was a major determinant of who lived and who died. Of the female passengers travelling first class, only three per cent were lost, while sixteen per cent of females travelling second class and forty-five per cent of females travelling third class perished (Thio, 1989). Income and wealth bring access to food, shelter, education, medical care, and power and influence. Social class affects both the 'quantity' and 'quality' of life.

Income is earned in the form of wages, salaries, and returns on investments. In Britain, most people rely on wages and salaries for their income, so the occupational structure is the most significant means by which people access goods, services, resources, status, and self-esteem. The occupational structure and an individual's occupation are important because of the differential value placed on occupations. The result is different levels of material rewards and status connected to occupations. This relationship between income, status, and occupations is demonstrated in governmental attempts to quantify social classes in Britain. Occupations, according to their similarity of qualifications and skills, have been equated with social class by the Registrar General, as indicated in Table 4.1.

There are a number of problems with this classification scheme because it tends to hide the extent of income inequality. For example, by basing social class position on occupation, some groups are left out of these classification schemes, such as the wealthy who may not have occupations. Nor do these scales take into account differences in income and status within each occupational group. Differences in income and status between hairdressers and police officers (class III) or teachers, nurses, and MPs (class II) are significant.

Table 4.1 The Registrar General's Scale of Social Classes

	Social class	Examples of occupations
I	Professional (upper middle class)	Accountants, solicitors, doctors, architects
II	Intermediate (middle class)	Nurses, teachers, managers, MPs
III	Skilled non-manual (lower middle class)	Clerical workers, sales assistants, estate agents
III	Skilled manual (upper working class)	Electricians, bricklayers, hairdressers, police officers
IV	Semi-skilled manual (semi-skilled working class)	Postal workers, farm workers, telephone operators
V	Unskilled manual (lower working class)	Cleaners, driver's mate, labourer

The Registrar General's system of classification was replaced in 1998 by the National Statistics Socio-economic Classification (NS SEC) as in Table 4.2.

Table 4.2 National Statistics Socio-economic Classification (NS SEC)

1. Higher managerial and professional occupations
   1.1 Higher managerial and managers in larger organisations
   1.2 Higher professionals
2. Lower managerial and professional occupations
3. Intermediate occupations
4. Small employers and own account workers
5. Lower supervisory, craft and related occupations
6. Semi-routine occupations
7. Routine occupations
An additional category for those who have never been in the paid work force and for the long-term unemployed will be added as needed when compiling government statistics.

This new system is also based on occupation. It identifies class position, not with skill, but with conditions and relations of employment including such factors as salary scales, possibilities for promotion, sick pay, and discretionary power of use of time and task planning. However, even this new scheme does not give an accurate picture of the distribution of income in Britain, and we need to look beyond broad occupational classifications that tend to obscure real differences in class and status positions (Table 4.3).

These figures tell us that of all the income earned in Britain in 1994/5, forty-three per cent was earned by only twenty per cent of the population. That is, nearly one-half of the income earned in Britain during this period was shared among only one-fifth of the population, while the same size group, the poorest fifth of the population, shared among itself only 6.3 per cent of total earned income. Another way to understand these data is to realise that the income, including unearned income, received by the richest fifth of the population is more than that of the bottom three groups combined. These data also show that the richest fifth of the British population increased its share of total earned income during the 1980s and 1990s, while all other groups have lost ground. And those groups with the least have lost the most.

Table 4.3 Distribution of income by fifths of population, United Kingdom, 1979–1994/5

	1979 %	1994/5 %
Richest fifth	35.0	43.0
Fourth fifth	23.0	22.0
Middle fifth	18.0	17.0
Second fifth	14.4	11.7
Poorest fifth	9.6	6.3

Source: *Households Below Average Income: A Statistical Analysis 1979–1994/5,* Department of Social Security, 1997

Wealth can be defined as assets that can be sold or invested to benefit the owner. Wealth brings power for several reasons. Firstly, the ownership of wealth means it is not necessary to rely on others for income so that the occupational structure becomes essentially meaningless as the major mechanism for purchasing life-chances. Secondly, wealth generates income and more wealth. And finally, wealth can be transferred from one generation to the next, giving new generations a 'head-start' on their access to life-chances. Wealth is more difficult to measure than income, and data often underestimate the true extent of inequalities in wealth holdings. The Inland Revenue compiles official statistics on wealth, and the wealthy have an interest in hiding their worth to avoid taxes. Nevertheless, the data show us (Table 4.4) that while income is unequally distributed, wealth in Britain is much more unequally distributed.

Table 4.4 Distribution of wealth for adults aged eighteen and over, United Kingdom, 1979–1994

	1979 %	1994/5 %
Most wealthy 1 per cent	21.0	19.0
Most wealthy 5 per cent	38.0	38.0
Most wealthy 10 per cent	50.0	51.0
Most wealthy 25 per cent	71.0	73.0
Most wealthy 50 per cent	92.0	93.0

Source: *Households Below Average Income: A Statistical Analysis 1979–1994/5,* Department of Social Security, 1997

What this table shows is that half the population of Britain owns ninety-three per cent of all the wealth, while the other half of the population shares among itself only seven per cent of the wealth. A quarter of the population owns nearly three-quarters of all wealth.

Wealth in Britain has traditionally been associated with the aristocracy, a hereditary and exclusive élite whose privilege and power were based on property and title. The most notable member of this aristocracy is the Queen, with a fortune worth over £6.7 billion (Devine, 1997). Yet, much aristocratic wealth and privilege has been steadily eroded during this century, and the aristocratic élite has gradually been replaced by an upper class of capitalists with 'gentlemanly characteristics' who now dominate Britain financially and politically (McDonough, 1997). A total of seventy-eight individuals, including Richard Branson (Virgin) and Anita Roddick (The Body Shop), have fortunes over £100 million, while 118 families are worth more than £50 million and 192 families have fortunes of more than £20 million (Devine, 1997), including Paul McCartney, worth an estimated £42 million (Browne, 1998). The relatively new British capitalist élite, like the aristocracy, is based on individuals with similar backgrounds and close social contacts (McDonough, 1997). Power is in the family and its connections, and inheritance is the most important mechanism by which wealth is transmitted from generation to generation (Devine, 1998). For example, over sixty per cent of the 500 richest people in Britain inherited their wealth, and forty-five per cent of bank directors with a listing in *Who's Who* have fathers with a previous entry (McDonough, 1997).

Wealth confers privilege, and the wealthy enjoy an exclusive lifestyle that they demonstrate through the possession of multiple properties and art treasures as well as particular leisure activities such as hunting, polo, breeding horses, and yachting. Private education at Eton, Harrow, Rugby, and Winchester is usually followed by higher education at Cambridge and Oxford and membership in the 'gentlemen's clubs' (Whites, Jockey Club, and the Garrick). These lifestyle characteristics and institutional mechanisms play a central role in the maintenance of kinship and social exclusivity and networking among the wealthy (Devine, 1998; McDonough, 1997). However, wealth alone is not sufficient for admittance to this exclusive group. Much of British business is in the hands of family-run companies established over a hundred years ago. The Anita Roddicks and Richard Bransons of British business, who were not born wealthy, are not automatically embraced socially by the established capitalist élite. The British upper class has the power to confer social, economic, and political advantages – or withhold them because of inappropriate accent or educational pedigree – in order to maintain its privilege.

The impact of race and ethnicity on life-chances

Data on income and wealth distributions give an overall picture of the unequal distribution of life-chances in Britain, but the answer to the question of who gets what is more complicated. For example, look at the distribution of income by racial and ethnic groups in Britain shown in Table 4.5.

Table 4.5 Distribution of equivalised disposable income by ethnic group, 1995/6

	Bottom fifth %	Top four-fifths %
Pakistani/Bangladeshi	66.0	34.0
Black	30.0	71.0
Indian	26.0	74.0
White	19.0	81.0
Other ethnic groups	27.0	73.0

Source: *Social Trends 28*, HMSO, 1998

We can see from this table that blacks are one-and-a-half times more likely to find themselves in the bottom income quintile than whites, while Pakistanis and Bangladeshis are nearly three-and-a-half times more likely than whites to be in the lowest income quintile. That is, of the total black population in Britain, thirty per cent are found in the lowest income quintile; of the total Pakistani and Bangladeshi population, sixty-six per cent are in the bottom income quintile. Since blacks comprise only 1.5 per cent of the population of Britain, Indians 1.6 per cent, and Pakistanis and Bangladeshis only 2.6 per cent (*Labour Force Survey*, 1996), it is clear that these groups are disproportionately represented among Britain's poor.

Members of racial and ethnic minorities in Britain are under-represented in managerial and professional occupations and in government. They are more likely than whites to work long and unsociable hours in semi-skilled or unskilled occupations, and more likely to be unemployed. The unemployment rate for members of racial and ethnic minorities has been about twice that for whites since 1984. Youth unemployment rates for those sixteen-to-twenty-four years old show that nearly forty per cent of young blacks, thirty-one per cent of young Bangladeshis and Pakistanis, and twenty-five per cent of young Indians are unemployed, compared to nineteen per cent of young whites (*Social Trends 28*, 1998). While the Race Relations Act of 1965 made it illegal to discriminate in employment and housing on the basis of race or ethnicity, there is considerable evidence of continued discrimination. In fact, complaints of racial discrimination to the Commission for Racial Equality, created in 1976, have doubled in the past decade.

Gender and inequality

Women are more likely than men to experience low income and its consequences. In 1997, approximately sixty per cent of those receiving income support benefits were women. In 1994, sixty-four per cent of low paid workers in Britain were women. The Council of Europe's decency threshold defines low pay and in 1994 this threshold was £221.50 per week or £5.88 per hour. Britain's new minimum wage was introduced in 1999 at £3.60 an hour (£3.20 for those under twenty-one years of age), considerably below the threshold set by the Council of Europe. There is a strong relationship between low pay and part-time work. In 1994, 4.83 million women were employed part-time and seventy-seven per cent of them were low paid (Oppenheim and Harker, 1996). Women are also more likely than men to work a second job. Yet in all categories of occupations, women's earnings are less than men's (*Social Trends 28*, 1998). Women's full-time equivalent gross weekly earnings are seventy-two per cent of men's earnings. The table below from the *New Review of the Low Pay Unit* (1996) illustrates pay differentials.

Not only are women in Britain paid less than men for equivalent work, they are also disproportionately under-represented in top professional jobs. For example, women comprise only nine per cent of senior civil servants, eight per cent of high court judges, eighteen per cent of barristers, four per cent of directors and senior managers in the top 2,300 British companies, seven per cent of university professors, and six per cent of university chancellors and vice-chancellors (*Labour Research*, 1997).

While women receive less for the work they do, they are at the same time more likely than men to be 'lone' parents, responsible for raising children on their own. In fact, nine out of ten lone parents in Britain are women (Oppenheim and Harker, 1996). The demands of sole responsibility for children further limit women's employment options and earning potential. And while women as a group tend to be economically disadvantaged, these problems are exacerbated for women who belong to racial and ethnic minorities (Table 4.6).

Table 4.6

	Men £ per week	Women £ per week
The best paid jobs		
Company finance manager	935.80	605.60
Medical practitioner	852.70	706.90
Investment analyst	790.90	464.50
Legal professional	727.30	517.30
The worst paid jobs		
Shelf filler	206.80	161.40
Cleaner	201.50	166.10
Bar staff	186.60	152.60
Laundry worker	182.90	162.30
Catering assistant	176.10	162.90
Kitchen hand	164.40	142.90

Social class and health inequalities

In spite of Britain's National Health Service and welfare state, there remains a close correlation between health and life-expectancy on one hand, and social class on the other. Both the 'quantity' and 'quality' of health are significantly affected by social class position. For example, the mortality rate for those in the Registrar General's social class V (unskilled manual workers) is twice that of social class I (professional), and those from class I live, on average, seven years longer than those in class V. Those in social class V are much more likely to die from injuries and poisoning, respiratory diseases, heart and circulatory diseases, cancer, and cerebrovascular diseases than those in social class I. The infant mortality rate is twice as high among those born into social class V than those born into social class I. Twice as many children from class V die before the age of five than children from class I (*Population Trends 80*, 1995).

There are a number of factors associated with low income that explain why the poor and working class suffer from greater ill-health. For example, lower income means poorer diets and housing, overcrowded and polluted living environments, and greater demand on limited and overextended community services and resources, including healthcare services. In addition to living conditions, conditions of work also place these groups at greater risk for health problems. Accidents and industrial diseases, longer working hours, overtime, multiple jobs, shift-work, lack of paid holidays, lack of paid personal time, and chronic and periodic unemployment are characteristic of the working conditions of the poor and working class. Stress-related illnesses brought about by economic uncertainty and the material and psychological conditions of poverty are greater among the poor and working class.

Poverty in Britain today

Poverty is an economic condition, but it is also more than that. While the lives of the poor are regularly and severely constrained by their lack of social, political, and economic resources, the conditions of poverty also affect their feelings of self-worth, aspirations, and expectations.

In Britain today, approximately thirty-five per cent of children are living in, or on the margins, of poverty. In fact, more children in Britain live in poverty than in any other European nation. One in ten children under the age of five in low-income families goes hungry at least once a month. In the population as a whole, approximately thirty-two per cent of Britons live in, or on the margins of, poverty (*Households Below Average Income: A Statistical Analysis*, 1997). One in five poor parents go without food regularly in order to feed their children. Lone parents comprise approximately twenty per cent of Britain's poor. Most lone parents are women who, as noted above, receive lower pay than men. To compound this, lack of affordable childcare means that work is often not possible and when it is, part-time work, which itself is lower paid, is the only option. Nearly twenty-five per cent of those in or near poverty in Britain today are the elderly who rely on state pensions. Since women live longer than men, they are disproportionately represented among the elderly poor because they are less likely to receive occupational pensions from employment and less likely to have savings to augment their standard of living. And while we often associate poverty with an unwillingness to work, one-third of those living in poverty in Britain are employed, working long hours for low pay.

Among the necessities they felt no-one should have to go without, two-thirds of the British public included items such as beds for everyone in the home, a refrigerator, self-contained and damp-free housing, a warm coat, three meals a day for children and two for adults, fresh fruit, toys for children, two pairs of shoes, enough money for celebrations on special occasions, a washing machine, extra-curricular activities for children, and regular savings of £10 a month. However, approximately twenty per cent of the British population, or 11 million people, lack three or more of these 'essentials': 7 million people do not have adequate clothing, 10 million people lack adequate housing, 5 million people lack adequate food, 2.5 million children do without enough food, lack toys, and cannot participate in extra-curricular activities because of financial constraints (Browne, 1998).

Regional inequality

Inequalities in Britain exist not only between groups of people but also between different geographical regions. Before World War Two, certain regions were defined by their dependence on particular industries: coal and steel in south

Table 4.7 1997 United Kingdom unemployment rate by region

	%
United Kingdom	7.1
England	6.9
North East	9.8
North West	6.3
Merseyside	9.6
Yorkshire and Humberside	8.1
East Midlands	6.3
West Midlands	6.8
East	5.9
London	9.1
South East (excluding London)	5.2
South West	5.2
Wales	8.4
Scotland	8.5
Northern Ireland	7.5

Source: *Social Trends 28,* HMSO, 1998

Wales and central Scotland, cotton textiles in the north-west of England, woollen industries in Yorkshire, and the automobile industry in central England. However, with the shift away from an industrial economy, regions that relied on mining or manufacturing have suffered economic decline. In addition, in the 1960s and 1970s employers began to locate outside the major industrial areas, taking jobs with them. There has traditionally been a north-south economic and status divide in England, with the southern part of the country generally more affluent than the north. There is also an economic difference between England on the one hand and Scotland, Wales, and Northern Ireland on the other. An example of regional inequalities in Britain is demonstrated in the unemployment rates, indicating regional differentials that persist even in times of falling unemployment (Table 4.7).

Institutional arrangements and inequality in Britain today

Individuals do not live their lives in a vacuum. Rather, they exist in a world in which social institutions play a fundamental role in structuring nearly all aspects of their lives. This includes the distribution of opportunities and rewards. Three such institutions are education, the occupational structure, and healthcare.

Education

Until the end of World War Two, free and compulsory elementary education was available to British children only up to the age of fourteen. Education beyond that age was private and fee-paying, so that education and its subsequent occupational opportunities were clearly allocated along the lines of social class and ability to pay. In 1944, the 'Butler' Education Act initiated a major reorganisation of education. The philosophy behind the Butler Act was that free education should be available to all children based on merit and ability, not income. Children attended primary school from ages five to eleven and then compulsory secondary school. Secondary school was divided into three separate and distinctly different types, each designed to provide particular kinds of education. Grammar schools provided academic courses of study, technical schools trained children for occupations such as engineering, and secondary modern schools gave children a general education aimed at lower ability students. The results on a standardised examination called the 11-Plus, taken at the end of the primary school years, determined which of the three types of secondary school a child would attend. Approximately fifteen per cent of children passed the 11-Plus and went on to grammar schools, where they were given the opportunity to sit further examinations, preparatory to higher education and higher-level white collar careers and professions. Most children, about seventy per cent of them, failed the 11-Plus and were placed in secondary modern schools, finishing their formal education at the age of fifteen.

While the intent was to provide each child with an education suited to abilities, it became clear that there was a class bias to 11-Plus examination results. Middle-class children were much more likely than the children of the poor and working class to pass the examination and go on to grammar school. While the intent of the Butler Act was to provide education based on merit and ability, the system that evolved as a result actually reinforced existing class divisions. In the 1960s, in an attempt to address this problem and provide equality of opportunity in education, comprehensive secondary schools were introduced. In this system, all children attend the same type of school, where they may be streamed according to performance and share the same potential opportunities. The philosophy behind this system is to provide flexibility to meet children's differing and changing abilities, aptitudes, and interests.

However, even in an educational system designed to provide equality of opportunity, there are significantly different educational outcomes according to social class. Poor and working-class children are disproportionately under-represented in higher education. For example, nearly three-quarters of university students are middle class (*UCAS Annual Report*, 1996). Reasons why poor and working-class children underachieve in school are complex. Certainly home environment plays a role, but the curriculum of the formal system of education itself continues to disadvantage poor and working-class children since it emphasises the cultural capital (Bourdieu and Passeron, 1977) and elaborated language codes (Bernstein, 1973) of the white middle class. In other words, the curriculum of the classroom reflects a world and experiences unfamiliar to poor and working-class children. Their inability to understand and articulate the cultural 'language' of the classroom results in poor educational performance and outcomes. This problem is much worse for children who are members of racial and ethnic minorities. Location is also important to the quality of education, and schools located in poor and working-class areas are characterised by poorer physical facilities, overcrowding, and greater demands on limited resources. However, in addition to the state-funded system of education, there remains a tradition of private, independent, fee-paying schools where the wealthy can purchase educational and career networking opportunities for their children. Only about five per cent of British children attend such schools, yet they ultimately comprise over fifty per cent of places at Oxford and Cambridge (McDonough, 1997).

The changing occupational structure

Most people in Britain rely on income earned through work to purchase their life-chances. Under a capitalist form of economic organisation, the way in which work is organised, what kinds of jobs are available, and what they are worth in the market result from the drive for maximum profit. The formal system of education trains future workers to take their places in the occupational structure and from childhood we are socialised to participate in the workforce. Even childhood play is often the acting out of various occupational roles. Later, most adults derive much of their sense of self-identity from the jobs they do. This means that the organisation of the occupational structure impacts individuals on both material and psychological levels.

Since the end of World War Two, the occupational structure in Britain has undergone important changes that affect both the objective conditions of work and subjective work experiences. For example, there has been a significant growth in both the service and information sectors of the economy. At the same time, there are fewer and fewer manual jobs available. Table 4.8 shows this trend.

Table 4.8 Employees by Gender and Industry

	Males		Females	
	1978	1997	1978	1997
	%	%	%	%
Distribution, hotels, catering, repairs	15	20	24	26
Financial and business services	9	16	11	19
Transport and communication	9	9	3	3
Other services	16	19	38	40
Energy and water supply	5	1	1	–
Construction	8	7	1	1
Manufacturing	35	26	22	10
Agriculture	2	2	1	1

Source: *Social Trends 28,* HMSO, 1998

Yet while more of the workforce is employed in 'white collar' work in the service and information sectors of the economy, increasingly many of these jobs are low skill, low status, low paid, temporary, and part-time. Over the past twenty years, there has been a trend on the part of employers towards 'flexibility'. That is, employers are engaging in 'just-in-time' hiring strategies, taking on workers when the economy is strong and demands for production high, and firing them when demand for production is low. This contingent workforce is primarily made up of women and racial and ethnic minorities, but increasingly white males find themselves employed as temporary workers. In fact, in 1993 only 3.7 per cent of all male workers in Britain were employed in temporary positions, but by 1997 this figure had risen to 6.6 per cent.

Healthcare

Healthcare is a finite resource. It can be distributed in two possible ways. Firstly, healthcare can be distributed based on ability to pay. That is, those who can afford to purchase healthcare receive it, and those who cannot pay do without. Secondly, healthcare can be distributed based on clinically assessed need. This is a triage system of resource allocation where those with the greatest need are treated first. In 1948, the National Health Service, or NHS, was created in Britain. This is a state-funded public health service that is free to all at the point of use, and care is allocated based upon need. While the intent behind the creation of the NHS is to provide healthcare services based on need rather than ability to pay, there are problems of inequality built into the structure of the NHS, and it fails to provide all groups in the society with equal access to healthcare services.

Two major problems of unequal allocation of healthcare are regional variations and variations according to social class. While each region can boast its 'mega' hospitals, populations in Wales and the north of England, for example, are also likely to suffer from fewer, older hospitals, fewer medical specialists, higher doctor/patient ratios, longer waiting lists for treatment, and generally greater demand on limited healthcare resources. This has contributed to higher mortality rates in these regions. The regions with the most limited healthcare resources are also those areas of Britain with a higher proportion of poor and working-class people whose need, because of their living and working conditions, is greater. But just as with the educational system, there is also privately funded healthcare available for those who can afford to bypass the long waiting lists and overextended resources of the National Health Service.

The extent of social mobility in Britain today

Measures of social mobility indicate the degree of 'openness' in a society. In a truly open society, people would achieve a place in the reward structure according to individual merit, talent, and motivation. Their position would be a result of individual effort, free from the influence of structural forces. Social mobility refers to movement within the class structure, and occupation is the most common measure of social mobility. But as noted earlier in this chapter, using occupation as a measure of social class is somewhat problematic because certain people are excluded from the occupational structure and because the nature and status of occupations change and cannot always be so neatly categorised and compared.

With these limitations in mind, it is still possible to make some general observations about movement within the British class structure. For example, over half the adults in the working and middle classes were born into families in the same class. Where there is mobility, most of it is limited to a class level or two. Instances of long-range mobility are rare. And at both the top and bottom of the class structure, there is very little movement at all. To be born poor is to stay poor, and the best way to achieve wealth in Britain today is to be born into it. Women and members of racial and ethnic minorities have poorer chances for upward mobility than white males.

Certainly, levels of upward mobility have increased somewhat this century, but there are structural factors quite beyond the control of individuals that affect their movement in the reward hierarchy. A number of these have been discussed throughout this chapter (changes in the occupational structure in which many jobs now designated as 'white collar' are routinised and low paid; a formal system of private and state-funded education which reinforces the existing class structure; institutional and cultural racism in education and employment; and obstacles to employment in higher level occupations for females, who though they tend to outperform males in school, receive a much lower return on their educational 'investment'.)

Conclusions

While only a very brief and introductory survey of social and economic divisions in Britain today, this essay gives some indication of the extent to which structural arrangements affect the lives of people in significant ways. On the most fundamental level, these societal arrangements impact both the 'quantity' and 'quality' of life for every member of society. We may like to believe that individuals attain their positions in society through a combination of inherent talent and motivation, but this is to ignore an important fact: the 'playing field' of social structure on which people compete for societal rewards and resources is not a level one, and individuals are placed at birth on the field according to social characteristics that provide advantages or disadvantages. Among the most important of these characteristics are social class, race and ethnicity, and gender. They affect opportunities and outcomes and the ways in which people in Britain live and experience their lives. Certainly one way to explain the patterns of inequality revealed in the data is to suggest that members of certain social groups such as women and members of racial and ethnic minorities simply lack what it takes to 'make it' in British society, that perhaps they are not as talented, motivated, intelligent, or hardworking, or that biology places them at a competitive disadvantage. Yet such an individualistic explanation fails to recognise systematic social forces that shape differential opportunity structures available to members of various social groups; it is these forces which are largely responsible for the patterns of inequality in Britain today.

Bibliography

Bernstein, Basil, *Class, Codes and Control,* Paladin, St Albans, 1973.
Bourdieu, Pierre and Jean-Claude Passeron, *Reproduction in Education, Society and Culture,* Sage Publications Ltd, London, 1977.
Browne, Ken, *An Introduction to Sociology,* 2nd ed, Polity Press, Cambridge, 1998.
Devine, Fiona, *Social Class in America and Britain,* Edinburgh University Press, Edinburgh, 1997.
Households Below Average Income: A Statistical Analysis 1979–1994/5, Department of Social Security, 1997.

Labour Force Survey, 1996.

Labour Research, Department of Education and Employment, Jan 1997.

McDonough, Frank, 'Class and Politics' in Mike Storry and Peter Childs, eds, *British Cultural Identities,* Routledge, London and New York, 1997.

New Review of the Low Pay Unit, No 42, Nov/Dec 1996.

Oppenheim, Carey and Lisa Harker, *Poverty: The Facts,* 3rd ed, Child Poverty Action Group, London, 1996.

Population Trends 80, HMSO, 1995.

Social Trends 28, HMSO, 1998.

Spybey, Tony, *Britain in Europe,* Routledge, London and New York, 1997.

Thio, Alex, *Sociology: An Introduction,* 2nd ed, Harper and Row, New York, 1989.

UCAS Annual Report, 1996.

Further reading

Mirza, Heidi Safia, *Young, Female, and Black,* Routledge, London and New York, 1993.

Storry, Mike and Peter Childs, eds, *British Cultural Identities,* Routledge, London and New York, 1997.

5
The British Cinema
Ken Nolley

Cinema and society – some introductory thoughts

We are encouraged to think of the cinema as an entertainment medium, and, indeed, we usually go to the movies looking for diversion and pleasure. Yet it is clear that the movies influence us in other ways as well, subtly shaping our lives and perceptions of the world. The influence may be relatively superficial in that it sparks a fad for a kind of clothing or a particular hairstyle popularised by a current star. Or, as most film critics would argue, the influence might be subtly very powerful and pervasive, helping to construct and maintain hierarchies of gender, race, and social class, often in ways that we do not notice particularly in individual cases, but which are very powerful in the aggregate, and which, when taken together, constitute the particular constellation of attitudes, assumptions and actions that go to make up a culture.

British film critic Laura Mulvey, for example, in perhaps the most influential critical essay on film from the last quarter of a century (originally published in *Screen* in the autumn of 1975), argues that classically narrated films, particularly Hollywood films, are constructed primarily by males for males – that the plots of conventional films are nearly always defined in terms of male projects, whether those projects be getting the cattle to market, capturing the bad guys, or defeating the evil empire. And at the same time, she suggests that the women who appear in these films generally do not further the action of the plot so much as interrupt it; the women in the film, she suggests, function principally as objects of visual pleasure for the men in the film, for the film crew that lovingly photographed them, and for the male spectators in the audience.

The result, she suggests, is a kind of double alienation for female viewers, who must set aside their own female identity and identify with the male protagonist both in following the plot and in enjoying the visual pleasure afforded by the display of the female characters in the film. Thus, Mulvey would have us believe, the cinema may well have significant social consequences for women, encouraging and naturalising a sense of the world in which men are encouraged to see themselves as active subjects and women are encouraged to imagine themselves as objects of a male's desiring gaze.

In certain ways, arguments such as Mulvey's fly in the face of many people's common-sense assumptions about the cinema. 'It's only a movie', it is often argued, 'and since I am quite aware of the fact that what I saw on screen was not real, it can't affect me very seriously.' And in any case, most of us normally think of our encounters with the cinema in largely private terms – we chose what film we wanted to see, we sat alone (it seemed) in the darkened theatre, or in company of a small group of our own choosing. And increasingly, of course, many of us experience films on video within the deeply private spaces of our own homes.

In these terms, it seems normal to imagine this encounter as a relatively simple and straightforward one which might be represented thus, implying that we look at and consume a story appearing on screen:

the image

us   >>>>>>>>>>>>>>>>>>>>>>>>>>>>>>>>   **or**

the story

But this sense that the encounter is a private one, even when it occurs in our own home, may in many ways be quite illusory. Though nothing appears to be standing between us and that lighted rectangle, either in the movie house or in our own home, in fact the image itself is constructed and mediated by a complex and substantive process. The movies, like all of the mass media, in certain ways represent a particular kind of conversation writ large in which the society talks to itself – or more precisely, in which certain segments of the society speak to as many people as they can manage to reach.

Thus, we might do better to represent the cinematic experience like this, implying that we are on the receiving end of a complex message system:

		Distribution	Production
	the images	System:	Apparatus:
us <<<	or <<<	distributors, <<<	producers, directors,
	the story	theatre owners	editors, genre, camera,
		TV networks	actors, script

The images and stories we encounter in the dark, then, may not so much be happy and idiosyncratic accidents as the deliberate product of a highly organised system through which various interests and concerns are expressed.

Film critics have traditionally lumped those interests together into two main areas. First, it is clear that films are the marketable product of an industrial production system. Thus it makes sense to try to understand the market forces at work that drive the industry to produce certain kinds of products, certain kinds of commodities, at certain times. On the other hand, at least since D W Griffith's *Birth of a Nation* sparked race riots in 1915, it has also been clear that films may form or at least galvanise social attitudes and influence public behaviour. Filmmakers, investors, activists, and government officials have thus been consistently interested in the content and shape of films as an instrument of social policy, wishing to encourage certain kinds of representations and to discourage or even to proscribe others. In some measure, these two kinds of interests are at odds with each other, of course. Films which represent a society quite inaccurately or which provoke reactions that economic interests or social hierarchies find disturbing may still achieve substantial market success.

It makes sense, then, not only for us to attempt to analyse and understand the images and stories we encounter in film, but also for us to ask questions about whose images and stories these are, as well as why those images and stories seem to be popular, and with whom. The answers to these questions will help us to understand better, not only what a society is saying about itself through its cinema, but also who is speaking to whom, and with what agenda.

The investors looking for profits from the cinema are drawn from the upper end of the social spectrum. Film audiences, on the other hand, are a rich mix, including a large percentage drawn from the lower end of society. In this sense, the cinema differs substantially from the theatre, which (like classical music, opera, and ballet) is pitched at a relatively small, elite audience. In certain ways, the cinema reaches audiences comparable to those reached in the nineteenth century by the popular novel, though one must remember that the 'great' novels of that period have been identified and preserved as such by the same elite establishment that maintains the theatrical, musical, operatic and balletic canons.

Thus, in some measure, the cinema provides a platform from which those with money can speak to a mass public. And if the green fuse that drives this flower is economic, there is also a constant ideological temptation to use films as a device of social engineering. During certain periods, particularly the 1930s when the British Board of Film Censors was established, or during the Second World War, the social consequences of the cinema were taken almost as seriously as the economic consequences were.

The British cinema certainly can tell us a great deal about British society, though we must not assume that what it says is necessarily true or representative of what the British experience is like most of the time. Watching the cinema of another culture or another country is a little like walking into a party and overhearing a variety of occasionally conflicting conversations between partygoers. If we truly wish to understand this place, our job is not only to try to find out what is being said, but also to try to figure out who is talking to whom, and to what end.

A short history of British film (or the shape of the conversation as we come in)

Most Americans are probably only vaguely aware of the British cinema, though the reverse has never been true. This fact has never been lost on British filmmakers. Indeed, throughout much of its history, the British film industry has worked on various schemes intended to preserve a British place in a marketplace that has been dominated by American products, as well as to provide a British voice in the cinema, particularly for British audiences. The financial interest has probably been the primary concern most of the time, but cultural concerns have undoubtedly helped to fuel the efforts to maintain and preserve British filmmaking. The hegemony that Hollywood has exercised over film everywhere, but particularly over film in the English-speaking world, has certainly hampered and challenged British filmmakers, even as it has probably reinforced some tendencies which often make British films discernibly different from their American cousins. In certain ways, these differences reveal important cultural differences between Britain and America; in other ways, these differences are also undoubtedly the product of this imbalance of cinematic trade. But these differences, whatever provoked them, are substantial, and, in many ways, the British cinema constructs a vision of the world quite at odds with that presented by most of the American cinema.

The roots of the cinema, of course, are in the nineteenth-century development of photography, long before there was an American presence to be dealt with; the competition at that time was between France and Britain, and photography was invented at about the same time in both countries. In France, in the 1830s following upon the earlier experiments of Joseph Niepce, Louis Daguerre developed a method for capturing images of the world on copper plates coated with a silver solution. Daguerre's earliest successful image was made in 1837, though he did not announce the invention until 1839.

In Britain, working sometimes in consultation with John Herschel, William Henry Fox Talbot had begun in 1835 to make images on paper coated in a silver solution. Though Talbot's images were initially less clear than Daguerre's, his were to pioneer the process of negative reversal and the printing of photographs on paper.

For the next forty years, photography would continue to develop as a more sophisticated and flexible medium so that images could be registered in fractions of a second, rather than the exceedingly long exposures required by the first experiments of the late 1830s and 1840s. These faster films, in turn, would lead to experiments in capturing images of bodies in motion, initially by groups of cameras operating in rapid sequence, and eventually through the operation of a single camera that could record multiple images one after another. The invention of the motion picture camera, like the invention of photography, may have occurred almost simultaneously in various places, though it is usually credited to Thomas Edison (or more properly, perhaps, to William Dickson, who worked for Edison) around 1890. From that point, things moved quite quickly, and the first movies were projected for public audiences by the Lumière brothers in Paris in 1895. The Lumières drew enthusiastic audiences to see their early films, which were principally documentary, or perhaps we might say 'home movie' style records of human-centred events – a train arriving at a station, a baby's meal, a parade, children playing with boats in a park, and so on.

The British cinema got an early start as well, though in some ways a different one from the Lumières'. In 1895, an English inventor named Birt Acres made a camera with which he filmed the Oxford-Cambridge boat race and the Derby. And the competition with American films that would preoccupy much of British cinema for the next century began to emerge in 1896 when a British entrepreneur named Robert Paul began by pirating Edison's early work, and went on to develop his own competing material, including a filmed version of the 1896 Derby, which he managed to project to audiences the same night.

From this point on, British filmmakers were locked into a fierce competition with filmmakers from abroad, particularly those from America, whose products needed no translation for British audiences. The Mutoscope and Biograph Company, which would bring Griffith to the attention of the world a few years later, opened a studio in London in 1897, as did a number of new British companies. By far the most important turned out to be the Hepworth Company, run by Cecil Hepworth. His 1905 film, *Rescued by Rover* – the story of a baby kidnapped by gypsies from a distracted nurse and eventually saved by the actions of the family dog – was probably the most sophisticated narrative film made to that date.

The next two decades, however, would be difficult ones for the British film industry. Early on in 1910, the British film market was dominated principally by the French, followed by American and Italian productions, with British films accounting for only fifteen per cent of the films screened (Chanon in Curran and Porter, p49). At the beginning, this state of affairs was probably normal for the emerging market; no single country could produce enough films in the early days to satisfy audience demand, so everyone depended heavily on imports.

But things would get much worse, and it would soon become apparent that the dynamic forces in the industry lay elsewhere. 'By 1926 of 749 films available only thirty-four were British and less than five per cent of screen-time was filled by British material' (Perry, p47). This drastic decline was driven by the emerging power of American production, partly because of the sudden rise in quality of American films after Griffith became active as a filmmaker, and partly because of the effectiveness of American distribution practices, which forced exhibitors to purchase films in large blocks if they were to get the major releases that they wanted. At the same time, Perry argues that 'the British industry tended to be complacent and unambitious, and spent far too much time in local squabbles instead of developing overseas markets' (p33). In consequence, British screens would have to be occupied with a great number of American films, even mediocre ones, if distributors hoped to bring the newest hits to their audiences.

The British film industry responded to this state of affairs in several ways. Throughout the period, they began one practice that would distinguish the industry in the future – they turned to traditional subjects that they thought might appeal particularly to British audiences, such as stories of Henry VIII or Queen Victoria. And in the Cinematograph Films Act of 1927, they outlawed block booking and established a minimal quota of film-time that had to be devoted to British cinema, beginning at the very modest level of five per cent, with the expectation that this was to rise each year until it reached a level of twenty per cent by 1936 (Murphy in Curran and Porter, p47).

Given this less than ideal state of affairs, some promising British performers, lured by the money and market power of the American cinema, took off for Hollywood, leaving fewer talented and creative individuals behind to develop an independent British film vision. Charlie Chaplin, one of the first to go, had already made the jump by 1913. Two distinct talents did emerge in the decade of the twenties, however – Anthony Asquith and Alfred Hitchcock (who was already giving evidence of his remarkable talent and vision in the second half of the decade). But overall, there was soon mounting evidence that the quota system was not producing exactly its intended effects; the changing market conditions of the beginning of the sound era in the late twenties also initially encouraged conservatism in film style and substance. As a result, much production time went into cheaply produced 'quota quickies,' which met the letter of the law and filled the required screen time without developing a voice and vision that would attract British and other audiences. One could say clearly that the quota quickies were particularly meant for British audiences, though perhaps they functioned rather like the 'uuuuummm' sounds people make when they don't quite have anything to say but wish to signal that they still have the floor.

The most interesting national cinemas during the decade of the 1920s probably were those in Germany and the Soviet Union. The German cinema of the period developed a particular pictorial style that depended upon the tight control of lighting afforded by studio production and the integration of camera movement with the movements of subjects of the film, producing dramatic, often dreamlike effects that led critics to associate these films with the movement of expressionism. The Soviet cinema, on the other hand, tended to shoot films in real locations and to use editing as their primary constructive tool; not surprisingly, the Soviet cinema had its roots in Russian constructivism and the result was a mastery of editing, or montage, that transformed people's sense of how movies might set about telling their stories.

The British cinema of the 1920s did not produce anything so distinctive as either of these other traditions, though undoubtedly Hitchcock's success was partly due to the fact that he had so thoroughly absorbed and learned the lessons that both the Germans and the Soviets had to teach. He became both a master of *mise-en-scène* (or the photographic design of the image within the frame) as well as a master of montage (or editing), and it was his ability to combine these two tendencies so well that led to his great successes in the 1930s and later.

In this rather dark time for British filmmaking, however, one of the most distinctively British developments in film was to emerge, not so much in the mainstream area of feature films, as in the invention of an entirely new genre of film – documentary film. Working initially with the Empire Marketing Board in 1929, and later with the General Post Office, John Grierson, and a group of people largely influenced by his vision, began to produce films whose goal was to bring to audiences images of a real world outside of the theatre, quite apart from the fictional worlds that people had come to expect to encounter on screen.

In a series of quite remarkable films, this group of filmmakers provided the principal impetus for an entire school of filmmaking that was to come, and which would particularly flourish later in the era of television. The most distinguished examples – *Industrial Britain* (dir Grierson, 1933), *Song of Ceylon* (dir Wright, 1934–35), *Housing Problems* (dirs Anstey and Elton, 1935), *Enough to Eat* (dir Anstey, 1936), *Coalface* (dir Cavalcanti, 1936) and *Night Mail* (dirs Wright and Watt, 1936) – made under the sponsorship of various organisations, peered closely at the fabric of British life, particularly the lives of working people, in the midst of the depression. To be sure, the films bore the marks of their sponsors – the EMB for *Industrial Britain*, the Ceylon Tea Board for *Song of Ceylon*, the GPO for *Night Mail,* the Commercial Gas Association for *Housing Problems* – and brought commercial and political sponsorship overtly into the area of filmmaking. But they also pointed toward a quite different role for film in a society, one in which film attempted to represent an actual world rather than to construct an imaginary one, one where film sought to inform and to teach more than to entertain. The legacy of the movement, which includes everything from films like *Hoop Dreams* to the television news, is perhaps the greatest and most pervasive gift from the British cinema to the world.

Though the documentaries were not hot commercial properties in their own right, they were clearly intended as a device to sell Britain and things British to the world. At the same time, the control exerted over their messages by their private and public sponsors was also a means of social control, using film to manage and ameliorate class tensions during the depression, just as the British Board of Film Censors, which became firmly established during the decade as well, attempted 'to control the power of the [commercial] cinema to affect the political outlook of uneducated people, especially those who went to the cinema regularly in the 1930s: the urban working class' (Pronay and Croft in Curran and Porter, p145). Though the board did not have the power to ban films outright, its recommendations were accepted everywhere by local councils, who did have that power. The result was a severe restriction on representations of class tensions, and all British films, fiction and non-fiction, tended, as a result, to suggest a world where class and racial tensions were non-existent.

The decade of the 1930s was a period of enormous market expansion for film globally. The coming of sound, once its technical demands had been mastered, helped to bring increasing numbers of film patrons into the theatres. And given the fact that movies now had to be shot in a particular language and that translation of a film from one language to another was a considerably more daunting task than merely rewriting a set of title cards, sound also gave something of a boost to many national cinemas; Britain, of course, did not get that break, and continued to struggle with the large influx of American films.

Clearly the most distinguished fiction films of the decade to be produced in Britain came from Hitchcock. *The Thirty-Nine Steps*, which he released in 1935, is perhaps his most enduringly respected film of the period, not only for the taut, economical narrative style that he had perfected, but also for the rich ways in which he interlaced humour, particularly sexual humour, with his suspense story. And Hitchcock's effective mastery of sound is commented upon again and again by critics, particularly, perhaps, in the moment when he cuts from a close-up shot of a landlady, who screams as she discovers a body in one of her flats, to a driving locomotive, whose piercing whistle merges perfectly with her voice, even as the train carries the prime suspect northward toward Scotland.

The coming of sound also brought some important new blood to the British film; perhaps most visible of the new group was a Hungarian immigrant named Alexander Korda, who came to England to direct films for others, but who quickly founded his own production company. After a series of low budget 'quota quickies', Korda produced a racy, irreverent film called *The Private Life of Henry VIII* in the autumn of 1933, which turned out to be remarkably successful with British, American, and indeed global audiences. Although the other work coming out of his company, London Films, was not so uniformly successful, Korda did strike a formula that seemed to work relatively well, and London Films produced a series of films particularly relying on historical subjects and novelistic adaptations.

This formula led to considerable success in the domestic market for Korda and others who followed his lead; by 1936, British production totals reached 212 feature titles. But still, British films were not having much success in breaking into the international market, although when the Cinematograph Act came up for renewal in this era, it was widely felt that the quota system had at last begun to work. The argument was made by some that quality controls should be added to the quotas so that in order to qualify for quota protection, a film would have to be judged to have met certain minimal standards of quality. But in the end, the act was left largely unchanged, and when the new version went into effect in 1938, a modest quota of fifteen per cent for exhibitors and twelve and a half per cent for producers was retained. Furthermore, new policies in the act actually turned out to encourage American producers to set up shop in Britain, in order to slip past quota restrictions. MGM was the earliest and most visible presence, and they began a practice of bringing American directors across the Atlantic to direct British productions, often the sort of novelistic adaptations that Korda had made successful. King Vidor, who had already made a substantial name for himself in America, was called over to direct a treatment of A J Cronin's novel about a young doctor setting up in a practice in Welsh mining country – *The Citadel* – in 1938, and Sam Wood directed the classic *Good-bye Mr Chips* in 1939.

In the hands of American directors who had grown up with Thomas Jefferson's suggestion that 'all men are created equal', the class tensions inherent in works like *The Citadel* were not likely to get rich and detailed treatment; at the same time, as we have already noted, the British cinema of the decade had been subordinated by the censors to its own rather limited portrayal of class and class difference. 'Cinema goers were quite simply prevented from being subjected to "the powerful impact of images and stereotypes designed to undermine their faith in the intentions of their rulers and in the beneficial effectiveness of the political system under which they lived"' (Aldgate in Curran and Porter, p260). Thus, class differences were systematically muted and sentimentalised in 1930s' Britain, just as American films of the period sought to maintain myths of racial harmony with their portraits of happy 'darkies'.

The outbreak of World War Two brought a new wave of trouble and complex challenges to the British film industry. Initially, the government tried to shut down the theatres, fearing the effect on morale, should a bomb strike a crowded theatre, but they soon came to feel that the movies actually served well to keep people's spirits up (Perry, p87). And, given the lack of other diversions, attendance at the pictures actually increased during the war. At the same time, however, rationing, conscription, and rising costs all combined to limit filmmaking possibilities, and production slipped substantially, to 108 films in 1940, and on down to forty-six in 1942, the low point of the war. Exhibitors made up the shortfall in films with reissues of pre-war features and longer runs. In 1940, Hitchcock was finally lured to the US by the budgets and resources Hollywood offered, and he would not return to work in the UK again until *Frenzy*, which he made in 1972.

The war again tended to focus the attention of British filmmakers particularly on the British experience as a morale concern, and away from the struggle to find markets and screens for its films. The documentary went into an entirely new phase, as the government funded films whose expressed aim was to energise and unify the country in support of the war effort. And fiction filmmakers tended to focus their stories more closely on the war and its effects, producing a series of studio features that were, in essence, war propaganda.

Many of the war films dealt directly with the contemporary situation in a way that had been impossible before the war due to censorship restrictions on the direct portrayal of living persons (Pronay and Croft in Curran and Porter, pp150–1). Likewise, rules requiring positive treatments of British soldiers were relaxed to allow more realistic portrayals of wartime realities, and together these led to many treatments of war themes. Pronay and Croft also suggest that even the pre-war ban on depictions of class antagonism began to break down somewhat during the war, though the changes were slight.

Perhaps the most famous and marketable of the wartime films was not overtly focused on contemporary events; Laurence Olivier's 1944 version of *Henry V*, which, like Sergei Eisenstein's Soviet film, *Alexander Nevsky* (1938), used a traditional story to stir contemporary patriotism. The appropriation of Shakespeare under such circumstances, however, brought Olivier's film substantial international success, both in America and in Europe, a success he would again find with his screen version of *Hamlet* after the war in 1948.

Other major international successes of the era also tended to draw upon well-known and respected novels or plays, or otherwise to appropriate the 'higher' arts. Gabriel Pascal made a film version of George Bernard Shaw's *Major Barbara* in 1941; Michael Powell and Emeric Pressburger produced a surprisingly popular ballet film in 1948 – *The Red Shoes*. David Lean adapted two of Charles Dickens' novels to great praise – *Great Expectations* (1946) and *Oliver Twist* (1948). Lean also teamed up with one of the most successful contemporary playwrights – Noel Coward – and worked on four films with him during the decade, the most successful of which was *Brief Encounter*, a richly understated (except for the Rachmaninov score) study of a hastily terminated affair between two quite ordinary people in the drabness of post-war Britain. The effect of much of this work was to continue to construct a vision of the traditional British experience as solid, wholesome and worthwhile, subordinating, particularly as it occurred in *Brief Encounter*, the will and desire of the individual in favour of that social whole, as stratified and class-ridden as it might have been.

George Perry refers to these few years after the war as the golden years for the British film industry. One new development was the emergence of a group of quite charming and popular comedies from Ealing Studios, many starring Alec Guinness (who would become known to another generation as Obi Wan Kenobe in the first *Star Wars* trilogy). In most of these films, the social convention that triumphed in *Brief Encounter* was gently mocked, certain kinds of social tensions and social divisions were admitted, and social unity was subverted by eccentric, dissident individuals and small groups – particularly in *Whisky Galore* (1948 – decorously retitled for American audiences as *Tight Little Island*), in which a Scottish village unites to relieve a wrecked freighter of its load of Scotch, much to the dismay of the English customs officials; and *Passport to Pimlico* (1949), in which a London neighbourhood secedes from the UK and establishes itself as an independent entity. In a manner typical of the period, the latter film redefines, restructures and contains very real class tensions in post-war Britain as comically resolvable when the heatwave that precipitated the rebellion ends in a thunderstorm. Riding the crest of the popularity of its post-war production, led by the infusion of new British capital, particularly from the studios of J Arthur Rank, and nurtured by rapidly rising gate receipts, the industry might have seemed poised to make a substantial leap forward. But it was not to be so easy.

The ongoing struggle between US and British filmmakers would become increasingly sharp in the post-war years, as the initial surge in ticket sales was followed by decline, and television began to compete seriously with cinemas for an audience. In the debate before the 1948 renewal of the Cinematograph Films Act, the government placed a high duty on American films; the American industry retaliated by boycotting British films. Both the duty and the boycott were quickly withdrawn, and when the act was renewed later in 1948, an effort was made to establish a much higher quota for British film – forty-five per cent. Quickly this too was watered down, but the effect of much of the jockeying was to bring a new infusion of American capital and control into the British film industry.

These rapidly changing conditions led to a wholesale collapse of much of the traditional British film industry, and throughout the 1950s, British film and American film became increasingly difficult to tell apart. Even as early as 1949, Carol Reed's *The Third Man* was made with substantial backing and influence from David Selznick (and central roles for Orson Welles and Joseph Cotton). Later, Hollywood's presence spread, with John Huston directing *The African Queen* (1952) and *Moby Dick* (1956) as joint American-British productions, as did Lean, whose *Bridge on the River Kwai* (1957) began to look more like an American-sized production for the collaboration than had any of his earlier pictures. Indeed, it served as a model for his later highly polished, large-scale productions. And Hollywood particularly came over the ocean to work on their own projects in the lower priced and underused British Studios, especially when those projects were of a certain type – usually literary, or having to do with traditional or historical British subjects – *Anastasia*, *The Barretts of Wimpole Street*, *Ivanhoe*, *Rob Roy*, *Treasure Island*, and *Captain Horatio Hornblower*. This pattern substantially undermined any distinctive character that the British film might have demonstrated in the 1950s – a time when Italian, Swedish and Japanese films were distinguishing themselves in the world cinema by facing and representing bleak post-war realities.

By the middle of the 1950s, movie-going was in sharp decline in Britain, due in significant measure to the competition from television. Cinemas began to close throughout the country, leaving many neighbourhoods and small towns without easy access to films, often for the first time in thirty years. At the height of the post-war boom, there were nearly 5,000 cinemas in Britain; by 1960, the number had dropped to about 3,000, and it would continue to fall to about

1,500 by 1970 (Perry, p170). In Britain, the decline was more substantial than it was in America for a variety of reasons. Given the fickleness of British weather, even in summer, and the cost of land, drive-ins never developed as an alternative to walk-in cinemas as they did in the US; former movie-goers simply gave up the habit and switched to television.

In spite of the decline, however, there were some promising stirrings in the British cinema late in the decade. Initially under the support of the British Film Institute, a movement known as Free Cinema began featuring a group of documentaries by young aspiring filmmakers, particularly three young men named Lindsay Anderson, Tony Richardson, and Karel Reisz. Their films got screenings at the National Film Theatre and attracted considerable attention. With this beginning, Richardson joined together with John Osborne, whose *Look Back in Anger* was the current talk of West End theatre circles, and other investors to form Woodfall Films, which would fund a number of the films that were to come from the group.

The earliest manifestations of their success came in a batch of relatively inexpensive, frank and gritty films about problems in contemporary Britain. Deliberately lacking the studio polish of the work of preceding generations, much of this work was shot on location, often in unglamorous and depressed areas, in a style that came to be known as 'kitchen sink realism'. (See also Harry Eyres' discussion of the theatre of this era.) These films expressed much more sharply than had the Ealing comedies, a significant sense of disenchantment with the Establishment and the terms of the social contract that had dominated visions of British life expressed in earlier British films. Among the earliest to emerge was Richardson, whose film version of *Look Back in Anger* was made in 1958 and was followed by a series of successful films, often dealing with class issues – particularly *A Taste of Honey* (1961) and *The Loneliness of the Long Distance Runner* (1962). The latter ends with a talented distance runner from a reform school (or Borstal), who refuses to cross the finishing line of a cross country race after he has soundly defeated his rivals from a posh public (Americans would say private) school, thereby humiliating them and simultaneously frustrating the authorities at his own school, who are attempting to steer him toward a life of accommodation with the way things are. (See Jean Elliott's discussion of this incident.) Three other directors of considerable importance to this period were Reisz, particularly for *Saturday Night and Sunday Morning* (1960), Anderson, notably in *This Sporting Life* (1963), and John Schlesinger, notably in *A Kind of Loving* (1962) and *Billy Liar* (1963).

Perhaps this quite remarkable flowering owed a great deal to the belated influence of the Italian neo-realists of the late 1940s and early 1950s; certainly it was made possible in part by the relaxation of censorship restrictions already referred to that occurred during and after the war; another factor was probably the French New Wave (particularly the work of Jean-Luc Godard and François Truffaut), that also emerged in 1959. Clearly the New Wave did not create or inspire the British film flowering of the period, but just as clearly, it reinforced its tendencies toward smaller, often independently produced works with a greater sense of spontaneity.

Television, which had so effectively helped to sink much of the traditional British cinema, actually came to play some role in this movement as well. Early in the 1960s, the BBC had decided to shake up its documentary production unit, and had hired a number of promising new directors. One of the most outspoken of this group was Peter Watkins, who in his first film for the BBC, *Culloden* (1964), made a blistering *cinema verité* recreation of the final victory of the Hanoverian troops over Scottish rebels under Charles Stuart at Culloden moor in 1746. In its own gritty realism and its serious questioning of the traditional ties that bind the UK together, Watkins' film was perhaps the most radical expression to date of the questioning that came out of the British cinema of the period. And he would carry it even further – in 1965, he made *The War Game*, a simulated documentary focusing on what a nuclear war, using current arsenals, would do to Britain. Partly influenced by political concerns voiced by the government, the BBC placed the film under a world-wide television ban which lasted for twenty years, though they finally agreed reluctantly to release it in 16mm in 1966, through which it earned a world-wide (though often a non-cinema) audience.

In spite of the decline in venues and the collapse of many British studios, the infusion of American capital continued through the 1950s and into the 1960s, a period when the American market, intrigued by British pop music, was absorbed with British culture; such popularity attracted American movie investors particularly because the deepening crisis in movie-going was now beginning to hit Hollywood hard, and traditional Hollywood films were not making good returns on investments. The combination of factors led them to support and distribute this quite remarkable resurgence in what remained of the British cinema. With such support, Richardson's films, particularly, changed focus to some extent later in the 1960s, beginning perhaps with *Tom Jones* (1963), a loose adaptation of Henry Fielding's eighteenth-century novel that became enormously successful internationally.

Later, Richardson, Reisz, and Schlesinger would all make films in Hollywood (even Watkins made *Privilege* in Britain for Universal in 1967), while from the other side, American-born Joseph Losey, thrown out of work by the Hollywood blacklist, would move to Britain, where he began a successful collaboration with British playwright Harold Pinter in films like *The Servant* (1963) and *Accident* (1967). Likewise, the American Stanley Kubrick would move to England, where he would make *Lolita* (1962), *Dr Strangelove* (1963), and *2001* (1968).

By the late 1960s, with American capital providing ninety per cent of the funding of British films, the national anger expressed in these films was being systematically replaced by more glamorous or exotic subjects. Some experimental projects did slip through – like Peter Brook's *Marat/Sade* (1966) – but generally these were, like this one or Lean's *Doctor Zhivago* (1965), exotic in some way and adaptations from stage plays or novels – the old staples that had sustained the industry so often in the past. And by the end of the decade, the American cinema was finding formulas that seemed to work with younger film goers again, with the result that much of the capital that had come to Britain at the beginning of the decade now returned home.

In the 1970s, production in England had dwindled and exports had again fallen off. Most of the inventiveness of the decade of the 1960s had been dissipated, though a few new faces and styles had appeared. Ken Russell made a stylish and effective adaptation of D H Lawrence's *Women in Love* in 1970, and later directed an outrageous series of films, mainly about music and artists. Beginning with a 1960s' icon, Mick Jagger, in *Performance* (1970), Nicholas Roeg went on to make the supernatural *The Man Who Fell to Earth* with David Bowie in 1976. And the Monty Python troupe made the jump from television to feature films in this decade.

By 1981, the collapse of the traditional British film market was nearly complete. Cinema attendance, which had stood at better than 1.6 billion admissions in the great year of 1946, slumped to just over 60 million, less than five per cent of the admissions to films the year that *Brief Encounter* was released. More and more, what was left of British films fell into a handful of quite clearly defined categories.

The grand traditional pictures celebrating an epic past and often based on famous novels continued (and still continues) to attract audiences. In 1980, Roman Polanski made *Tess*, a successful adaptation of Thomas Hardy's novel. In 1981, Hugh Hudson's nostalgic and patriotic *Chariots of Fire* attracted large audiences, and it was followed almost immediately by Richard Attenborough's *Gandhi* (1982) and Lean's *Passage to India* (1984), both of which revisit the grandeur and guilt of the old empire. And the products of this tradition of British filmmaking continue to attract audiences, with a lavish style that in some ways has richly merged with television. This is especially true of the novelistic adaptations that British television has done for America's PBS television series *Masterpiece Theater*, which provides lavish co-funding and American marketing for British serialised adaptations of works of fiction, particularly of classic or period novels. Television and film production quite literally merged recently in a spate of Jane Austen adaptations, several of which enjoyed lives both on the small screen and in release to cinemas.

On the other end of things, modern Britain has developed a small, but reliable space for some experimental and independent productions that challenge easy assumptions about the nature of the world and the film-going experience. Some space is provided by government financing, which continues to be available in small amounts that support marginal and experimental work. More is provided by a fragmented market, which makes small, cheap, niche productions profitable. And yet more becomes available through shrewd attempts to combine markets of traditional film, television and video distribution, an approach which has brought the resources of the independent television channels into film production as well.

Perhaps foremost among Britain's recent independent voices was Derek Jarman, who developed, in films like *Sebastiane* (1977), *Jubilee* (1978), *The Angelic Conversation* (1985), *Caravaggio* (1986), *The Last of England* (1987), and *War Requiem* (1988), a unique and often apocalyptic vision of British life. In a slicker and more cynical vein, Peter Greenaway developed a series of films that Bruce Kawin characterises as 'at once cold and sensual' – *The Draughtsman's Contract* (1982), *The Cook, the Thief, His Wife and Her Lover* (1990), and *Prospero's Books* (1991).

And there are still pockets of filmmaking, often independently produced, which confront directly issues of sexuality, class and race in contemporary Britain. In a somewhat paradoxical way, the collapse of the British film industry, which has provided more opportunities for small-scale independent production, has provided opportunities for voices to be heard that never could get funding before. Stephen Frears made *My Beautiful Laundrette* (1985), *Prick Up Your Ears* (1987) and *Sammy and Rosie Get Laid* (1987). More recently, Mike Leigh has also produced a striking series of unsentimentalised small films about modern British life – *Life Is Sweet* (1991), *Naked* (1993), *Secrets and Lies* (1996), and *Career Girls* (1997).

And occasionally other such films peek through, like *The Crying Game* (1992), their international success being much more likely if they are comedies like *Brassed Off* and *The Full Monty* (both 1997). But increasingly, as production has become more open and decentralised, previously marginalised or silenced voices are being heard, even when the product is not marketable in the traditional way. For example, Ngozi Onwurah, a female, Anglo-Nigerian filmmaker, has made several films about the Afro-British experience, most notably, perhaps, a short film called *The Body Beautiful* (1991).

Still, what is left of British filmmaking now exists mainly under the umbrella of a market dominated increasingly by a few enormously powerful production entities that are driven by the imperatives of the Hollywood market. Guy Ritchie's first film, which came out in 1999 – *Lock, Stock and Two Smoking Barrels* – offers an example; it was described this way in a *Village Voice* review: 'First-time director Guy Ritchie shows there's still wit and verve in the Tarantino tough-guy formula.' And as I have been writing this, in the early days of the release of *The Phantom Menace*, the new Star Wars release, this description of the rental contract for the film in Britain came over H-Film, a discussion list of film scholars that I co-moderate, from Leo Enticknap, a graduate student in film who is also a projectionist in Exeter, a cathedral city in the west of England:

1) It [*The Phantom Menace*] must be shown in the theatre's largest auditorium, at least four times per day, for at least seven weeks.

2) Eighty per cent of the box office goes to the distributor.... A typical figure for the average distributor contract is thirty-five per cent.
3) The only food (e.g. popcorn) and soft drinks which can be sold for consumption in the auditorium and during performance are those supplied and licensed by the distributor, who gets eighty per cent of the retail price. In other words, the only things cinemas can make any money on are sales of alcoholic drinks in the bar (if they have one).
4) The exhibitor must agree to a two-week run of two other films specified by the distributor (translation: enable them to offload some turkeys). At the Exeter Picture House, they were *The Honest Courtesan* and *Best Laid Plans* ...

The result of all this is that exhibitors are going to have to play very safe with their other auditoria, during the *Star Wars* run.

At the start of the new century, the British cinema is poised between two forces. On the one hand, there is the dominant, homogenising force of American-dominated English-speaking production that treats British audiences as only a small part of their intended market. Insofar as that side of the cinema treats British themes at all, it does so increasingly within the limits of Hollywood formulas that become increasingly influential, since they reach the overwhelming number of cinematic admissions. On the other hand, there is a quite small but vital number of local productions offering perspectives on British society that have never been available to cinema audiences before. Unfortunately, these productions are seen by quite limited numbers of people. Anyone interested in British film and British society will find uncommon reason for both hope and despair in this state of affairs.

A few more words about the cinema and society

So where does this hasty survey of British film leave us, and how can it be of some assistance to us as we encounter recent British films, particularly in helping us to understand a bit more of the significance of what it is that we are seeing?

There can be little doubt that a number of forces have worked to shape the British film and its history. Undoubtedly, the pressure of large-scale American production driven by immense American markets has forced the British cinema into a defensive posture almost from the beginning; since the two countries shared a language, the problem was much more intense for Britain than for most of its non-English-speaking European neighbours, where American films had to appear with the limitations either of subtitles or dubbing. Likewise, it seems clear that as the forces of American capital have pretty thoroughly subverted traditional British filmmaking, conditions have been created which have allowed a more diverse, innovative and vital cinema to emerge in the margins.

If we turn from the conditions of production to analysing the works themselves, what we might call content analysis, several concerns seem to run through the British cinema from early to late. One of those concerns emerged clearly in the post-war era, as the powerful consensus-building, propagandistic role of the wartime industry began to give way increasingly to views of the society that admitted of schism, unresolved tension, and difference. The Ealing comedies implicitly raised questions about the repressive qualities of the United Kingdom, questions that the films mainly contained within the larger consensus created by shared laughter. But later films, like the films of the kitchen sink period or like Watkins' *Culloden* or *The War Game*, confronted directly and even angrily problems concealed by the usual rhetoric of society. The British cinema, particularly in the second half of the century, struggled to define itself in terms of this tension, and to find a role for itself, whether that role was one of attempting to shore up and maintain old understandings upon which social order rested, or whether it was to question the very basis and legitimacy of that order. As is usual with such tensions, mainstream films (funded as they are by upper-middle-class investment) have tended to opt more often for the former role, and marginal and independent films have tended more often to adopt the second, made as they might well be by people from classes traditionally shut out of the filmmaking process.

Britain is also a society everywhere saturated with a sense of social class. It permeates the language one hears, the cut of people's clothing, the very nature of their thoughts, of their hopes and dreams. It is possible to see, for example, in the tradition of the British novel (that inspired so many of Britain's films), how, before Dickens, the novel had been musing, with some significant consistency, upon class relations between the old aristocracy, largely rooted in the countryside, and those classes immediately beneath them in the social hierarchy – either those partially disenfranchised elements of the landed classes, who for lack of ready cash or an inheritance had drifted into the church, or the newly rising bourgeois interests whose fortunes had been established in the cities and towns. And it is possible also to see that Dickens tends to reformulate and refocus much of the energy of the novel from being an instrument of middle-class aspiration to being an instrument of middle-class conscience, as he redefines class conflict away from the aristocratic/bourgeois axis toward the tensions experienced between the middle classes and the working classes. The films that set out to retell these traditional tales are also revisiting these old conversations.

Likewise, while the classic British novel tended by tradition to end with a marriage that symbolically united classes initially revealed by the narrative to be divided, many of the more recent novels and films reject such hopeful forms of closure, concluding in much more pessimistic ways. Indeed, the rejection of such structures of hope and reconciliation has been a part of an occasionally heated discussion in Britain over films like *Trainspotting*. Because Americans tend emotionally to want to look past issues of class, or to wish them away, we are almost certain to miss much of the texture and nuance of class at play in British film, unless we train our ears and our eyes to notice better how class is implicated in both the content and the narrative structure of the films we watch – if we are to understand what is at issue in these films for British audiences.

At the time of the rise of the cinema, Britain was still in control of a global empire. Some of the early uses of the cinema in Britain were to record the pageantry of the empire; in fact, one major stimulus to the spread of television in Britain even in the early 1950s was the broadcast of the funeral of George VI and the coronation of Elizabeth II. The loss of many of the major colonies, particularly after World War Two, led to a substantial redefinition of what Britain was and should be in the world. And while that subject was avoided initially after the war, such considerations also began to surface in many British films in the second half of the century, which in one way or another, considered Britain's past in the world, even as they implied various possible futures. Such considerations were for a long time quite foreign to the American conscious-ness, at least before the disaster of Vietnam.

There are other abiding concerns in British films as well, and we can use this sort of content analysis reasonably as one sort of entry point into all those concerns. At the same time, however, the discussion we have just had should serve to remind us of several basic considerations – that old stories retold might well be analysed, not only on their own merits, but also with some considera-tion of who is now talking to whom, and in service of what end? We can do some useful analysis of historical issues (insofar as they are accurately reproduced) in films like Richardson's *Tom Jones* or Lean's *Passage to India*, but it is also useful to ask some questions about why this particular story was unearthed for revival at this time, just as it is useful to ask who is speaking through the film – that is, whose interests are being furthered.

Likewise, it is important and instructive to try to determine the degree to which we, as Americans, are the intended audience of the film, or at least a major element of that audience, as opposed to being merely silent outside observers who are privy to a private conversation going on between and among British folks. It is difficult even for an American audience not to conclude that the *Masterpiece Theater* school of filmmaking has as its primary target audience a collection of Yank Anglophiles; once one knows the troubled history of British filmmaking, one can begin to appreciate how richly calculated the message is for American ears. Of course we can learn a great deal from discussions about Britain that are designed particularly for foreigners like us, but we can also learn other different and quite important things by listening quietly to conversa-tions not necessarily intended for our ears.

Bibliography

Barr, Charles, ed, *All Our Yesterdays: 90 Years of British Cinema*, British Film Institute, London, 1986.

Barr, Charles, *Ealing Studios*, Woodstock, The Overlook Press, New York, 1980.

Chambers, Iain, *Popular Culture: The Metropolitan Experience,* Methuen, London and New York, 1986.

Curran, James, and Vincent Porter, eds, *British Cinema History,* Weidenfeld and Nicolson, London, 1983.

Dickinson, Margaret, and Sarah Street, *Cinema and State: The Film Industry and the Government 1927–84,* British Film Institute, London, 1985.

Durgnat, Raymond, *A Mirror for England: British Movies from Austerity to Affluence,* Faber and Faber, London, 1970.

Giannetti, Louis, and Scott Eyman, *Flashback: A Brief History of Film,* 3rd ed, Simon and Schuster, Englewood Cliffs, NJ, 1996.

Haworth-Booth, Mark, *The Golden Age of British Photography 1838–1900,* Aperture Books, New York, 1984.

Mast, Gerald, and Bruce Kawin, *A Short History of the Movies,* 5th ed, Macmillan Publishing Company, New York, 1992.

Miles, Peter, and Malcolm Smith, *Cinema, Literature and Society,* Croom Helm, London, 1987.

Mulvey, Laura, 'Visual Pleasure and the Narrative Cinema' in *Visual and Other Pleasures,* Indiana University Press, Bloomington, 1989.

Murphy, Robert, *Sixties British Cinema,* British Film Institute, London, 1992.

Perry, George, *The Great British Picture Show: From the 90s to the 70s,* Hill and Wang, New York, 1974.

Schaff, Larry, *Out of the Shadows: Herschel, Talbot, and the Invention of Photography,* Yale University Press, New Haven and London, 1992.

Sorlin, Pierre, *European Cinemas, European Societies 1939–1990,* Routledge, London, 1991.

Williams, Raymond, *The Country and the City,* Oxford University Press, Oxford and London, 1973.

— *Television: Technology and Cultural Form,* Schocken Books, New York, 1974.

— *What I Came to Say,* Hutchinson Radius, London, 1989.

Winston, Brian, *Claiming the Real: The Griersonian Documentary and Its Legitimations,* British Film Institute, London 1995.

6
Post-war British Theatre – A London Perspective

Harry Eyres

The period since 1945 – and especially since 1955 – has been one of the most vital and productive in British theatre history. This second Elizabethan age does not perhaps quite match the first one in brilliance – at least, it has not produced another Shakespeare – but future historians may come to compare it not unfavourably with that heyday in terms of quality and variety of drama.

If theatre always reflects its age (which is not to deny its poetic and prophetic functions), holding a mirror up to the individual and society as much as nature, then post-war theatre in Britain has reflected and responded to the dominant events of its era: the dissolution of Britain's overseas empire and, at home, the building, flourishing and partial dismantling of the welfare state. State funding or public subsidy has been of central importance in the development of post-war British theatre. This period has seen the creation of two of the world's most important subsidised theatre companies, the Royal Shakespeare Company (RSC) with no fewer than five theatre spaces, three in Stratford and two in London's Barbican; and the National Theatre (NT), more recently and in the opinion of many unnecessarily renamed Royal National (RNT), with its triple-auditorium concrete art-palace on the South Bank.

The importance of public subsidy stretches far beyond these twin flagships. A complex system of subvention, from both central and local government revenue, has enabled the development of an extensive net of regional repertory theatres, as well as a mix of smaller art theatres in the capital such as the Royal Court, the Young Vic, the Almeida (currently perhaps the most influential theatre in the country), the Tricycle, the Bush and the Gate (specialising in neglected European work). All of these houses have seen it as their mission to promote a theatre not of escapist entertainment but of intellectual challenge and quite frequently of social, political, philosophical and spiritual enquiry, accessible and available to a very wide audience.

This resource of public theatre buildings and companies – hugely admired by such American luminaries as Arthur Miller, who has passionately protested against its undermining in the Thatcher-Major era – has in turn provided the stage for a post-war dramaturgy which, unfettered by purely commercial demands, has been able to risk going against the grain of the cosy assumptions of 'Middle England', aspiring to set audiences thinking and feeling, sometimes delivering a radical political message (and sometimes also descending to forms of propaganda).

The plays that set British theatre ablaze in the late 1950s – John Osborne's *Look Back in Anger*, Shelagh Delaney's *A Taste of Honey* and Arnold Wesker's *Roots* to name only three – were revolutionary in giving voice to characters from classes hitherto largely excluded from the stage (except as comic relief) and the auditorium (except as ushers or vendors). The 1960s and 1970s brought the dark territorial studies of Harold Pinter, the witty philosophical comedies of Tom Stoppard, the anarchic, epigrammatic farces of Joe Orton, but also saw a polemical political theatre often with a Marxist colouring – the early work of Edward Bond, David Hare (who later metamorphosed into a reformist anatomist of national institutions), Howard Brenton, Trevor Griffiths, Caryl Churchill and David Edgar. The abolition of censorship in 1968 freed British theatre from its remaining vestiges of prudery and, for the first time since the Restoration period, unleashed nudity and sexual explicitness onto the stages.

That the political theatre fizzled out in the 1980s, the decade when some of its darkest prophecies were being borne out under Margaret Thatcher, has mystified many commentators. Part of the reason may have been that theatre managements, increasingly strapped for cash as subsidy decreased in real terms, were forced in a more conservative direction. Certainly, Thatcherism evoked a more muted reaction from oppositionist playwrights than might have been expected. The end of the 1980s, of course, saw the collapse of communism in Russia and its remaining European strongholds, and the triumphalist announcement of the end of history – events that could hardly fail to shake what had in the previous decade become something of a cosy leftist theatrical establishment.

The 1990s saw theatre struggling in what some have termed a post-political environment – a new consensus marked by a softer rhetoric than that which prevailed in the 1980s but also by an unquestioning surrender to the hegemony of the global market. Compared with their condition just after the war, theatre-writing, acting, theatres and audiences are certainly far more diverse and plural. The more fragmented or kaleidoscopic politics of feminism, gay liberation, ethnicity, and the green movement have been reflected to some extent in theatre – more perhaps in the spaces of community and educational theatre than in the mainstream.

London's West End, which in 1945 more or less defined the British stage, is now only one among many theatre sectors in the capital, not to mention the scores of others up and down England, Scotland, Wales, Northern Ireland and Ireland. For a while now, the West End has had more of a name for large-scale, long-running musicals offering little in the way of intellectual challenge than for serious new plays or revivals – though these regularly occur, in many cases transferred from subsidised houses and companies.

Even the big national subsidised companies, which set standards for thoughtful productions of Shakespeare and introduced important new writing during much of the post-war period, are now perceived by many, for instance the critic Michael Billington, to have lost much of their inspirational importance. When the RNT occupies its biggest stage with revivals of *Guys and Dolls* and *Oklahoma!* and the RSC gears its Shakespeare productions to tourists, while both complain of economic pressure, big questions are raised about the case for subsidising theatres which espouse commercial values.

The Royal Court, despite a temporary change of address, and a couple of misfires in its first season back at Sloane Square, is one institution that seemed as alive and kicking at the end of the 1990s as it was in the late 1950s, still blazing the trail for new theatre-writing. Apart from the Royal Court, London's most innovative theatres in terms both of revivals and new writing are those which form the 'off-West End' sector (a term only recently introduced by the listings magazine *Time Out*) – the Donmar Warehouse, the Almeida, the Bush, the Tricycle, the Young Vic, the Gate. Other important innovative houses in the rest of the country include the West Yorkshire Playhouse in Leeds, the Royal Exchange, Manchester, the Traverse, Edinburgh, the Citizens, Glasgow, and many others.

London also, of course, has a Fringe. This term originated as a description of the mushrooming unofficial theatre at the Edinburgh Festival in the 1960s, and was quickly transferred to the English capital's extensive network of small theatre spaces, often attached to pubs, offering professional-quality theatrical fare in non-deluxe surroundings.

Equally important, if not more so, are the touring theatre companies that have increasingly set standards for innovation and challenge in production. Three of the leaders are Cheek by Jowl, Shared Experience, and Théâtre de Complicité, all of which have highlighted actors' physicality, and in some cases skills learned from mime, challenging the predominance of the traditionally conceived text and speaking voice.

All this diversity of theatre spaces, companies, actors and writers no doubt reflects the pluralism of contemporary Britain. For some, the fragmentation of both the society and the theatre audience does not bode especially well for theatre, which has flourished most vitally when diverse audiences have been able to come together in one auditorium. It is difficult to imagine any play written now carrying such weight as, and embodying a national mood in the same way as, for instance, Osborne's *Look Back in Anger* in 1956. New technologies, enabling vast apparent choice in terms of televised entertainment, also pose either a huge threat, or a huge challenge, to theatre. But given all the uncertainties surrounding this ancient, apparently anachronistic art-form at the millennium, theatre in Britain appears to be not just surviving but living with some vigour.

Before *Anger*

The years between 1945 and 1955 are often regarded as little more than a prelude to the explosion of new energy in the theatre to be detonated by Beckett and Osborne. The verse dramas of T S Eliot and Christopher Fry, which enjoyed great success in this period, have not on the whole aged well. Other dramatists highly regarded at the time, such as John Whiting and the absurdist, N F Simpson, have enjoyed very occasional revivals. A fine and now fairly frequently revived dramatist, specialising in the costs of English emotional repression, came to prominence in Terence Rattigan. However, the most significant theatrical figure to emerge in this period may well have been the young Peter Brook, by far Britain's most important and visionary director, in both practical and theoretical terms, since 1945.

Brook's precocious talent burst on the theatrical scene with productions of Shakespeare's *King John* and *Love's Labour's Lost*, Jean Cocteau's *Machine Infernale* and Christopher Marlowe's *Dr Faustus* in 1945–46, when he was only just out of his teens. That Brook's liberties with the Shakespearean text infuriated critics now seems rather quaint, since Brook's most celebrated single production is the circus-inspired 1970 *A Midsummer Night's Dream* for the RSC.

Brook soon showed that (unusually for a British director) he was as interested in contemporary currents in the European theatre as in reinvigorating Shakespeare with new theatrical languages. In fact, these two sides of Brook's work clearly interpenetrated and cross-fertilised each other. His questing theatrical spirit later took him into the further reaches of experimentalism and multi-culturalism, exemplified by his Artaud-inspired RSC Theatre of Cruelty season, the documentary *US*, about the Vietnam War, and the nine-hour Indian epic *The Mahabharata*. Brook's subsequent move to Paris, where funding from international foundations and the French government enabled him to set up his International Centre for Theatre Research and later found his theatre, Les Bouffes du Nord, seems one of the gravest losses to British cultural life since the war.

Apart from the launch of Brook's career as director, the period 1945 to 1955 can be seen in retrospect to have been preparing the way for the excitements to come. A greatly gifted generation of actors, including Laurence Olivier, John Gielgud, Ralph Richardson, Alec Guinness and Peggy Ashcroft was in its prime. Just as important, the foundations for state subsidy of theatre were laid. In 1946 the wartime Council for the Encouragement of Music and the Arts was renamed the Arts Council, and established itself as a government-appointed but independent body through which a relatively modest amount of government revenue was channelled to the arts, in particular the performing arts. The Bristol Old Vic was one of the first fruits of this policy, and several important touring companies were founded.

Godot, *Anger* and after

Peter Hall's 1955 production of Samuel Beckett's *Waiting for Godot* and the 1956 English Stage Company premiere of Osborne's *Look Back in Anger* at the Royal Court are rightly seen as two of the seminal happenings in post-war theatre. With the benefit of hindsight, they can be seen to signpost two distinct paths, the former that of a more abstract, non-naturalistic theatre, concerned with the problematics of language, which inspired such different playwrights as Pinter and Stoppard, the latter that of a realistic theatre of social comment and protest.

Not surprisingly perhaps, given English culture's unease with the philosophically abstract, it was the second path that proved the more productive in terms of quantity if not quality of dramaturgy. It has become fashionable to point out the formal and ideological conservatism of Osborne's supposedly radical drama, but the sheer liberation of energy represented by Jimmy Porter's dyspeptic tirades should not be underestimated.

Look Back in Anger provided the springboard (or should one say ironing-board?) for a plentiful succession of what later became known as 'kitchen-sink' dramas – realistic plays dealing frankly with the concerns and aspirations of characters from milieux, classes, ethnic or other groups previously neglected by the theatre. Examples included Wesker's *Roots* trilogy, about a family of Jewish Communists, and Delaney's *A Taste of Honey*, written when the author was seventeen and fiercely critical of provincial narrow-mindedness. Such plays were performed with enormous gusto by a new generation of mainly working class, though still classically trained, actors led by Peter O'Toole, Albert Finney, Tom Courtenay, and Rita Tushingham. This new generation of British actors was the first to be influenced by the famous Stanislavskian 'Method' developed at the Actors' Studio of Elia Kazan and Lee Strasberg, though British actors from this time on aimed to combine psychological realism with the formal demands of verse-speaking.

After the 1960s, television and film tended to claim the area of social realism, deploying the talents of gifted writers and directors, Delaney, Ken Loach and others. The theatre director Mike Leigh showed the versatility of his improvisational techniques of extreme naturalism by making successful feature films in the 1980s and 1990s.

A third path, distinct from the Godot and Anger routes, should also be mentioned: the Brechtian one. Bertolt Brecht's epic theatre with its famous 'distancing effect', encouraging audiences to make connections between events on stage and the conditions of their own lives, provided inspiration for a number of young dramatists including John Arden, whose anti-militarist

Serjeant Musgrave's Dance (1959) is one of the most important post-war British plays, and the Irish playwright Brendan Behan, author of *The Hostage*, a tragi-comedy about IRA activities set in a brothel.

The sixties – from the rise of subsidised theatre to the abolition of censorship

Whatever the sixties represented – the last flaring up of the human spirit before its definitive quenching by a totalitarian world capitalism, as the avant-garde American theatre director Andre Gregory claims in the film *My Dinner with André*, or a hedonistic, antinomian movement in music, politics, sexual mores and fashion – they were undoubtedly a time of creative ferment when boundaries were challenged and almost anything, for a while, seemed possible. This bubbling energy was reflected in British theatre, which enjoyed one of its most effervescent decades.

A ten-year span graced by the theatrical maturity of Pinter, Stoppard, Bond, Arden, Osborne, Peter Nichols and Peter Shaffer was obviously rich in diverse playwriting talent. Vigorous new writing was matched, encouraged and sustained by generous and imaginative public subsidy, brilliant acting and directing talent and a newly exploratory public taste.

The 1960s saw the long-awaited creation of the National Theatre and the transformation of the Stratford Shakespeare Memorial Theatre's part-time company into the permanent Royal Shakespeare Company, with Brook and Hall at the helm. These two great national arts institutions, granted sufficient levels of subsidy (still way below those enjoyed by continental equivalents) to ensure very high artistic and technical standards and affordable seat prices, gave an incalculable boost to the nation's theatrical life.

The RSC obviously had, and continues to have, the nation's premier poet-dramatist at the centre of its activity, while at the same time being committed to the production of new work and the revival of plays by Shakespeare's contemporaries and other classic writers. Under Hall's successor, Trevor Nunn, it enjoyed what many remember as a vintage period in the 1970s when it seemed able to combine searching productions of Shakespeare with romantic but far from mind-numbing epics such as the adaptation of *Nicholas Nickleby*. The subsequent reign of Adrian Noble, widely admired as a commanding Shakespearean director, has attracted widespread accusations of lack of vision and purpose.

The mission of the National – where Hall succeeded (Lord) Olivier as director in 1973 – was from the beginning to be a broader one, encompassing a wide range of contemporary and classic writing. The move to the grand premises on the South Bank, and in particular the unwieldiness of the Olivier Theatre, received considerable criticism in the late 1970s. This criticism was more muted during the highly successful stewardship of Richard Eyre, who seemed able to keep the flame of experimentation burning without emptying the auditoria. In 1997 Eyre completed his term and Nunn became the RNT's fourth director.

Both companies obviously provided splendid opportunities (as well as unprecedentedly comfortable conditions) for what has been Britain's prime theatrical resource since the time of Shakespeare, its fund of gifted actors. The RSC in particular, employing actors for periods of a year or longer, has been able to approach the close-knit, ensemble way of working more familiar on the Continent. The National has not generally been able to offer the same continuity to actors, but in the 1960s under the direction of Olivier saw the creation of a repertory company graced by the presence of Olivier himself, Richardson, Gielgud, Ashcroft, Irene Worth, Judi Dench, Eileen Atkins, Dorothy Tutin and many others. Nunn has now returned to this policy.

It was not until the mid-1970s that the National moved from the Old Vic to its vast new concrete location a few hundred yards away on the South Bank. Outside the capital, however, there was much innovative new theatre building in the 1960s. The shift from the proscenium theatre, which originated in North America with such stages as the Guthrie in Minneapolis and the Arena in Washington, DC, was picked up in Britain with the construction of thrust and in-the-round stages at Chichester, Scarborough, the Elizabethan-style Mermaid at Puddle Dock in London and elsewhere.

The new subsidised theatre companies and stages galvanised and transformed the whole nature of theatre in Britain – not just writing, acting, directing and designing, but also theatre-going, the audience's role. The new, more open stages encouraged experimentation in writing from playwrights as different as Bond, Stoppard and Alan Ayckbourn. There was also a shift in the audience's relationship with theatre.

Fashion and public taste have always played a huge, if not easily analysable, part in determining theatrical success or failure: theatre, even if not quite so modish as pop music or short skirts and tight jeans, was definitely 'in' during the sixties. Young playwrights like Pinter and Stoppard and actors including O'Toole, Finney and Vanessa Redgrave became famous, even rich. The theatre had cast off its somewhat staid image of the 1940s and 1950s, and attracted the kind of young, diverse, lively audience playwrights, actors and directors dream of.

This was, of course, an anti-authoritarian decade. The Conservative Establishment, weakened by the Suez disaster and the sex scandals that rocked the Macmillan administration, seemed ripe, or over-ripe for toppling. The new Labour administration of Harold Wilson, with Jenny Lee as arts minister, embodied for many a spirit of hope. Even before the anachronistic censorship of theatre by the Lord Chamberlain was finally abolished in 1968, the defences of hypocritical prudery (memorably attacked by George Bernard Shaw) were already crumbling.

Despite not featuring full frontal nudity or four-letter words, plays such as Pinter's *The Homecoming*, in which the American wife of an East End Londoner comes back to his father's house where she becomes a kind of willing prostitute, and Bond's *Saved*, in which a baby is stoned, are more profoundly shocking than the sexually explicit show *Oh Calcutta*, from the pen of the critic and dramaturg Kenneth Tynan.

Perhaps the most valuable achievement of the 1960s in retrospect was the freedom and generosity of spirit that allowed so many different kinds of theatre to flourish simultaneously. At the beginning of the decade, audiences might choose between *Ross*, Rattigan's sympathetic, romantic play about T E Lawrence, and Pinter's *The Caretaker*, which showed the playwright's concern with language as mystification. Later the dandified elegance of Stoppard's fantasia on themes from *Hamlet* in the style of Beckett, *Rosencrantz and Guildenstern are Dead*, co-existed with Nichols' excoriating play about a handicapped child, *A Day in the Death of Joe Egg*, Shaffer's epic *Royal Hunt of the Sun*, about the end of the Inca Empire, and Joan Littlewood's satirical World War One musical, *Oh, What a Lovely War!*

The 1970s – political polemics and sardonic comedies

The 1970s were marked by economic and political uncertainty and pessimism: the Middle East oil crisis and miners' strike of 1973–74 put a sudden stop to a period of economic expansion. At the same time impending, or already occurring, ecological crisis became an unavoidable theme of the time. Attacks on what seemed a moribund and destructive white, male, patriarchal civilisation were mounted by feminists and campaigners for racial and sexual tolerance. Not surprisingly, these events, movements and feelings were reflected, in part, by what Benedict Nightingale, echoing the playwright Howard Barker, has called a political 'theatre of cataclysm'. But political theatre was by no means all that the 1970s produced. There was also a flourishing movement in satire and sardonic comedy, whose leading lights were Ayckbourn, Simon Gray, Alan Bennett and Michael Frayn. And possibly, the most important plays of the period were the strange, uncategorisable, minimalistic late works of Beckett.

The leftist political theatre of the 1970s, like the fiercely critical West German cinema of Rainer Werner Fassbinder and others, was an offspring of state subsidy. Some of its apocalyptic critique of the British state and late capitalist society now seems to lack subtlety and accuracy: David Edgar's 1976 play *Destiny*, about the rise of the National Front, for instance, looked less than convincing when revived at the end of the 1980s. Brenton's *The Churchill Play* (of 1974), set in a 1984 Britain which featured concentration camps for dissidents, though vigorously polemical, did not quite hit the prophetic mark.

Still, the 1970s produced at least one masterpiece of a political play in Griffiths' *Comedians*. Unlike some of the work of Edgar, Hare and Brenton, this play achieved prophetic resonance in a more oblique way, by exploring the political implications of stand-up comedy. The heatedly poetic work of Barker (a prophet little honoured in his native land) also seems more likely to last than some of the more doctrinaire political theatre of the period. Another major dramatist – one of the few important female writers for the stage to emerge at this time – was Churchill, whose sharp critical intelligence and theatrical ingenuity were immediately apparent in her plays such as *Softcops*, a Foucauldian piece about the intensification of social control, and *Cloud Nine*, a study of gender and colonialism.

Theatrical ingenuity is put to very different ends in the plays of Ayckbourn, the beady-eyed chronicler of middle-class manners. Ayckbourn's long associa-tion with the in-the-round Stephen Joseph Theatre in Scarborough (where he is director) shows in his inventive stagecraft, though his view of character is sometimes marred by a condescending knowingness. Gray's focus seems to be even more on middle age than the middle classes; he has written well and unpretentiously about those characteristic post-war British themes of failure and decline (also treated by the satirist Bennett), often beautifully served by the actor Alan Bates. Gray is also an intelligent playwright who has managed to thrive in the commercial theatre.

A further, very different strand in 1970s theatre should also be mentioned: this was a period when many performers turned their backs on drama in favour of performance art and other forms of avant-garde experimentalism. Performance art still has its enclave at the Institute for Contemporary Arts (ICA, the last bastion of the avant-garde) and groups like DV8 and Volcano Theatre Company continue to offer exciting, physically adventurous work. All the same, this does not at the moment seem like a movement with the tide behind it.

Theatre under Thatcherism – the decline of subsidy, the rise of touring companies

Thatcherism as a political movement was a reaction to what many saw as the negative effects of the Welfare State – the excessive power of trade unions, the sapping of self-reliance and entrepreneurialism in a cosily declining polity.

Subsidised theatre was always going to live uncomfortably with the indi-vidualism (summed up by Thatcher's cry 'there is no such thing as society') and harshly monetarist economics of Thatcherism. The 1980s and 1990s saw a gradual, slow erosion of public subsidy of theatre (now to some extent offset by contributions from the National Lottery). So-called standstill grants have in fact represented a steady reduction in levels of funding in real terms: by 1998, the situation had reached a point where one of the nation's most lavishly subsidised arts institutions, the RNT, saw fit to send out begging letters to theatre-goers (who were already supporting the institution through taxes).

The 1980s and early 1990s were not a great period of theatre-writing – at least of the traditional male authorial variety (Hare's state of-the-nation trilogy, Tony Kushner's epic *Angels in America*, Billy Roche's Wexford trilogy and late work from the inexhaustible Arthur Miller excepted). Much of the new life that came into theatre during this period sprang from other sources. Several innovative new touring companies were established, bringing approaches to acting distinct from the classically British, text-based school. An example was Théâtre de Complicité, whose founders trained with Jacques Lecoq in Paris and drew inspiration from continental traditions of clowning, commedia dell'arte and mime. Both Complicité and another touring company, Shared Experience, tended to look for material outside the frame of mainstream drama, which gave more freedom for their innovative styles of acting and production. A route favoured by both companies – and pioneered by the RSC with its magnificent dramatisation of *Nicholas Nickleby* directed by Nunn and John Caird in 1981 – was adaptation of classic (and more obscure) nineteenth- and twentieth-century novels.

For Edgar, the playwright and co-dramatiser of *Nickleby*, the 1980s were above all the decade when women finally achieved something approaching parity with men in the fields of playwriting and directing. Certainly playwrights Churchill, Timberlake Wertenbaker and Winsome Pinnock and directors Deborah Warner and Katie Mitchell were responsible for some of the most resonant plays and productions of the decade.

A more controversial trend of the late 1980s and early 1990s was towards directors' and designers' theatre. Probably the single most talked-about and successful production of the early 1990s was not of a new play; it was Stephen Daldry's expressionistic revival, designed by Ian McNeill, of J B Priestley's *An Inspector Calls*, a play seen by many as a dated piece of theatrical sermonising. Daldry was accused of using second-rate plays (he also revived Sophie Treadwell's *Machinal* and Wesker's *The Kitchen*) to impose an overbearing aesthetic. Many actors voiced concern about designer-dominated productions that impeded the free movement and expression of players. A certain directorial arrogance, more often associated with continental theatre, was also apparent in 'conceptual' productions of Shakespeare such as Jonathan Miller's *Tempest* with Max von Sydow, which saw the play almost exclusively as a parable about colonialism.

A postscript on theatre in the Thatcher-Major years would need to say something about purely commercial, unsubsidised theatre during this period. On the whole, though by no means exclusively, the West End proved reliant on the subsidised houses for transfers of intellectually challenging plays, while musicals monopolised many playhouses. These included but were not confined to the musically and intellectually vapid confections of Andrew Lloyd-Webber and Tim Rice: several new works by Stephen Sondheim also saw the light in this period (but usually in subsidised houses). Ventures such as Kenneth Branagh's Renaissance Company and the Peter Hall Company, based first at the Old Vic and later at the Piccadilly Theatre, seemed a not unwelcome throwback to the age of the great actor-managers and impresarios.

The future of theatre

Theatre, once described as the fabulous invalid, is the most surprisingly resilient of valetudinarians. Who would have predicted a fashionable wave of new theatre-writing in the mid- to late-1990s, a time when many had written off the whole medium as hopelessly anachronistic, doomed to more or less complete extinction in the age of multi-channel digital TV? It is perhaps too soon to make confident judgements about the work of such still young writers as Martin McDonagh, Jez Butterworth, Jonathan Harvey, Mark Ravenhill and Sarah Kane (who committed suicide in 1999). It could certainly be regarded as 'post-modern' in its stylistic eclecticism, tendency to pastiche, and scepticism – verging on nihilism – about the possibility of social and political progress. In their favour, the fair-minded commentator could cite their plays' proven attraction to younger audiences.

Another remarkable achievement of the late 1990s was the completion of Sam Wanamaker's Globe Theatre project – the painstaking reconstruction of one of Shakespeare's theatres close to its original Bankside site. Under the mercurial direction of Mark Rylance, the Globe has proved far from a stuffy museum-piece: the relationship between actors and groundlings has worked well and freshly to revitalise comedies and history-plays; Rylance himself has led the move into tragedy, playing Cleopatra in 1999 and Hamlet (a role he performed memorably for the RSC a decade earlier) in 2000.

A considerable part of the money needed for the Globe's completion came from the National Lottery. Lottery money has also been used to maintain and repair the fabric of several other theatre buildings, and to fund individual projects under the Arts for Everyone scheme. At the same time, the government's 1998 spending review included a booster for the arts, easing the drought in funding of the Thatcher-Major years.

At the end of the 1990s theatre in Britain was certainly not in the state of collapse some darkly predicted a decade before. New writing, after a disappointing decade in the 1980s, appeared to be resurgent – though black and Asian writers have been slower to emerge in theatre than in fiction. The best of the new generation of actors deploy greater resources of physical expressivity and emotional openness than their predecessors – the peerless verse-speakers of the generation of Olivier, Gielgud, Ashcroft and Richardson. When these physical and emotional resources are combined with acute sensitivity to text, as in the case of such actors as Stephen Dillane, Kathryn Hunter, Clare Holman and several others, the results are surely as fine as any achievements in the British thespian tradition.

No young director of the stature of Peter Brook may have emerged, but Warner, Mitchell, Matthew Warchus and Sam Mendes all in different ways put their gifts at the service of re-appraising the play rather than promoting their egos. We have also been enjoying a vintage era, not much sung, of theatre design. The best theatre design does not impose alien or overbearing 'concepts' on plays, but sensitively counterpoints its own expressive language or languages with the verbal text. The financial and practical constraints on touring companies such as Cheek by Jowl (designer: Nick Ormerod) have encouraged flexible, mobile and economical designs (a fine example being those for Kushner's *Angels in America*) whose influence has spread to larger houses.

There is no doubt about the variety and quantity of British theatre. About theatre's larger role in the culture and its future there are inevitably questions to be asked. Thirty years ago, in *The Empty Space*, Peter Brook divided theatre into categories of Deadly, Holy, Rough and Immediate. Neither the aspirations of Holy Theatre, to fill the spiritual void of modern life, nor the political and social missionary work of Rough Theatre seem closer to realisation: in fact even to talk of theatre in such terms could seem inappropriately grandiose. Against the enormous noise generated by the mass media of television and film, the unamplified, undigitalised sound of the human voice in a live theatre could appear hopelessly weak and small. Strangely enough, the power of theatre to make audiences feel and think, to think feelingly and feel thoughtfully, and so ultimately to effect change, seems out of all proportion to the numerical insignificance of those audiences. Theatre in Britain as elsewhere can only be one of many artistic and cultural fora: but it seems likely that it will continue to be a vital and important one, whatever the digital age brings.

Further reading

Barker, Howard, *Arguments for a Theatre*, Manchester University Press, Manchester, 1997.

Brook, Peter, *The Empty Space*, Penguin, Harmondsworth, 1972.

Nightingale, Benedict, *The Future Of Theatre*, Phoenix, London, 1998.

7
The Government of Britain
Martin Upham

Introduction

While leading his 'New Labour' Party in Opposition, Tony Blair described Britain as an 'old' country that he was going to make 'young'. Mr Blair's ambitions may have ranged more widely than politics, but visitors cannot fail to be impressed by the powerful evidence of *tradition* shaping Britain's political system itself. A constitutional monarchy that yet remains grand, the use of the Crown as camouflage to legitimise political acts, a parliament building that – though not old – consciously evokes the medieval and early modern, antiquely named offices of state and antiquated procedural practices: all seem to suggest a grandly remote, even quaint, power structure. Only with difficulty can teachers explain any legitimate democratic reality behind the ceremonial charade of such grand rituals as the State Opening of Parliament. This, like lesser occasions, serves too often to reinforce the notion that the British state, like Britain itself, is hopelessly out of date.

Yet tradition does not sweep all before it in shaping the British political system. A visitor might be just as powerfully impressed by the ample evidence of *centralisation* that it offers. The electoral system, the absence of entrenched constitutional rights, the commingling – rather than separation – of powers, the absence of any formal procedures to ratify executive decisions, the doctrine of parliamentary sovereignty and the unregulated sprawl of patronage: all contrive to deal most of the cards in the political pack to whoever takes office after the breathtakingly fast transition of power that follows a general election. The ability of the British state – and its temporary elected custodians – to get its way has few, if any, parallels in the Western metropolitan world.

Centralisation is deplored and admired in equal degree. Things get done, but they are not always the right things. Critics of the British system find it the more obnoxious for the power it gives to a victorious political party. *Partisanship* is evident at almost every level of the political system reinforced by habit, the electoral system, the enduring influence of class in British society, parliamentary procedure, press bias and the power of patronage. Parties, largely unregulated in their behaviour patterns, are the only path to a political career. The loyalty they attract from adherents is almost tribal. Yet their central political presence goes largely unquestioned: it does look very much as though the British themselves would not have it any other way.

But if tradition, centralisation and partisanship have their critics, there is a wide acknowledgement that the political system has demonstrated its robustness. Even its detractors agree (while often suggesting that it is in peril) that the British polity has a high degree of *legitimacy*. This it derives from its longevity, its stubborn refusal to collapse in times of national crisis, its ability to accommodate change and its demonstrable ability to attract citizen involvement, especially in general elections. But the legitimacy of the country's political arrangements is increasingly disputed. The call most insistently heard from the New Labour administration which took power following a landslide victory in May 1997 was for 'modernisation', a slogan which may not be new but has already proved fecund in institutional change. Three years on, Britain is experiencing the most profound constitutional alterations for more than three centuries. By a startling paradox, the new administration is using the centralised powers it, like any other British government, possesses, to push through constitutional reform; in such a context the doctrine of parliamentary sovereignty, normally conservative in its impact, becomes a potent weapon for change. Tradition, centralisation and partisanship, while they may combine to frustrate reform can also be catalysts. To lay bare the enduring features of British government and politics in this time of uncertainty is the object of this essay.

The monarch

'New wine in old bottles' was the happy description applied to British institutional arrangements in one standard textbook of bygone days. The phrase combined two thoughts: the durability of the institutions themselves, and their adaptability to altered circumstances. Ancient institutions are being invoked but so too is their ability to accommodate change. Tradition clearly is the starting point in Britain, even if some practices turn out to be not as old as many believe.

The most famous embodiment of tradition is the monarch. British monarchy has been constitutionally limited since late in the seventeenth century; its pretensions to absolutism were lost in the reign of Charles I (1625–49). The impact of dependence on parliament and the rise of electorally-backed executive power slowly but irrevocably robbed the Crown of power and most of its influence. Charles' successors are heads of state but not of government.

Today the monarchy lends dignity to state occasions, most colourfully at the state opening of each new parliamentary session where the Queen's presence and her voice reading a speech of legislative intent written by her prime minister signal to observers the acceptability and legitimacy of change. This can be taken to extremes as when, in November 1998, she read out a speech which included proposals to bar hereditary peers from the House of Lords, even though she herself is the most famous embodiment of the hereditary principle. At the state opening and on countless less significant occasions, the monarch is subordinate to the head of government, as no elected head of state would agree to be. Moreover many facets of the monarchy (including its funding, the number of royals the public is prepared to bankroll, primogeniture – succession through the male line – and its position as 'Supreme Head' of the Church of England) are under review, apparently with the Queen's blessing, even possibly at her instigation.

Today the first principle any government student needs to master is the crucial distinction between monarch and Crown. The first is a person who in Walter Bagehot's phrase may 'encourage, advise or warn' but whose continuance on the throne depends crucially on her *not* exercising those powers she may in theory possess: it is quite inconceivable that Queen Elizabeth might dissolve parliament against the wishes of her prime minister, dismiss him, or refuse to sign a properly-made piece of legislation. On the contrary, her aim in almost half a century has been to avoid becoming an obstacle to what is perceived as the expression of the popular will: since this is usually taken to be the government of the day, conflict can scarcely arise. There remain only those infrequent occasions where the popular will cannot readily be divined: a split in the governing majority party, an indecisive general election outcome. In such cases the monarch will proceed with the utmost caution and under heavyweight constitutional advice. Her aim will be to avoid controversy because only on that condition can a non-elected head of state survive.

The Crown and the prime minister

But if the monarch is not personally powerful, what of the Crown? This is quite another matter. The Crown is a convenient fiction for the brutal exercise of executive power in Britain, an activity led by the prime minister of the day. Constitutional doctrine, such as it is, defines sovereignty as being exercised by the Crown in parliament. Since Her Majesty's role is so diminished it is the prime minister, elected head of government, leader of the majority on the House of Commons, who determines: in the name of the Crown he makes governments and exercises vast and largely unchecked powers of patronage. If a Committee of Inquiry is appointed or a Royal Commission set up, if parliament is bullied or judges are made, it is usually as the result of the exercise of Crown powers, a pretence which can extend to the very letter of appointment.

Aided by this contrivance, the office of prime minister concentrates impressive power in the hands of the occupant. He (and one she, so far) faces colleagues, parliament, party and public opinion. One approach to the study of the office is to contrast dynamic occupants of it with consolidators but *any* prime minister must master an enormous range of powers. The remarkable thing is how little structural change has been introduced into the way he wields them. In the absence of a codified constitution, the powers of a prime minister are what a prime ministers does, but this itself makes a list so daunting that some commentators describe incumbents as unelected monarchs.

Patronage is the heart of prime-ministerial power. Its most dramatic demonstration comes when a new government is formed. He appoints all members of the new government, who can number as many as ninety, most of them members of the House of Commons and therefore politicians with a personal electoral base. They stay in office if they perform competently and retain the support of the majority party. The power of dismissal also rests with the prime minister. It is used routinely to refresh an administration, or at least to give the appearance of rejuvenation, to retire ministers who are no longer needed and to gain new blood from the parliamentary party. None of these appointments is subject to a formal endorsement: nomination by the prime minister is enough.

Yet this power to appoint and dismiss is not exercised in freedom. Every prime minister, even the most powerful, inherits a collective party leadership, those he dare not fail to appoint; in such cases his influence is demonstrated by the choice of post offered, which may not be to the recipient's liking. The corollary of this is that he may not stack his administration with favourites. Only after a period in office may new prime ministers advance to high (i.e. Cabinet) office their closest allies, as did Margaret Thatcher with Norman Tebbit, and Mr Blair with Peter Mandelson. Dismissals, especially of high-ranking ministers unwilling to go, have to be handled with extreme care. Any sacking reflects on the man who made the original appointment and the parliamentary tradition, now invoked by even the obscurest resignee, of making a 'personal statement' to the House of Commons following one's resignation, gives the aggrieved former minister an early opportunity to exact early and punishing vengeance. Unmuzzled, he or she can give a personal version of the events that ended a career; it is often not charitable. The personal statement of former Chancellor of the Exchequer Norman Lamont gravely wounded the premiership of John Major; that of Sir Geoffrey Howe signalled the end of Mrs Thatcher's.

Centralisation and its constraints

For most of his time in office, a British prime minister is running the country. He chairs regular meetings of the Cabinet, that leading committee of British government, which brings all heads of department together, he dictates its agenda and writes the minutes. In all he does as government chief, he is assisted by the Cabinet Secretary, who also heads the Civil Service. Even here party politics intrudes: for the faces the prime minister sees around the Cabinet Table are elected politicians of weight in the ruling party. Each heads a large department of state with its own civil service, traditions, budget and agenda.

Some (like Social Security, Health and Education & Employment) are spending departments; they are opposed by the most powerful department of all, the Treasury, which has to find the money. The tension between the need to spend and the need to raise revenue can determine the fate of governments.

Government works by delegation; no prime minister can expect to run every minister's department. Most of the time members of a government are in any case united around broad objectives: they are members of the same political party and share a core ideology. In normal times each department will pursue policies which are a mixture of policy and response so a conflict will not arise. Despite this, it is remarkable how robust the tradition of ministerial independence is: even so dominant a prime minister as Margaret Thatcher suffered two years of growing disagreement with her Chancellor of the Exchequer over that most fundamental of all questions, exchange rate policy.

There are conventions to enforce coherence or, failing that, to maintain a fiction of unity. 'Collective responsibility' enjoins all those in office (even those in attached unpaid posts such as a minister's Parliamentary Private Secretary – PPS) to toe the government line in public. There are arguments of course – they are the lifeblood of government – but once policy is set it must be respected and the minister who cannot live with it must depart. This can be a harsh doctrine, for each is expected to support in public, or at least not to oppose, policies which he or she may have had no part in making. Worse yet, the minister may be on the record as opposing the very policies he or she must now implement. The potential for embarrassment is great. But *Questions of Procedure for Ministers*, the recently revised guide to conduct in office handed to each new appointee, presents it differently. In its pages, collective responsibility becomes a device facilitating good government; it allows each minister to consider every possible solution to a problem in the secure knowledge that he won't be demonised in the press for thinking the unthinkable.

The remarkable thing is just how robust this convention is. It applies not only to the Cabinet, but to all ministers; and not only to ministers but to their PPSs. It has also crossed the floor of the House of Commons and turned up as a device to give coherence to the Opposition. In a House of 659 members the number unable to speak freely because they hold office comfortably exceeds 100. Unfortunately for this doctrine, it can be difficult to establish just where the line is drawn: a powerful minister can get away with a great deal. The New Labour government is unprecedentedly sensitive to press coverage and the use of ministerial press secretaries to 'brief' on behalf of their masters against other ministers caused a flurry of resignations just before Christmas 1998. The press assiduously follows each turn in an unfolding news story and they are getting it from somewhere. Moreover, in these days of instant memoirs and ministerial diaries, the public learns the inside story from protagonists – or a least one version of it – much sooner than the official thirty-year bar on publication of Cabinet Papers would allow.

Party and country leader

A prime minister finally must face his party and the country. He owes his office to being leader of the party that won the most recent general election. As long as he looks like doing it again he will retain its support. Prime ministers expect and demand loyalty, and receive it for much of the time. A competent performance and the appetite for office will do much to keep party members onside. But the expectation of victory is critical in Britain, where there is no separation of powers and a government win is a win for a majority of parliamentarians as well. In the past, a prime minister was most at risk when – as was the case for the Conservative Party between 1965 and 1997 – the election of the leader is in the hands of the party's MPs alone. Edward Heath in 1975, and Margaret Thatcher in 1990 were given brutal lessons in how quickly opinion can crystallise against an unpopular incumbent. Today's Conservative and Labour leaders answer to a much wider electorate of their entire party including members outside parliament: sacking them before they are ready to retire is likely to be much more difficult.

As for the country, the prime minister is always news. His presence and words are continuously reported by the media. To much of the public he *is* the administration, just as an American president is; unlike his American counterpart however he has to present policy formulated in part by strong and sometimes fractious colleagues, each of whom has his own electoral base. It is hardly surprising that so much effort goes into securing a favourable press. Bernard Ingham, press secretary to Mrs Thatcher and Mr Callaghan before her, and Alastair Campbell, who acts in the same capacity for Mr Blair, gained reputations for tirelessness in this cause. Yes such efforts can be unavailing, as they were from September 1992 when the papers began to sniff the disintegration of the Conservatives and hastened it with relentless hostile reporting. Small wonder that the Blair administration – the first Labour government ever to win with a majority of the press in support – massages the press more assiduously than any previous government. It has had to endure charges of an improper closeness with News International, the powerful media group which owns *The Times*, *The Sun* and Sky TV. Yet by the end of 1998 there were unmistakable signs of press disillusionment with New Labour, suggesting that the papers were preparing to take up the opposition role the Conservatives, for the present, were unable to prosecute. In the two years following, the press became much more critical, first over specific – notably European – issues, and then in levelling the damaging charge of 'control freakery' against Blair.

Whether dominant like Lloyd George (1916–22), Churchill (during his first spell 1940–45), Wilson (in his first period of office 1964–70) and Thatcher (1979–90) or collegiate like Major (1990–97), a prime minister is famously the 'first among equals'. He leads, yet faces elected colleagues. Members of the British government are, by definition, also Members of Parliament. They too, once appointed, must make policy within the broad guidelines established by the party; like him, they must explain their policies to the House, smite the opposition, retain the confidence of the government benches and persuade the media. A British minister is responsible for his own policy, its coherence and efficient execution. A second convention, ministerial responsibility, expresses the accountability of individual government members to parliament. It is a shadow of its nineteenth-century self when policy was more personally defined and resignations were considered the honourable response to failure. Today the extent of a minister's personal responsibility is more narrowly defined: an errant minister may retain office if the party backs him. It is the *absence of party support* which spells his doom and has compelled the resignation of many ministers whom the prime minister would rather have kept.

From central to local

It would be wrong to conflate the centralisation of power in Britain with the office of the prime minister. It extends more widely. All ministers, indeed government as a whole, have a wide range of unrestrained action. Two central government relationships, those with local government and with the judiciary, illustrate this well. The case of the judiciary will be considered in the context of legitimacy below. British local government, which is examined here, has a long history. In the nineteenth century it was the instrument which brought civilised life to the masses in the cities; from the middle of the twentieth it was one of the two principal means (the National Health Service – NHS – being the other) whereby the welfare state extended its care to the entire population. At the dawn of the twenty-first century, elected local councils still dispensed educational, housing, planning, environmental and social services to the whole country.

Yet the framework and content of these services as well as the structure of local government itself has been under constant revision. Each service is dispensed within a statutory framework, that is to say within margins set down by parliament. Since no one parliament can bind its successors, this context can change, and it frequently does. Thus from 1945 to 1980 central government pressurised councils to build high-standard, affordable accommodation for rent to their local populations; from 1980 the pressure of central government has been exactly the opposite – a legislative impulse to *sell* council rented accommodation to sitting tenants. Education services consisted for most of the twentieth century of local initiatives, albeit qualified by nationally imposed obligations to educate up to the school-leaving age. But from the 1960s the central state has intervened ever more brutally – to hasten comprehensivisation (1965), to impose a national curriculum (1989), to prescribe a daily 'Literacy Hour' to primary schools (1998), and likewise a 'Numeracy Hour' (1999). In a speech of June 2000, Education Secretary David Blunkett seemed to envisage a further shrinkage in local authority spending powers over schools.

Parliament has always reserved for itself the right to define the nature of local government services. Essentially it imposes responsibilities on councils to provide the services it wants delivered while still insisting on their form. Thus parliament defines the qualifications required of a director of planning, social services or education; it requires sufficient school places to be available for all children between the ages of five and sixteen whose parents require them; it insists on adequate refuse disposal.

No entrenched local powers

The last two decades have seen the role of local government within the state questioned, perhaps for the first time. During the premiership of Mrs Thatcher, strenuous efforts were made to challenge the assumption that its growth was automatic as people's expectations of public services rose. Her determination to 'roll back the frontiers of the state' cut across the usual central-local tensions, substituting a new dichotomy: private versus public. Councils were discouraged from seeking to offer services directly; their role would be as managing agents, awarding contracts to private providers and monitoring standards thereafter. Like so many initiatives of the Conservatives, this trend has not been reversed by New Labour. Today local government's interests are as wide as ever, but its role as a direct *provider* of services has shrunk and is set to diminish.

But perhaps most revealing of all is the impact of central government on the very structure of local councils. The 1972 Local Government Act turned the shape of councils upside down, establishing six huge metropolitan councils in England's largest connurbations (a similar authority appeared in central Scotland) to match the Greater London Council (GLC), which had been created seven years earlier; outside these areas a two-tier system was established with county councils (some of them newly defined) delivering education and personal social services and district councils (in the metropolitan areas, boroughs) responsible for housing, environmental services and planning. Yet in 1986, all six metropolitan councils and the GLC were abolished by Parliamentary Act, the clearest possible demonstration of where power ultimately lay. In the most populous areas of the country, many functions (such as the emergency services) were as a result not under democratic control at all.

Nor did the process stop with Mrs Thatcher in 1986. Subsequent Acts of Parliament have abolished the more unpopular of the new counties; in many places the two-tier system has been replaced with unitary authorities (which deliver all services from one elective base). The Government of London Act 1999, endorsed in lacklustre fashion in a capital-wide referendum, restored elected local government to the capital. In this instance, New Labour modernisation took the form of a directly elected mayor and a new twenty-five-member Greater London Authority (GLA). The mayor's budget and powers are modest, but in his first month of office from May 2000, the first incumbent, Ken Livingstone, suggested the possibility of powers of persuasion and symbolism beyond his formal functions. It is too early to say what the implications are of combining such a powerful personal mandate with diminutive powers: Labour's original intention to bring in executive mayors in all major conurbations, and perhaps the whole country, may falter on this contradiction.

The only exception to this catalogue of irresistible interference is in the interesting sphere of taxation. Until the Scottish parliament opened in 1999, local councils were the only level of government in Britain outside parliament which could raise a tax. For centuries, this tax was a property-based levy, the rates. Taxing property had never been popular with the Conservative Party but this distaste did not lead to action until the advent of Mrs Thatcher's radical administration. She was concerned about the inflationary impact of local government spending and frustrated at the ability of some Labour councils to maintain social programmes in cheerful defiance of central government edicts. This was possible because they could raise the rates to compensate for the shortfall in grants paid out to councils by central government. 'Rate-capping' (whereby excessive rate levels attracted financial penalties) proved only a partial success and increased her sense of exasperation. Her solution in 1990 was to introduce a flat rate Community Charge (or Poll Tax), an equal amount to be levied on all persons eighteen years old and over in a local government division. The rates had been rough and ready but they had been paid. The Community Charge, however, actually criminalised large numbers of natural Conservatives who just could not afford to pay. It aroused such opposition in 'middle England' to its perceived unfairness that it was repealed within two years, the clearest case of administrative failure, said one critic, in post-war British history, and one which certainly hastened the demise of Britain's radical prime minister. Today the local tax that Britons pay is the 'Council Tax', an apparently acceptable marriage of individual liability and property market values.

Unitary government

It is obvious that central government, using the authority of parliament, intervenes freely if not always with wisdom. That is the meaning of unitary government where all authority flows from the centre. But 1999 brought the first significant fissure in the system. Until the 1970s, the trend of British politics had been overwhelmingly unionist, the yielding of all power to legislate and decide to parliament. Parliament might entrust this power to others, local government for example, but there was no other source of authority. Scotland, Wales and Northern Ireland were all represented in government and in parliament by secretaries of state with enormous strategic powers. MPs from all three territories (the term used by political scientists to describe the minority nations) are elected to Westminster. Indeed, on a strict numerical calculation, each is over-represented. House of Commons committees of several kinds reflect their national concerns.

But the last quarter of the twentieth century saw the principle of a sovereign (Westminster) parliament in a unitary state under challenge from nationalism and a growing interest in federalism (the division of power between different levels of government). An earlier attempt to achieve devolution (whereby the centre yields powers to a lower regional tier of government) failed to command sufficient support, but it remains a priority for New Labour, which is intellectually convinced of the need to pass power to the United Kingdom's constituent parts and which is the overwhelming majority party in both Scotland and Wales. Labour has used its power in the Westminster parliament to cede authority. And so in 1999 Scotland became the second legislative and the third tax-raising level of British government. Its new parliament has the power to pass laws shaping most Scottish internal affairs and to vary the UK rate of income tax by up to 3p in the £. Scotland by this means became largely self-governing: it achieved administrative 'home rule' within the United Kingdom, though the contradictions of devolving while retaining most financial power at the centre remain to be addressed. To Wales, where nationalism is less assertive, 1999 brought something less: an elective assembly to monitor the affairs of a newly-elected executive and first secretary. Northern Ireland too has a newly-elected assembly, counterpart to its emerging power-sharing executive. This was not part of the grand devolutionist design but the outcome of the peace process initiated in 1993; nevertheless it clearly dovetails with the Scottish and Welsh initiatives.

This uneven distribution of power offends some minds. It is partial federalism, for the Welsh and the Irish – for quite different reasons – will not be able to legislate or indeed to tax. Many critics of devolution, interpreting it as a breach in parliamentary sovereignty that must widen, believe that the position of England, largest of the UK nations, will become anomalous. New Labour has a formal manifesto commitment to regional assemblies. This would make for greater constitutional tidiness, but it is not clear that they are desired by the populations of the regions concerned. The boundaries of English regions are difficult to define (which is not a problem for the Scots or the Welsh) and various non-elected agencies (water companies, tourist boards, government statisticians to name three) administer them on different boundaries. Yet there are bound to be changes as the implications of Scottish home rule sink in. The Conservative opposition, seeking to adjust to the new constitutional realities, at one point contemplated the idea of an *English* parliament; its leader rejected this idea for the alternative of allowing English MPs alone to vote on English laws. Others, looking to British governmental tradition, are relaxed about anomalies: consistency has always been elusive. Whatever the outcome of a debate that is only beginning, it is important to emphasise one underlying fact:

the United Kingdom – despite the constitutional changes of 1999–2000 – remains intact. It is *one* state, with *one* sovereign parliament responsible for the foreign policy, economy and defence of the country. Perhaps in the future there will be an independent Scotland, and Northern Ireland will vote to leave the UK, but that moment has not yet arrived.

Party organisations and funds

The wheels of British government are greased by party politics. Rivalries between the parties are supported in almost every institutional corner. British party politics, like a gas, has no fixed volume: it simply expands to fill the space available. There was once a tradition of 'independence' in local government, but that is virtually dead. Though arguably in generic decline, Britain's political parties are discovering ever new arenas of activity. For the best part of two centuries, Britain has had a two-party system and it remains powerful. But the dominance of Conservatives and Labour is today rivalled – if not yet toppled – by the Liberal Democrats and, in minor key, by Welsh, Scottish and Irish parties.

It is remarkable that organisations possessing so much power remain largely unregulated. The leader of a party victorious in a general election becomes prime minister, yet the state has never specified the process whereby the party makes its choice. It has taken the Conservative Party only one-third of a century to move from allowing its leaders to 'emerge' (without a vote following con-sultations among its elders) via an election (under vague rules) by MPs alone, to a wider all-party ballot; other parties may have mocked the outcome but they have always accepted the result. Today it is possible to discern structural trends common to both major parties, each of which has reshaped itself to concentrate more power in the hands of the leader, a shift motivated by the lack of electoral success.

In either case this trend offends tradition. Labour's internal constitutional changes have increasingly challenged its traditional federal character as it moved from a triangular power structure (of affiliated trades unions, MPs and members) to one where individual members alone have a relationship with the leader. The Conservative shift has been more abrupt, and collided with the traditional independence of local Conservative Associations, but no less certain. The growing influence of both leaders within their party may increasingly be a cause for concern due to changes in the electoral process itself: the June 1999 elections to the European parliament were held under the 'closed list' system, by which voters chose between parties rather than candidates. The power to influence, or even ordain, this list is a major lever of party power: it offers great scope for leader influence.

One area of party activity that has attracted concern is funding. In the twentieth century, the flow of funds reflected the contrasting composition and programmes of Conservatives and Labour. The Conservatives, always the highest spenders in the past, attracted an almost absolute monopoly of corporate backing; Labour was correspondingly dependent on its affiliated unions for support. Labour's massive election victory of 1997 was anticipated and followed by major success in persuading businesses to fund it. Union backing, though still the principal source of Labour funds, is now rivalled by fund-raising, membership contributions, and donations from individuals and companies. The Conservatives, by contrast, have failed to find easy replacements for the company and private donors who defected during their decline of 1992–97. Their last five years in office were pockmarked by financial irregularities, some of which suggested that donors could buy party or government influence. One consequence was the establishment of a Committee on Standards in Public Life whose reports, difficult to oppose, have radical implications for political conduct. The Committee's Fifth (October 1998) Report recommended clear rules on disclosure of donations, an end to donations from abroad, a limit of £20 million (exceeded by both parties in 1997) on *national* election spending, and an Honours Scrutiny Committee with powers to investigate suspected links between an honour (a title, possibly conferring entry to the House of Lords) and a partisan political donation. During the 1999–2000 session, parliament considered legislation incorporating many of these recommendations. In the absence of any really generous system of state-funding, such changes will make for a tough regime.

The rise of New Labour

The public knows little of party funding and structure but is much more aware of the parties' programmatic commitments. Here the evolution of the two main parties has been remarkable by any standards. Essentially each has repositioned itself ideologically during the last quarter-century and (unless the Conservative debacle of 1997 turns out to be permanent) done so while remaining a major force. Of course, the circumstances were different in each case. The Conservatives' adoption of what became known as Thatcherism took place largely in office, fuelled by confidence that it brought unstoppable electoral success. Labour's reinvention, more complete than that of the Conservatives for it did not even disdain rebranding as 'New Labour', was powered by eighteen years of electoral failure. If the purpose of New Labour was to achieve electoral success (and its many critics believe New Labour *has* no other purpose), then the 1997 general election result was its ultimate validation.

Yet great tensions persist. From its foundation in 1900 as the Labour Representation Committee, Labour was a socialist party, committed to a redistribution – through taxation, egalitarian organisations like the NHS or state-run schools – of income and wealth. If no longer the working-class party of the first half of the twentieth century in character, it retained a pronounced working-class outlook. It proposed and defended state ownership, sought to reduce poverty and sympathised with the influence of the unions that its federal character allowed to affiliate. It was also unafraid to embrace potentially unpopular left-wing policies such as renouncing Britain's nuclear weapons. However, under Tony Blair and his two predecessors, Neil Kinnock (1983–92) and John Smith (1992–94), all of this has been abandoned. Labour in office has accepted private ownership of Britain's utilities and proposes to extend it; it has only marginally mitigated the harshness of the Conservatives' industrial relations laws; it speaks the Conservatives' language of competition and measured outcomes in the public services; and it proposes no increases to the basic rate of income tax. Blair – of all Labour leaders the one least indebted to the past – speaks of a 'third way', an elusive formula which seems to owe little to Labour tradition and much to post-Conservative Party capitalism. Until Spring 2000, he successfully persuaded most party members to stay loyal, but a crop of poor election results prompted quite senior figures to warn of disenchantment in the party's 'heartlands'.

Thatcherism and after

If Labour's ranks stay loyal, it will be because the Blair approach has delivered electoral success. Thus it was also with the Conservatives under Margaret Thatcher. Hesitatingly, and then with increasing vigour, she assaulted the consensual heritage of the 1940s and broke with the 'One Nation' Conservatism of the 1950s. During those decades – and for some time after – the party had accepted the mixed economy and the welfare state and come to terms with the legitimacy of unions and their demands for a role in national planning. The party's leaders emphasised continuity and patriotism but of a socially inclusive kind. However, Mrs Thatcher, and her successor John Major, sold off most state industries, radically reshaped the public services, sharply lowered the basic rate of income tax and passed no less than eight major statutes regulating (effectively weakening) the position of unions within the law. There were major economic successes, notably in reducing the rate of inflation to what looks like a permanently low level of around three per cent. High public spending proved more intractable, for the harsh economic regime produced heavy social casualties for which the welfare bill was enormous. Unemployment rocketed during her first years in office, and it is now beyond doubt that poverty increased. For such a determined opponent of the 'dependency culture', this was a bitter blow, and ultimately it was to doom her hopes of cutting the growing total of public spending.

The Conservative Party is frequently accused by its opponents of 'wrapping itself in the Union Jack'. But Mrs Thatcher's nationalism seemed shrill by comparison with that of her predecessors. Under attack for her leadership style at home, she experienced during her last years in office a sense of isolation on the world stage she so impressively strode. If she expected electoral credit for the end of the Cold War she had waged with such vigour she did not receive it; as the more prescient commentators noted at the time, the mood at the end of the 1980s was to reject all strong leaders. For years she was the most awkward European head of government, and the discomfort many Conservatives felt over this turned opposition to her into a critical mass. In November 1990 she fell, like Lucifer, and just as fast. Perhaps it was because of this that the Conservative Party paid the electoral price of Thatcherism only seven years later. In the years after this defeat, the party did not decisively indicate whether it would commit itself to return to her policies or to those of earlier Conservative leaders. Its young leader, William Hague, sought out populist issues with some success in the June 1999 European parliament elections, where its sceptical platform brought the party its first nation-wide victory in seven years, and again in the local and London elections of May 2000.

The role of parties

Despite Labour's 1997 landslide, the two-party system still seems powerful. In the House of Commons, 583 of the 659 MPs are Labour or Conservative. But the Liberal Democrats (LDs), with forty-six members, and more numerous than they have been since the days of Lloyd George, have made great electoral strides: twice their strength of recent years in parliament, they now have representation in the European parliament and have roughly the same number of councillors as the Conservatives. The LDs are untroubled by splits over the benefits of the European Union (EU), a great advantage when the historic and imminent decision to take up membership of Economic and Monetary Union (EMU, the use of a single currency, central bank and interest rate policy by EU member states) is in the balance, but they have yet to shape a clear course that will define them against Labour, whose constitutional reform project is close to the Liberals' own. The future may bring fusion: LD leaders sit on a Cabinet Committee on constitutional change with Labour ministers and actually govern Scotland in coalition with Labour. But many Labour MPs (and some ministers) oppose a close relationship between the parties, and the thirst for independence among the vociferous and active LD rank and file is unassuaged.

Territorial parties are also present in the House of Commons. The Scottish Nationalists (SNP) are the most formidable separatist force in the United Kingdom. Their small Westminster presence of six MPs belies their powerful position in Scotland, where they advocate independence within the EU. In the first ever Scottish parliament elections of May 1999, they ran a respectable second to Labour which has dominated Scottish politics for forty years. Welsh nationalism also has a party political vehicle in Plaid Cymru (PC), but one which does not command the same territorial support as the SNP and advocates more modest goals, promoting greater self-determination for Wales rather than separatism. Yet it too securely established itself as Wales' second party in the first ever National Assembly elections, also held in May 1999. The 'two traditions', as they are misleadingly called, of Northern Ireland are also reflected in the House of Commons by political parties; indeed the Northern Ireland party system is now quite distinct from that on the mainland. Unionists (mainly Protestant) vote for unionist parties (those who defend the union of Great Britain and Northern Ireland, sometimes described as loyalists), above all for the Official Ulster Unionists who have cautiously embraced the peace process underway since 1993; Nationalists (entirely Catholic) divide between those (like Sinn Fein) for whom reunification with the Republic is the dominant political objective and those (like the Social Democratic Labour Party, SDLP) who may be content in the medium term to win closer links with Dublin.

From this survey, it may readily be appreciated that the ideological terrain of British politics is changing. Former debates, which reflected the dominance of class in British society, seem to have waned; in their place have emerged concerns that express doubts about the place of Britain in the world, anxieties about the viability of the United Kingdom itself, sharp policy differences over the robustness of traditional British institutions, and the path to economic renewal. Britain seems to have moved away from a class-based party political system, but each of the parties is struggling – for different reasons – to find a focused identity. Whether they remain efficient vehicles for the issues that will exercise the public from 2000 on remains to be seen.

As a species, Britain's political parties are in long-term decline. In the summer of 2000, new estimates put Labour's membership at 360,000 and that of the Conservatives at 320,000: each had lost two-thirds of its membership during the second half of the twentieth century. They both bring together leaders, members and voters and when they work well the tension between these three levels can be creative. But there is internal dissatisfaction with each main party leader, and voluntary party activity has none of the magic for the young that is held by short-term or single-issue pressure groups, notably those active on environmental issues. And the electors themselves seem not only more volatile in their loyalties but also less committed. Though 33 million people voted in the 1997 general election, the turnout of around seventy-one per cent was one of the lowest for many years. To put it another way, more than ten million did *not* vote, and the evidence seems to suggest that they are concentrated among those who have benefited least from the actions of governments of every persuasion. Participation in the devolution and European parliament elections of 1999 (the latter with a turnout below twenty-five per cent) offered few grounds for complacency. The May 2000 election of London's first mayor, intended in part to ignite public interest in local government, lured a pitiful one-third of eligible voters into the polling booths. During the local elections held nation-wide on the same day a number of experimental measures intended to raise access to (and participation in) the electoral process were introduced.

Challenges to the electoral system

But many pillars support the party system. Among the most robust are the electoral system, the role of the press and the business arrangements of parliament itself. The electoral system has undoubtedly been a major influence for retaining the duopoly, since it tends to over-reward the winner of a general election and penalise losers, at least in terms of numbers of seats gained in the House of Commons. But this electoral system has not only been in force in the House of Commons; it applied until recently to the whole British body politic. Its critics argue that its disproportionality (the lack of clear correspondence between the share of votes and the share of seats) diminishes the legitimacy of the entire political process; defenders point to the high degree of accountability over elected representatives it affords and the way it rapidly expresses change or conservatism according to the people's will.

The Commons – the powerful lower chamber of Britain's bicameral parliament – is elected by 'first past the post'. To win a seat, a candidate need only gain the highest number of votes in small single-member constituencies which average 69,000 voters. This system puts a high premium on local representation, emphasised by the Commons' custom of referring to MPs as the 'Honourable Member for' rather than by his or her name. Voters have no difficulty in gaining access to their MP and most know the name in any case. They vote primarily for a party – candidates' names and party affiliation are printed on the ballot paper – though evidence abounds of them rewarding or punishing a particular MP if they think fit. Nationally the system can facilitate change, as the 1997 election showed, though it can also sustain long periods of one-party rule, such as the 1950s or the 1980s. In either case it is difficult to resist the conclusion that such outcomes reflected the contemporary popular will.

And yet the case against first-past-the-post has gained a powerful momentum. Initially this was because of the experience of 1979–97, during which the Conservative Party remained in power to implement its radical programme though in four general elections it never gained more than forty-three per cent of the national vote. Opponents read this as a fifty-seven per cent majority *against* 'Thatcherism', but no other party came anywhere near the Conservative share. In any case, less has been heard of this argument lately: ironically, New Labour's share of the national popular vote is almost identical to that of the Conservatives before 1997. With forty-three per cent, New Labour nonetheless has *two-thirds* of the seats in the Commons; even Mrs Thatcher was not so generously served by the electoral system.

This may be an unduly narrow approach, for British governments *never* have fifty per cent of the popular vote. But there are further objections, for the 'winner's bonus' is achieved at the expense of most other parties that fail to gain their proportional share of seats. Currently, the Conservative Party, which took thirty per cent of the 1997 vote, has only one-quarter of Commons seats; most spectacularly of all, the Liberal Democrats – even though they doubled their number of elected MPs in 1997 – have only seven per cent of the seats for a seventeen per cent share of the popular vote. Small wonder they are the most prominent party critics, denouncing an electoral system which allows a party with only plurality backing to behave as if it had a genuine majority.

The drift to proportionality

First-past-the-post continues to operate in local council elections but the many constitutional changes implemented so far and yet to come in each case move in the direction of greater proportionality. The Scottish parliament and Welsh Assembly elections of 1999 were both held under variants of the 'Additional Member System' whereby the outcome of voting in single-member con-stituencies was corrected by a formula intended to smooth out disproportionalities. Thus for the Welsh Assembly the process had two stages: each *Westminster* constituency elected a single Assembly Member (AM), deter-mining the first forty of them. Then the share of votes gained by the parties in the Westminster constituencies that make up each of the five *European parliament* constituencies was the basis of allocating a further five blocks of four seats. Labour fell short of an overall majority, but it formed a single-party administration nonetheless, hardly a sign of the new politics a different electoral system was intended to inaugurate: as it transpired, the elections were the beginning of a troubled period for Labour in Wales. In Scotland, Labour also won fewer than half the seats in the parliament but here the outcome was different. A Lib-Lab coalition emerged with Jim Wallace, Leader of the Scottish Liberals, serving as Deputy First Minister, the first Liberal in government since before World War Two. The formation of the Scottish executive was preceded by several days of bargaining, a spectacle to which British voters – nurtured on the crisp outcomes of First-Past-The-Post – may yet have to become accustomed.

Nor does the shift in electoral arrangements stop there. The European parliament elections of June 1999 introduced the controversial 'closed list' system; voters could still read the names of candidates on the ballot paper, but their votes were counted by party. The share of the popular vote counted within each English region, Scotland and Wales determined the number of seats per party. Yet another variant appeared when London's mayor and GLA were elected in May 2000, the first by a preference system, the second by a combi-nation of direct and proportional list elections. Controversy attached to the methods by which Labour picked its mayoral hopeful and to the quality of all leading candidates. Once again, Labour, so recently impregnable in London, was humiliated, losing the mayoralty to an independent and reduced to level terms with the Conservatives in the GLA. One by-product of the new voting system was to disclose the widespread support for smaller parties one of which, the Greens, secured three GLA seats. Discussions are still proceeding on what to do about electoral arrangements for the rest of local government, but it is scarcely conceivable that it will resist the trend; *if* there is an elective element in the arrangements for the new House of Lords it will certainly be proportional in some wise. And, though it has attracted little attention so far, the introduction of *fixed-term* elections at the territorial level to join those already in operation at the local and European levels has great implications, especially for the government of the day.

But the government of the day gets its power from the House of Commons which does *not* have fixed-term elections, and the system in force there rightly attracts the most attention. The New Labour government is committed to a popular referendum on the electoral system. In Autumn 1998, a government-appointed committee under Lord Jenkins proposed that voters in this referendum be given a choice between first-past-the-post and its 'best alternative', unhappily baptised as 'Alternative Vote top-up' (AV top-up). AV top-up would allow eighty to eighty-five per cent of MPs to be elected as now but in rather larger constituencies, while the remainder would be elected on an open list allowing voters to choose candidates or parties. The British voter would thus vote twice during a single visit to the polling station and, crucially, instead of marking an 'X' next to his preferred candidate he would indicate his preferences one, two, three and so on. Most reformers, even those who favour 'purer' forms of proportional representation, fell in behind Jenkins whose recommendation, they claimed, would ensure Britain was never again governed by a minority. Some kind of electoral reform is clearly central to Mr Blair's personal project of ensuring that what he believes to be the country's natural anti-Conservative majority remains in power. The promised referendum cannot be held before the general election of 2001 or 2002, but if the electorate votes for change then there are fundamental implications for the entire political system.

Parliamentary sovereignty

And it is to the legitimacy of this system that we finally turn. Britain's political arrangements have evolved: there has been no violent transfer of power since the 1690s. The present dispensation arises from a series of adjustments made in response to popular pressure: the electoral system, for example, pre-dates the democratic age. The absence of some initiating act, some deliberate promulgation of basic law – means that Britain, unlike say Germany or the United States, makes no distinction between its constitution and its political system. Constitutional change – including the ambitious programme of New Labour – is achieved by putting bills through three 'readings' in Britain's parliament: there is no difference in the process of setting up a Scottish parliament or altering the speed limit in built-up areas. This paradox is achieved because the whole constitutional edifice is constructed on a single principle: that parliament is sovereign.

The doctrine of the sovereignty of the Westminster parliament dates from the end of the seventeenth century when parliament, dominated by the landed peerage, moved with the support of the judiciary and the hierarchy of the established Church of England to depose King James II and replace him with his Protestant daughter Mary and son-in-law William of Orange. By this aristocratic coup, dubbed the 'Glorious Revolution', parliament asserted its primacy in the political system and the subordination of the monarchy, which became more thorough with the passing of time. The doctrine has survived and in its modern form refuses to acknowledge limits to its power which it transfers anew to each incoming House of Commons (and therefore to whichever party commands a majority therein). In 1999 parliamentary sovereignty can simply mean majority rule, a dogma alien to any system with a codified constitution where the right to resist a majority is fundamental.

The sovereignty of parliament also means that it is the sole source of law, facing no judge of the constitutionality of its actions. British judges – the allies of parliament against the King in the seventeenth century – acknowledge the supremacy of an elected parliament in the twentieth. United States-style conflicts between the most senior courts and the government are unknown in Britain. Only if it can be demonstrated that a minister has taken powers that parliament did not vote to give him (that he has acted *ultra vires*) will the courts intervene: in such a case, they can argue that they are upholding the authority of parliament. As yet there are no authoritative proposals to re-found the constitution: major amendments are being introduced piecemeal, in what many might consider a peculiarly British way. Nevertheless, New Labour is introducing constitutional innovations that in other countries are normally associated with a basic law. Thus the European Convention on Human Rights has recently been incorporated and introduces the concept of positive rights, which is generally absent from British law. The personal freedoms historically enjoyed in the United Kingdom generally exist as spaces that are left after the law has pronounced; there is not, by and large, a rights-based political culture. Incorporation therefore has potentially revolutionary consequences. But how is a sovereign parliament – the only body which can agree to incorporate the convention in the first place – to be brought to agree to setting up a judge of the propriety of its own actions? By attaching to it a very British procedure whereby a judge will offer an *opinion* (non-mandatory) that the law has infringed an individual's civil rights. It will be many years before the implications of incorporation work through the legal system.

As a doctrine, parliamentary sovereignty has survived but it is encrusted with a significant amount of myth. Britain's global economic and naval primacy has, after all, been lost. The country's ignominious exit from the Exchange Rate System in 1992 rudely demonstrated the curtailed economic power of the nation-state. Since joining what was once the European Economic Community (EEC) in 1973, Britain has progressively accepted extensions to 'Community

Competence' (the ability of what is now the European Union as a whole to decide for the member states). Among the key EU institutions is its court of justice, whose judgements rank higher even than those of the Law Lords, once the final court of appeal (see below). A sovereign parliament in a non-sovereign country is a tricky paradox: whatever the internal constitutional position, powerful *external* forces contain Westminster's writ.

Reputation of parliament

But what of the institution itself? Of course, its legitimacy has been challenged from within Britain too. The socialist reformers of the Labour Party in the 1970s explicitly confronted the right of MPs to act as representatives (taking a considered but essentially independent view of the constituency interest) and not delegates (mandated by their local or national party). The Liberal Democrats have long argued that an electoral system that falsifies the popular will vitiates the standing of parliament. The hasty making of bad or incoherent law has done nothing to enhance Westminster's reputation: wise arguments against the Community Charge, or the emergency security regulations of September 1998 were easily shrugged off by powerful governments commanding Commons' majorities. To balance these collective, party-driven errors, many MPs bravely stand up to their party machines: the principled constitutional stand of 'euro-sceptic' Conservatives (those unhappy at Britain's increasing closeness to the EU) from 1990 to 1997, that of left-wing Labour rebels against proposals to reduce benefits to single mothers in December 1997 compel admiration.

In the 1990s, the standing of parliament was damaged by a stream of revelations concerning improper, and even corrupt, behaviour by MPs. The roseate ideology of New Labour (general election slogan: 'Britain deserves Better') cannot obscure the fact that this stream has continued since its return to office. Without doubt, there is a widespread view, fanned by sensationalist media reporting, that there is considerable venality in the House of Commons. In fact, MPs have taken considerable steps to define and enforce proper behaviour: there is a Register of Members' Interests, an activist Committee on Standards, and a Parliamentary Commissioner with wide investigatory powers. And one can only wonder at the stamina of those many activist MPs who work hard in their constituencies on social work for little electoral (and no other) reward. This may have a marginal effect in shoring up politicians' failing reputations.

Referenda

In one respect, parliament has very clearly acknowledged its limits and that is in the area of constitutional change. Today in British politics, the major innovation is the referendum. Pioneered during the 1970s in all three minority territories in the context of constitutional change and also to endorse Britain's terms of entry to the then EEC, the referendum was eschewed in the 1980s by a Conservative administration anxious to reassert parliamentary sovereignty. The 1990s however have brought its revival to the point of being an ineradicable feature of political practice. Euro-sceptic pressure to force a referendum on the outcome of the 1991 Maastricht Treaty, which set up the EU, did not succeed, but it undoubtedly made further integration impossible without a popular vote. In the middle of the decade Euro-sceptics pressed, and eventually obtained, commitments from both major parties that the next big step towards European integration – membership of Economic and Monetary Union – could only occur *after* a positive referendum result. (The LDs always favoured a referendum because they wanted popular endorsement of their long-standing *pro*-integrationist position.)

Then the 1997 election of New Labour extended the terms of the debate. Devolution for Scotland, Wales, London and Northern Ireland was preceded in each case by a referendum; the country also awaits a referendum on the electoral system. All these events and proposals have one thing in common: they represent resignation in the face of diminished parliamentary authority. Clearly some issues are just too big to be resolved by a simple House of Commons majority – parliament needs the extra endorsement of the people. In many countries this would be unexceptionable; in Britain it is revolutionary. The referendum has yet to intrude into those issues (capital punishment, abortion rights) where MPs traditionally exercise their consciences and do not vote at the behest of the whips but it seems likely to prove a drug whose dosage will grow in time. In its 1999–2000 session, parliament considered new legislation to lay down parameters for the conduct of future referenda, an acknowledgement that they are here to stay.

House of Commons

Parliament has been vulnerable to its critics for reasons other than the bullying of parties or the venality of individuals. Some of its customs are impenetrable and even absurd; its conduct of business can be slipshod; its ability to resist government is patchy at best; the unequal distribution of power between its two houses seems grotesque. But parliament of course means – most of the time – the House of Commons. The Commons is the only elected chamber and since 1911 has effectively exercised all powers. The Commons is the chamber which holds nearly all ministers, including the prime minister, to formal account: each of them must report to it, make statements, introduce legislation and answer questions of which no notice has been given. 'Questions to the Prime Minister' is a globally and justly famous weekly session where this powerful politician has to defend his policy before elected peers. Opinions differ as to the effectiveness of this particular scrutiny practice but there is general agreement that at its best the House of Commons is as impressive as any debating chamber in the world

But its weaknesses are also very apparent. Only in 1979 did it develop a comprehensive system of inquisitorial committees; it has only slowly increased the efficiency with which it processes legislation issued by the EU; most of its business is dominated by partisan directives; the opposition has no role in the making of law. Above all, the house seems impotent before an all-powerful government whose very power rests on a majority within it. This is the crux of the parliamentary system: the British people at a general election elect simultaneously a parliament and a government. The legitimacy of the British government and the legitimacy of the law itself spring from one single source: possession of control of the House of Commons, a prize gained by winning a majority of seats there at the most recent general election.

The defects of the House of Commons might be of less concern if parliament were more balanced. But its other two elements – the Crown (for reasons explained above) and the House of Lords are emasculated. The Parliament Act of 1911 (another instance of constitutional reform *sui generis*) removed the Lords' power to block money bills passed by the Commons: the budget deadlock experienced in recent years by the United States simply could not occur in Britain. To win a general election is to know that one can command parliament: when the Chancellor of the Exchequer in a majority government presents his budget, enactment is certain. This Act (embellished by further legislation of 1949) also reduced the veto of the Lords to little more than an invitation to the Commons to 'think again' about its decisions.

House of Lords

Readers might wonder that the lack of balance between parliament's two chambers has not been more controversial. But the Commons alone has democratic legitimacy; it is the chamber whose representative character validates the entire institution. How can one possibly extend the powers of the House of Lords as presently constituted? Its four elements, the hereditary peerage, life peers, the hierarchy of the Church of England and the Law Lords have one thing in common: none of them is elected. New Labour addressed one feature of this by legislating to remove most hereditary peers from the Lords: this was a major constitutional change that cut the size of the House by two-thirds. Under pressure – and in the face of accusations that it intended to replace the hereditary peers with cronies – the government agreed to set up a Royal Commission to look at the entire question of Lords' composition. The Commission, chaired by the Conservative Lord Wakeham, reported its very cautious conclusions in January 2000. By the summer of 2000, it was unclear whether the second stage of this reform would happen at all; if it does occur, and reflects Labour's intentions and the findings of Wakeham, there will – at most – be a partly-elected House of Lords. But one thing is sure: *any* reform of the Lords that introduces even a partially elective chamber must increase the Upper House's legitimacy. The excuse for keeping it powerless will have gone. Hence informed observers have always understood that reform of the Lords can only be the prelude to reform of the House of Commons. Its claim to have all the power in parliament will be destroyed by a legitimate second chamber and a new method of making laws will come. The cynical view persists that this factor alone may, ultimately, keep the Lords unelected.

Conclusion

Tradition and Centralisation, Legitimacy and Partisanship, these are the features of political life in Britain. The curious thing is the extent to which action for political reform seems to reinforce past trends as much as it innovates. If Britain is now in the process of major constitutional reform, it is only because of the speed and scale of the transition that followed the general election of 1997. It is, at present, the brutal power of a bullying government that is driving the reform process. New Labour's supporters argue that under its leadership parliament is finally using its power altruistically – to give up power. Its critics point to the accrual of power around the office of prime minister and say New Labour is building a permanent power base for itself. During 1998–99 the political world echoed misleadingly to language that recalled, in a minor key, the debates of 1909–1911 when a radical Liberal government stripped a then still-powerful British aristocracy of its power. It is reasonable to doubt whether such reforms as the removal of some hereditary peers really address the imperative question posed in every established democracy today: how is it possible to curb the power even of an elected executive?

Further reading

Dunleavy, P et al (eds), *Developments in British Politics*, **5**, Macmillan, London, 2000.

Jones, B, *Politics UK*, 4th ed, Pearson Education, London, 2001.

8
Britain and the World
Henry Davis

Britain's place in the world: a bird's eye view

This essay examines Britain's self-perceived and actual place in the world during the twentieth century: its changing defence policies; its relations with the lands of its former empire and present Commonwealth; with the European Union (EU) and with Europe in general; and with the United States of America with whom Britain has been said to have a 'special relationship'.

Though geographically a part of Europe, Britain has always kept the European continent at arm's length, not only because of its fortuitous separation from the mainland by twenty-one miles of the English Channel, though this is now spanned by a very useful tunnel, but because of intellectual and emotional characteristics sometimes wider than the Channel itself.

Historical and geographical circumstances have nearly always allowed Britain to choose the extent of its participation in European affairs without being forced to do so, like France. The last successful invasion of Britain was by the Normans in 1066, and although others have tried since – the Spanish in the sixteenth century, the Dutch in the seventeenth, the French in the eighteenth and nineteenth, the Germans twice in the twentieth – none has succeeded. On the whole, Britain has tended to sail to war rather than fight on its own doorstep.

From the sixteenth century Britain's (or, more precisely, England's) horizons became and remained global and imperial, as its navy and explorers sailed the world in search of territory and influence, trade, precious commodities and raw materials. International competition among European maritime countries was as fierce then as now, and England was going to be the leading imperial player – not to say imperious, because (in the words of a pre-World War One British army colonel, quoted by the actor/writer Peter Ustinov), 'to have been born British is to have won first place in the lottery of life ...', a commonly-held belief of the English upper classes. Through those centuries of expansion, Britain managed to spread its culture and language further than any of its imperial adversaries, to the extent that English (in its British or American version) is now the pre-eminent language in the world of technology, popular culture and overall communication, and is spoken more widely than any other tongue except Chinese.

Britain in the twentieth century

Despite the loss of thirteen of its North American colonies in the eighteenth century because of a catalogue of blunders and misunderstandings, Britain's empire continued to grow to an immense size. In 1900 Britain controlled a huge amount of the world's land surface, had the largest military and merchant navy, and as originator of the industrial revolution had the largest export economy, and boasted London as by far the world's largest city.

Britain was at that time perhaps the greatest of the world's great powers, had a domestic population of no more than 41 million (including the whole island of Ireland), yet it governed an empire of over 311 million people – twenty per cent of the world's estimated population – whose territory covered almost ninety per cent of the Earth's land surface, or 10 million square miles. As the old cliché said, the British Empire was so immense that the sun never set on it, and it became even more huge after World War One when the League of Nations gave Britain a mandate over former Ottoman Empire territories in the Middle East.

The scale of Britain's mercantile supremacy could be measured by the total tonnage of the British merchant navy: 15.4 million, which was only about three million tons less than the rest of the world's shipping put together. This compares during the same period with the USA's tonnage of just 3.8 million.

Britain's foreign trade was thus remarkably buoyant. As measured in pounds sterling at 1900 values, this amounted to twenty-one per cent of all international trade, while the USA, with a population nearly twice as large, shared only eleven per cent of the world's commerce (Bacon, 1908, p17).

Britain was therefore the world's supreme imperial and economic power up to around 1900, but its wealth was badly distributed. Even thirty years later, George Orwell could not help noticing in his investigation of workers' poverty in *The Road to Wigan Pier* how small, thin, sallow, rickety and generally unhealthy the average working-class person spectating at King George V's silver jubilee commemoration in London's Trafalgar Square appeared to be – a tragedy given that London was the world's greatest capital at the centre of the world's wealthiest empire.

While Britannia ruled the waves at the start of the twentieth century it had no fears of the USA as a rival (though perhaps it should have had, because the wealth of the United States had overtaken Britain's by 1900), nor of France, but was rightly starting to become very nervous of Germany as its most unrelenting economic, naval and imperial competitor. The turning point for Britain's traditionally anti-French foreign policy came around 1910, when plans changed towards defending the English Channel and the North Sea against the might of the German rather than the French navy. Though Germany was defeated after four years of World War One (1914–18), this 'war to end all wars', which destroyed the imperial German, Austro-Hungarian, Russian and Ottoman regimes, also began the process of undermining Britain's world-wide dominance; and World War Two (1939–45) completed this debilitation, largely because winning these wars cost Britain a formidable amount of her wealth as well as stimulating a desire for self-determination among the subjects of its colonial possessions.

World War Two and its aftermath

While at the start of World War Two Britain set up a Royal Naval defence of such size and sophistication that the German navy could not overrun it in the English Channel, and thus Britain's shores remained safe, a new and most severe challenge to Britain's safety came when Hitler's airforce relentlessly attacked and bombed England during the Battle of Britain between July and October 1940. The Royal Air Force managed to shoot down so many German planes – 1700 in all – that Hitler had to postpone his plans to invade Britain and, fortunately for Britain's safety, turned his attentions instead to conquering Russia. Happily for Britain, by December 1941 Germany had taken on the two much bigger forces of the USA and the USSR, without whose participation in the conflict Nazism might well have triumphed.

By the end of the war in 1945, Britain was virtually bankrupt with a war debt of $20 billion and, despite a large wartime subvention to the value of $44 billion from the USA, mainly in the form of 'lend-lease', the country became in 1948 the largest single recipient – to the tune of 24.4 per cent – of aid under the Marshall Plan, which provided $17 billion to Western Europe between 1948 and 1952 (Lloyd, pp271–2).

Notwithstanding its indebtedness to the USA and the heavy rationing that the British people had to endure, by 1950 Britain was able to produce half as much again as in its most productive pre-war year, though most of the goods went into exports, the national motto being 'Export or Die'. A larger and more consistent economic boom took off soon after, not just in Britain but throughout Western Europe, and even in the defeated Italy and Germany, not to mention the United States. The Germans elegantly called it the 'Wirtschaftswunder', or the 'economic miracle', and, fuelled by cheap oil, it effectively lasted throughout Europe until the Middle East oil crisis of 1973. The process of fast economic growth also embraced Communist-dominated Eastern Europe and the USSR, though not in the conventional capitalist sense, and standards of living, social welfare and education rose there too.

While Britain was in the process of adjusting to the new reality of its reduced situation during the immediate post-war years, the same period has been seen by some commentators as one of the most successful in British foreign policy history. Paul Kennedy has pointed out that Britain faced a horrific collection of problems – Europe in ruins, Palestine in turmoil, British imperial India on the brink of civil war, seething discontents in Egypt and other parts of the Arab world, insurrection in Malaysia, an alarming decline in relations with Russia, Communist pressure from Berlin to Hong Kong, American indifference to Britain's problems, and then, as it seemed, excessive American belligerence as a Cold Warrior, on top of 'ominous and persistent' economic pressures on sterling which was especially onerous in view of Britain's pretensions to run a sterling area in competition with the dollar. Yet despite all the terrible pressures, by the time the Conservatives came back to office in 1951, the Labour government had resolved many of these obstacles to the country's future security and prosperity.

But suddenly it was necessary for Britain to see itself as a medium-sized European state needing to divest itself of its expensive imperial possessions, needing also to take on more of a European rather than a global personality, and constantly – as still a great power (for example: still imperial and then nuclear, an occupier of Germany, one of the five permanent members of the United Nations Security Council) – being concerned to secure peaceful change and to prevent any major international crisis escalating into war (Kennedy, 1981).

Consequently, the new Labour government, elected in July 1945, embarked on the revolutionary programme of progressive decolonisation, a process which continued to the end of the 1990s, though it was already mainly implemented twenty years earlier.

The Suez crisis

As late as 1956, but well before the process of empire-dismantling had been completed, Anthony Eden's Conservative government, still wielding the stiff stick of imperialism, saw Britain as having a right and a duty to invade Egypt to prevent its leader, Abdul Gamal Nasser, from nationalising the Suez Canal and from attaining leadership of the Arab world, two events which would undermine Britain's political and economic stake in the Middle East. Eden vividly recalled that Adolf Hitler had not been stopped in the 1930s when he could have been, and such a mistake must not be made again. Although the precedent was not exact, and Eden perhaps showed some evidence of paranoia, Britain's ally, France, felt the same way, both countries being reluctant to forgo their traditional influence in the Middle East. Large-scale public opinion in Britain and France, however, thought otherwise, but this did not prevent an Anglo-French expeditionary force being sent to occupy Suez in an attempt to regain control of the canal, while Israel took this opportunity to invade Egypt pre-emptively. The Anglo-French operation lasted just over a week and failed, largely because of the resolute hostility of the US Secretary of State, John Foster

Dulles. It ended in an embarrassing withdrawal, stimulated by the dramatic collapse of the value of the pound sterling.

The Suez crisis had the sad effect of alienating not only the United States administration of President Dwight D Eisenhower, which was hostile to displays of old-fashioned imperialism by European countries who should have known better, but also of estranging almost all of the Commonwealth, who severely criticised Britain's seeming return to gunboat diplomacy; and it split the British nation thoroughly. Another crucial outcome was to provide an opportunity for the USSR to establish a large foothold in the Middle East through its willingness to support Egypt morally and – more importantly for Nasser's Aswan Dam project – financially.

The Suez failure so jolted the antiquated British conventional wisdom about foreign affairs that Harold Macmillan, Eden's successor, was able to haul imperialist pretensions right out of Britain's foreign and defence policy, realign it away from the grandiose ambitions of his Conservative predecessors, and place a new alternative emphasis on accumulating domestic prosperity. This attitude did not necessarily go down well in more traditional Tory circles, but after Suez, Britain began to enter the post-colonial world, while the Conservative intellectual, Enoch Powell, wrote in 1957: 'The Tory Party must be cured of the British Empire, of the pitiful yearning to cling to the relics of a bygone system.' Even so, as late as 1964, the incoming Labour prime minister, Harold Wilson, felt traditional enough to declare proudly: 'We are a world power and a world influence or we are nothing' (Robbins, 1994, p272).

Britain's painful readjustments

Macmillan was soon able to boast to the people in the 1959 general election campaign: 'Life is better under the Conservatives', which became popularly transformed to 'You've never had it so good'. 'Supermac' (as he was called, first in derision but then in admiration) also went to apartheid South Africa to inform his hard-line white audience bravely and effectively that a 'wind of change' was blowing through Africa which, if not heeded, would sweep aside the old order. He understood how to deal with Britain's post-war decline far better than earlier Conservative rulers had done, while at the same time was able to project himself as a world statesman – as Soviet boss Nikita Khrushchev discovered to his and Russia's discomfiture when Macmillan gently but properly ridiculed him for his coarse behaviour (banging on his desk) during Supermac's address to the United Nations General Assembly in New York.

Britain's overall attitude towards the Third World fluctuated after Macmillan. Sometimes governments were keen to show leadership in bridging the north-south divide – particular the Wilson and Heath administrations. But often the disposition seemed to be one almost of indifference, especially during Margaret Thatcher's stint as prime minister from 1979 to 1990. The motto 'charity begins at home' prevailed then, and Britain's governmental contribution to overseas benefit programmes continually fell well below the United Nations' guidelines for aid assistance by prosperous countries. Mrs Thatcher's ministers would insist that it was not the amount of aid that mattered so much as the effective targeting of aid, and according to that criterion the government would argue that British aid achieved better results than that of most other countries.

What Britain possessed and wanted to pass on was its know-how in the crucial fields of politics, administration, finance, law, education, technology and defence. The Thatcher government was prepared to aid the distribution of this knowledge and training for it, including talking about setting up a new Marshall Plan after 1989 in order to bring the former Communist countries up to Western democratic and economic levels. In due course, disillusion set in because not much of practical value appeared to come at the speed of change desired by the West or the East.

In a 1962 speech at West Point, former US Secretary of State Dean Acheson commented with vast prescience that 'Britain has lost an empire but has not yet found a role'. Certainly an air of vague bewilderment and indecision hovered over Britain for several decades after the 1940s while its rulers tried to make up their minds about what her place in the world should be. Acheson's speech thus struck a very sensitive chord at the time, and his words continued to ring true as Britain struggled with issues like an increasing loss of sovereignty if it were to throw its lot fully with the European Union in place of its historically independent and influential global vocation (Baylis, 1997).

Yet all the while from the 1950s onwards, by way of compensation, the standard of living of the British people was rising to unprecedented heights in real terms, and no doubt this new wealth helped the British a great deal to adjust to their country's modified post-war rank and position. In fact, Western Europe in general was wallowing in a new-found prosperity, and Britain was soon to be overtaken by many European states in terms of income per head.

The map of the world had changed substantially since the beginning of the twentieth century. By the end of the 1990s there were many more nation-states – nearly 200 compared to fewer than forty in 1900 – and Britain (with Europe) had to face serious economic competition from many newly-industrialised countries in other continents, starting with the USA in 1900, continuing with Japan from the 1950s, and on to Korea and the 'Asian Tigers' from the 1970s onwards.

By 1997, Britain's place among the world's leading economies had fallen to sixth – which though no longer first was still very respectable – while its standard of living in terms of GDP per head had become only a humble twenty-second in the world, with a per capita annual income of $18,500, compared to the USA's $26,000 (in seventh place) and Luxembourg's $40,000 (in first place) (*The Economist Pocket World in Figures*, 1998).

If Britain was to adapt to its newly reduced global circumstances, some serious thinking had to be made about where its future lay: whether as part of Europe, or in some kind of special relationship with the United States of America, or perhaps as a tenacious trader covering a territory that encompassed the whole world. After all, two-thirds of most British embassies' business by the 1990s dealt with commerce and export promotions, while Britain continued to prosper as a huge trading nation.

Being a World War Two victor and asserting itself as an important nuclear power early on in the post-war period, Britain had played an influential role: it was one of the four occupying authorities in Germany between 1945 and 1990, one of the five permanent members of the Security Council, a key player in the North Atlantic Treaty Organisation (NATO, formed in 1949), a leading participant in the Group of Seven (G-7, an association of the world's most important industrial countries), and therefore it continued to hold a prominent position at the international top table after 1945 despite its lessening of power.

Aside from the active use of British troops across the empire prior to colonial independence, and as a necessary adjunct of NATO's European deployments and other non-European military alliances in a peace-keeping capacity, Britain has engaged itself militarily in only five important conflicts since 1945: the Korean War as part of the United Nations force to push back Communist insurgents from the north, 1950 to 1953; the Suez Crisis to restore the Suez Canal to Anglo-French control after its nationalisation by President Nasser, July to November 1955; the Falklands War, April to June 1982, in which Britain's forces successfully regained its South Atlantic island colonies conquered by Argentina; the Gulf War, again as part of a UN-sponsored alliance, to liberate Kuwait from absorption by Iraq and to safeguard the Persian Gulf's oil supply routes, 1990–91; and, in 1999, as part of a NATO force, the bombing of Yugoslavia in defence of Kosovar Albanians.

The debate continues about what Britain's international role and self-perception ought to be, and what factors should characterise Britain's attitude towards Europe, the USA and the rest of the world. Writing in 1998, Peter Unwin, a former British Ambassador, argued that Britain's international policy has too frequently been:

> an unhappy amalgam of habit, emotional ties and short-term calculation; which is why so many British people assume that the United States is their best ally and the European Union a dangerous conspiracy.

Since World War Two, Unwin continues, the British have got into an emotional mess about themselves, and no longer behave like 'perfidious Albion' (a pejorative nineteenth-century French phrase). Faced with their country's decline relative to many rivals, the British have concluded that their country has not just declined but failed.

Yet, says Unwin, Britain remains one of the main players in the world's game, actively involved in the Atlantic and European worlds and connected by language, history and institutions to countries all round the globe. The British could not detach themselves from the rest of the world even if they wanted to. But they stand to gain most from a wholehearted commitment to Europe and the European Union (EU), using their weight to help keep the continent prosperous and secure, politically and economically liberal, an equal partner rather than an antagonist of the USA, open to the world, building links with the Pacific countries and generously, even altruistically, engaged with the developing world (*Hearts, Minds and Interests: Britain's place in the world*, 1998).

Dean Acheson's old barb about Britain not having found a role is still being addressed after all these decades.

Britain's foreign policy as linked to defence

It is not really possible to separate British foreign policy from its defence requirements: Britain's relations with the outside world are often determined by its stance on its defence insecurities at any give time. Since 1945, much of the approach by British governments has been based on the same triangle bounded by foreign policy needs, defence prerequisites, and budgetary considerations due to often sickly economic constraints. The latter point of the policy triangle has led to a consistent downsizing of Britain's pretensions, and an ongoing re-evaluation of what its place in the world should be, and this brings into focus Britain having to decide on whether its best and least grand option is to see itself as first and foremost firmly European, rather than global.

This self-assessment of Britain's role for the twenty-first century should engage its opinion-formers for many years to come, and the issue will remain crucial to Britain's future livelihood in view of the firm decision by EU member states to launch European Monetary Union (EMU) in 1999 whether Britain chose to join initially or not.

Between the late 1950s and early 1960s, Britain ceased to be able to think of itself as a great power with continuing global commitments. One unmistakable sign of this was the ending of National Service, a system that conscripted all fit young men to serve in the military for two years or more. This decision, based on grounds of military efficiency and economy, reduced the armed forces by half to 350,000.

Another connected decision of the time committed Britain's defence to more of a nuclear approach than a conventional one. Cutting back on conventional forces immediately confirmed Britain's decline as a world power, because, whereas the USA and the USSR could commit as many conventional forces as they wished to anywhere in the world, Britain had to decide that it could no longer afford to play in that league. This was a great contrast to Britain's perception of its position between 1945 and 1951, when it sought to be both a nuclear power and to enhance its world role. Instead it would now deploy nuclear weapons in submarines and use aircraft carriers more, while reducing and modernising its conventional forces and integrating them more fully into the essentially regional and not global NATO.

With this decision, Britain was forced to enhance its relations with the USA since, because of the vast expense of the nuclear option, it needed American assistance crucially. As a result of this cosier relationship Britain could deploy the latest American weaponry, including Polaris devices launched from submarines, which replaced Britain's own Blue Streak, its only home-manu-factured intermediate range nuclear missile designed in the 1950s, but abandoned in 1961. While Blue Streak was an accurate missile with a 2,000-mile range (that is, it could easily fly from Britain to Moscow), it took fifteen minutes to fuel up, which in an era of four-minute nuclear war warnings was somewhat too long.

The USA was also permitted to station a quantity of nuclear missiles on British soil, and Britain quickly became dependent on the USA's nuclear umbrella, especially when Cruise missiles appeared in 1980. These would help to counteract Soviet rockets that, if launched from the western USSR, would take only nine minutes to reach their British targets.

Britain's foreign policy thus continued to shrink fast into a primarily defensive role. The more dependent Britain became on the USA's protection, the weaker its resolve, and this turned into a controversial issue with the political left in Britain, especially with the foundation of the Campaign for Nuclear Disarmament (CND), a pressure group which demanded that Britain unilaterally give up nuclear weapons for its own best chances of survival, let alone for moral reasons.

The USA seemed cheerful about offering Britain a 'special relationship' as long as Britain was prepared to defend itself and to affirm the USA's dominance as leader of the Western world. In the early 1960s, at the height of the Cold War, the USA constantly consulted Britain, probably because of the personal warmth between President John Kennedy and Prime Minister Harold Macmillan; but the even-handed equality that had existed between Prime Ministers Winston Churchill and Clement Attlee and Presidents Franklin D Roosevelt and Harry Truman in the 1940s and early 1950s could not possibly be sustained.

The defence and foreign policy retrenchment continued in the post-1964 Labour government era. The key decision was taken to remove Britain's military presence from the lands 'east of Suez' by 1968, primarily because of the huge cost of not doing so. There were three main factors that led to the further retreat of Britain from world power status:

1. The end of empire in Africa, reducing the need for Britain's navy to patrol the Indian Ocean. The new Commonwealth nations of Africa did not need Britain to defend them, and as the government explicitly excluded the use

of force when Ian Smith's racist Southern Rhodesia illegally declared its independence in 1965, there was no longer any need for a British naval presence in that part of the world.

2. The recognition of Europe as an alternative to British world-wide activity. The Conservative government had applied for British membership of the European Economic Community (EEC) in 1961, and Labour Prime Minister, Harold Wilson, applied again in 1967, and on both occasions President Charles de Gaulle of France had exercised his veto. But Wilson was continuing to follow Macmillan's policy of fundamentally re-orientating British priorities so as not to require large forces overseas; NATO, Germany and, by 1969, Northern Ireland were becoming almost enough as permanent venues for British troops. From 1968, the only other troops east of Suez would be in Hong Kong, Belize, the Falklands and Cyprus.

3. Economic problems made it pressing for Britain to subordinate its foreign policy to urgent domestic needs, yet be able to continue to afford the nuclear option.

Part of a long-term trend since at least Suez in 1956 had been to rationalise Britain's defence by reducing conventional forces, developing the nuclear deterrent, and, overall, switching the emphasis from an active foreign and war-prepared policy to a reactive and defensive one. This brought Britain in under ten years from a world power to a regional power (Lee, 1996, pp274–5).

Although Edward Heath and the Conservative Party wanted to reverse Labour's 'East of Suez' policy when they came to office in 1970, in fact defence expenditure went up to only 5.75 per cent of GNP from Labour's five per cent. Britain's world role could not be revived because strong downward economic pressures forbade that, as demonstrated by the constant industrial unrest during the 1970s and early 1980s. Also, much more had to be spent on providing a strong military presence in an increasingly restive Northern Ireland, and, on top of that, Britain finally gained admission to the EEC in 1973 now that Charles de Gaulle had resigned from the French presidency. This would mean a policy geared more towards Europe than anywhere else.

Britain's economy worsened when the largely Arab-controlled Organisation of Petroleum Exporting Countries (OPEC) raised oil prices by seventy per cent partly in response to the USA's support for Israel during the 1973 Yom Kippur War: this finally ended Britain's lengthy era of economic growth based on cheap oil, and the ensuing economic crisis lost Edward Heath the 1974 general election.

With the return to power of Harold Wilson and Labour in 1974, defence expenditure was targeted as a way of paying for rising welfare state costs. A reduction would be made within ten years to 4.4 per cent of GNP, though money for the nuclear deterrent would be retained, as would payment for the British Army in northern Germany and its NATO commitments in the joint defence of Western Europe.

However, US President Jimmy Carter began from 1976 to retrench the USA's overseas commitments, a policy which alarmed the European members of NATO who promised to make up the shortfall in their defence against the USSR's increasingly exuberant military activity. Britain was reluctant to pay for the USA's shortcomings, and felt even more broke, as emphasised in a Central Policy Review Staff report in 1977 on Britain's diplomatic representation abroad:

> In the past twenty years ... our share of world trade has fallen by more than half. In today's world a country's power and influence are basically determined by its economic performance. Inevitably therefore the UK's ability to influence events in the world has declined and there is very little that diplomatic activity and international public relations can do to disguise the fact (Lee, 1996).

Foreign policy under Margaret Thatcher

In 1979, Margaret Thatcher became prime minister, with the firmest possible belief that the central purpose of British foreign policy should be to assert Britain's national interests. She turned nationalism into her main credo and, asserting Britain's intention to regain world power status, made defence a top priority, with the armed forces being awarded a one-third rise in pay. But one year later the old truisms had reasserted themselves: Britain's economic condition was such that a strong nuclear deterrent could be maintained only by cutting back on current conventional defence expenditure. This had been a factor since 1957.

Much more than her predecessors, Thatcher emphasised the threat from the USSR, and therefore her determination to modernise Britain's nuclear arsenal by having Polaris replaced by the more advanced American-made systems: Trident, which was British-controlled, and Cruise, which remained in US military hands. Her critics thought that the heavy presence of these missiles would make Britain even more vulnerable to attack, but she believed that the concept of MAD (the as yet untested theory of Mutually Assured Destruction) would prevail and keep Britain safe from nuclear war.

But in return for Thatcher's enhanced nuclear weapon expenditure, the government decided to decommission two-thirds of the Royal Navy's aircraft carriers. As ever, dramatic defence changes like these led to keen controversy at home, with scant agreement in parliament about how to prioritise huge yet shrinking defence funds.

The Falklands crisis of 1982

No sooner had HMS *Endurance*, the only Royal Navy vessel in the South Atlantic, been withdrawn from service as a result of these very cuts, than the military rulers of Argentina, interpreting this as a signal that Britain was about to pull out, ordered the invasion of the Falkland Islands. These islands, a small British possession in the South Atlantic that Argentina had claimed since the late eighteenth century, were among the last of the imperial outposts. Even if it had barely thought about their status, Britain could hardly allow the Argentinean dictatorship to get away with imposing their unpleasant rule over 2,000 British subjects.

For that reason and because of the potential for wealthy oil, mineral and marine reserves in the seas off the Falklands, which Argentina was not going to be allowed to sequester, Britain launched its first military attack since Suez. Two crucial matters had to be dealt with – gaining the approval and support of the US administration for the liberation of the Falklands, which, despite the Monroe Doctrine, was achieved largely because of Mrs Thatcher's excellent relations with President Ronald Reagan; and gaining the endorsement of fellow EEC members, some of whom like Spain and Italy had an historically senti-mental and ethnic attachment to Argentina. With both of these achieved, Britain launched an amazing armada from several thousand miles away to eject the Argentinean military from their bleak Falklands foothold.

The British forces won the war, although greatly outnumbered, because of their superior professionalism and equipment – not least a squadron of very effective Hawker Harrier jump jets. While victory was undoubted, there was little triumphalism at home because it was felt that intelligence reports about Argentina's intentions had been ignored and that the human and financial costs need not have been incurred. Nor should it have been necessary to sink the Argentinean naval vessel, the *Belgrano*, at a time when it seemed to be retreating, and thereby cause the loss of hundreds of young Argentinean sailors. In the war's aftermath, other problems emerged: deficiencies in Britain's weaponry; no effective counter to Argentinean missiles; the apparent pointlessness of conducting a near-anachronistic colonial war against a third-world dictatorship; and the strong possibilities of damaging relations with the USA, EEC member states, Latin American countries and third world states which saw the war as a north-south confrontation (a view enthusiastically endorsed by the USSR).

Needless to say the war also proved to be extremely expensive, costing £700 million, while the sum for maintaining the post-war garrison on the Falklands would total £5 billion – though much of this was subsequently recovered from the profits of oil and other finds in the British-protected seas around the islands.

Notwithstanding her critics, Margaret Thatcher's reputation and Britain's prestige swelled abroad and her foreign policy began to be even more assertive, persuading many that she was the scourge of the Argentinean dictatorship and the defender of democratic freedoms. In 1983 she was even able to win the next general election, largely on the basis of the 'Falklands factor', despite 1.5 per cent fewer of the British electorate voting Conservative than at the previous election of 1979.

The end of the Cold War

It was Mikhail Gorbachev, president of the USSR from 1985, who made it clear to the much more cautious leaders of the Soviet Union's Eastern European allies that the Brezhnev Doctrine ('together we stand, divided we fall') was now dead and that if they could not defend their governments against their own dissidents, he would not step in to prop them up; and they all duly collapsed because of absence of legitimacy and for economic reasons.

Hence in the famous year of 1989, one Communist government after another collapsed, and perhaps the most significant to fall was the government of the German Democratic Republic. When the people of the GDR began demanding unification with West Germany, Gorbachev did nothing to stand in their way. Thus in a series of swift moves spearheaded by the German Chancellor Helmut Kohl, arrangements took place very quickly to achieve the financial and political unification of the two Germanies with the blessings of the leaders of the four-power wartime alliance – Britain, the USA, France and the USSR.

Suddenly – and much more quickly than Thatcher herself might have expected – the Cold War with its forty-year tensions was over, largely thanks to the sound working and friendly relationship between Thatcher, Reagan, Gorbachev and Kohl.

However, Thatcher proved over-optimistic when she said in 1988:

I believe that Britain's role and standing in the world have increased immeasurably.... We are now able once again to exercise the leadership and influence which we have historically shown.

In fact any increases in Britain's world role were temporary, the result of Thatcher's own very 'special relationship' with Reagan; and because she could get on well with Gorbachev, the joint leadership of these three proved crucial in ending the Cold War. History will commend them more for that process than for anything else.

Thatcher was defeated in 1990 as Conservative Party leader by her own Conservative Party in parliament and therefore had to resign as prime minister, not least because of her unrelenting hostility to what was by then the European Community (EC). This was because of her extreme defensiveness about British government sovereignty, and her morbid fear of its vulnerability at the hands of the EC.

The Gulf War crisis

John Major, Thatcher's successor, had no particular foreign policy outlook and little experience in foreign affairs. Yet in no time at all he had to preside over Britain's second war in nine years – the Gulf War – when he sent 45,000 troops to the Persian Gulf to participate in the international (though US-led) effort to recover Kuwait from Saddam Hussein's invasion and incorporation of that country into Iraq.

Britain not only acted as the USA's most supportive ally, but did so on two principles: that stronger countries should not be allowed to get away with threatening – let alone eliminating – their smaller neighbours; and that Iraq should be prevented from controlling one-third of the world's oil supplies. Therefore the Gulf needed to be patrolled and protected to ensure the safety of the Western world's oil requirements. The USA and Britain felt absolutely as one over these issues, though it should be emphasised that eliminating Saddam was not seriously contemplated because he secured a stable Iraq in a region of the world riddled with instability. Indeed, he had once been seen by the British and the Americans as a friendly ally, especially during the long and ultimately pointless Iran-Iraq War of 1980–88, when he took on Iran's fundamentalist Islamic leader Ayatollah Khomeini, who was a keen opponent of the USA.

John Major and President George Bush were nowhere near as close to each other as Thatcher and Reagan, but Major handled Britain's war involvement well, was admired by Bush for doing so, and was never as popular with the British public again as in his moment of victory.

The Gulf War (and Britain's anti-Saddam alliance with the USA) was one of the most potent moments of British foreign policy in the 1990s; thereafter the usual demands for defence cuts resurfaced, fuelled by support for the 'peace dividend' of spare cash after the rapid collapse of the Communist bloc, the Warsaw Pact and the USSR itself. These were seen as opportunities for real defence cutbacks, and Labour left-wingers demanded (though of course failed to achieve) the cancellation of the Trident missile programme.

By 1996 defence expenditure had fallen to seventy-five per cent of its 1986 level, and had been cut from five per cent of GDP to three per cent. After reunification, the British forces in Germany could now be greatly reduced, and those who stayed did so primarily in their NATO role.

Foreign and defence policy under John Major and Tony Blair

John Major had to contend with a more uncertain Europe now that the Cold War was over, Thatcher having argued in 1990 for more preparedness, which was 'never more important than when Europe is convulsed by change'. A strong threat to peace and stability might come from a newly nationalistic Russia; and restraints previously imposed on their allies by the USA and Russia barely existed any more. Because of the 'spheres of influence' factor, whereby the superpowers tacitly agreed not to interfere in each other's back yards, and the concept of 'MAD/Mutually Assured Destruction', whereby a nuclear war would be bound to end in an utterly annihilating stalemate, perhaps the Cold War era had been the golden age of international stability, but the world seemed not to recognise this alarming notion at the time.

British foreign policy under Major was at a loose end; relations with Europe were poor and distant, mainly because of Major's apparent continuation of Thatcher's policy of opting out of any EU provisions disliked by the government. And with Clinton in power in the USA, the 'special relationship' merely simmered, to suffer a setback when the Democrat Clinton accused Major and his Conservative Party of blatant pro-Republican bias during the 1992 presidential campaign.

Criticisms continued on both sides. The USA would have wanted a firmer British military commitment in Bosnia-Hercegovina in 1993 during the Yugoslav Civil War; and Clinton angered Major when he approved a USA visitor's visa to the Northern Irish Sinn Fein (pro-IRA) leader Gerry Adams, despite advice to the contrary from the anglophile US Ambassador to London, Raymond Seitz. Clinton further annoyed Major in 1995 by suggesting that Britain should reduce its nuclear weapons stockpile in line with reductions already made by the USA and Russia.

Major's government seemed to be caught between European and American pressures. The prominent British foreign policy analyst William Wallace said in 1994 that the government 'had no foreign policy, no sense of Britain's place in the world or how best to use diplomacy to achieve national objectives' (Lee, 1996).

Major and Clinton patched up their relations, especially when Clinton in 1995 became the first US president ever to visit Northern Ireland, where he made some rousing speeches of reconciliation that satisfied both the Unionist Protestant and the nationalist Catholic sides of the community.

Major lost the 1997 election, brought down by vast dissensions in his party over Europe, not to mention the electorate's sheer boredom with the Tories. The new Labour prime minister, Tony Blair, not only saw Clinton as his best ally and personal friend, but set about repairing relations with Europe by being conciliatory towards the goals of what was now the European Union (such as opting back into the Social Chapter), though reserving his judgement about endorsing further integration and European Monetary Union until a later date (see section on 'Britain and Europe' below). Relations with the Commonwealth and with the Third World were also given a much higher priority.

The same problems relating to defence budget cuts continued with this new regime, and the 'New Labour' government announced that it was reshaping its armed forces to reduce expenditures and meet the increasing need for speedy and flexible deployment to trouble spots abroad. In plans that would trim $1.1 billion from the current $36 billion defence budget over the following three years, Britain proposed to reduce reserve troops, tanks, warplanes and submarines, while strengthening its super carriers, battlefield helicopters, amphibious forces, Harrier jump jets, transport planes and container ships (*International Herald Tribune*, 9th July 1998).

This time the government's defence and strategic review was heralded by experts as 'the most important in Britain in 30 years', allowing Britain's military responses to be far more flexible than before. There would be two deployable army divisions, one in Britain and 22,000 troops in Germany, and Britain would buy 232 Eurofighters, the standardised European-built combat plane.

Britain would now firmly be a 'middle power', enabling it to deal with two foreign crises at the same time, in contrast to the USA, which as a superpower could handle two full-scale wars simultaneously (*International Herald Tribune*, 9th July 1998).

Meanwhile Britain has held its position as one of the most vigorous sellers of weapons, and this has contributed greatly to the country's balance of payments. The government thought there was a moral dimension to arms dealing, pleading that it vetted prospective purchasers carefully to make sure that the weapons sold were not of the type to be used by governments against their own populations – a goal easier said than done, and a policy very difficult or even impossible to sustain.

The diagnosis of Britain's place in the world is permanent and ongoing. Every British government has seen it as a top priority to re-evaluate Britain's role, and this has often been a painful and puzzling undertaking.

Britain, Empire and Commonwealth

Even before the end of World War Two, it was becoming painfully obvious to Britain that the mighty British Empire was no longer the asset to the British 'Mother Country' it had only recently been: it was now a liability because of the impossible long-term cost of running and policing it, especially in the teeth of determined (and well-armed) local independence movements. From 1947 on, most of Britain's wars would be fought against the irregular liberation armies of its colonies and mandated territories – Palestine, Malaya, Kenya, Cyprus and Aden.

The post-war ethos no longer lent itself to empire and imperialism. Those millions of troops from the British Empire and Commonwealth who had fought to defend Britain's freedom and independence in two world wars had every right to ask why what was good for Britain should not be equally good for their people and nations too. The 1945 Labour government understood those ideals, but also looked at the balance sheets and saw that it was best for Britain's economy to decolonise as quickly as made sense.

Winston Churchill, as Leader of the Opposition after 1945, was not in favour of Labour's policy on colonial freedom. In 1946, he still felt able to say as part of his famous 'Iron Curtain' speech in Fulton, Missouri (in which he frighteningly predicted that the post-war world would now be facing a permanent East-West conflict):

> Let no man underrate the abiding power of the British Empire and Commonwealth ... half a century from now you will ... see 70 million or 80 million Britons spread around the world and united in defence of our tradition, our way of life and of the world cause we and you [the USA] espouse. (Baylis, p9)

In 1947, the granting of independence to India ('the jewel of the Imperial crown') led to a hasty partition between Hindus and Muslims, and in the ensuing fifteen-month war between India and Pakistan millions of people became victims. This was not the best of beginnings for the process of dismantling the British Empire but, nevertheless, Britain showed its willingness to disengage and to remain on friendly and co-operative terms with these new countries.

It does no harm to acknowledge that, of all Europe's imperial powers who were compelled to liberate their colonies – France, the Netherlands, Belgium, and later Spain and Portugal – Britain's decolonisation process worked the most smoothly, despite occasional rearguard military actions by British armies against impatient freedom fighters; the scale and sophistication of decolonisation was an extraordinary achievement, and relationships between Britain and former colonies stayed the friendliest among those of all European colonial powers.

Rather than vainly struggling to persist as the mother country of a great empire, as France was trying and failing to do in the 1940s and 1950s, Britain became instead a leading part of the Commonwealth of Nations, an association of sovereign countries from every continent that had once been governed by Britain and that chose to linger together in a co-operative fraternity after achieving their independence. Interestingly, the British monarch was accepted as titular head of the Commonwealth even by new republics such as India, and the Commonwealth evolved into the largest inter-state and multiracial organisation outside of the United Nations.

The Commonwealth of Nations was originally constituted alongside the British Empire by the Statute of Westminster in 1931, which redefined the relationship between Britain and its self-governing dominions of Canada, New Zealand, Australia, South Africa, Eire and Newfoundland as:

> autonomous communities within the British Empire, equal in status ... united by a common allegiance to the Crown and freely associated as members of the British Commonwealth of Nations. (Palmowski, 1997, p133)

The British monarch's role, in fact, is merely the nominal one of Head of the Commonwealth, and though the members have little in common apart from historical and linguistic ties to Britain, and the Commonwealth has little influence on the world stage, nevertheless it is a world-wide multi-ethnic voluntary community of countries that meet every two years to debate a wide variety of matters, and to offer one another north-south or south-south aid and collaboration. Queen Elizabeth II, crowned as long ago as 1952, is in the extraordinary position of having met and known every Commonwealth leader and every prominent British and foreign politician since then, and that has given her a unique role as fount of knowledge and adviser to present politicians should they find that useful.

The 1945 Labour government's blueprint for colonial freedom offered a programme for establishing a viable framework for independence, including a working economic, financial, governmental, administrative, military, educational, policing and legal system. This would take a few years to achieve while British rule prevailed, and national public opinion might become impatient, but a well-ordered system was worth inheriting. Britain would have very limited responsibilities after independence, so what happened then would no longer really be its concern. From the 1940s to the 1970s, Britain often had to engage troops in actions against local terrorists or 'freedom fighters' (in, for example, Palestine, Kenya, Malaya, Aden and Cyprus) who wanted independence more quickly than the timetable allowed. But, in due course, the Commonwealth achieved a membership of fifty former colonial territories and dominions, thirty-three of which became republics and only seventeen of which retained the British monarch as their head of state.

The Commonwealth has had its crises, as when India and Pakistan fought each other in 1947–48, 1965, 1970–71, and 1999 – often over unresolved territorial disputes involving Kashmir; or with sanctions against apartheid South Africa, which the Thatcher government refused to condone, and which could have resulted in Britain being expelled from the Commonwealth (and 'good riddance' might have been the attitude of many Commonwealth members). Expulsion would have had few practical drawbacks for Britain, since the majority of Britain's trade is with Europe, Japan and the USA, but it would have been a grave humiliation.

Some British prime ministers (notably Margaret Thatcher, from 1979 to 1990) sadly took little notice of the Commonwealth's measure as an influential world-wide network of friendly interlinked countries both rich and poor, while the Queen remained an enthusiastic (though discreet) champion of the Commonwealth.

Some former colonies and mandated territories (those given by the pre-war League of Nations to Britain to manage) refused to join: Burma in 1947, Israel in 1948. Another, Ireland, left in 1949, though it might well rejoin. Still others left under semi-duress: South Africa in 1961 though it came back in 1994; Pakistan in 1972 though it rejoined in 1989; and Fiji in 1987. Nigerian membership has been under threat because of the undemocratic nature of its political system. Membership applications continued to be received and were accepted from countries with scant British links – Mozambique, for example. Clearly, then, membership is seen as a good opportunity for countries to forge useful links with one another bilaterally or via the Commonwealth Secretariat in London.

By the close of the twentieth century, Britain's domestic population had increased to more than 58 million, while the empire – once Hong Kong was returned by Britain to China in July 1997 – had shrunk to fifteen tiny dependent territories, mostly islands in the Atlantic and Pacific oceans with a combined population of 200,000, the merest echo of what once had been (*Whitaker's Almanac*, pp1060–67).

Britain had governed its mighty empire with surprisingly few military and administrative personnel for such a vast overseas area and population, and had needed three state departments through which to conduct its foreign policies – the Foreign Office, the Colonial Office and the India Office. Now there is simply the Foreign and Commonwealth Office (FCO), in tune with today's requirements, though these include an establishment of 222 full embassies and consulates to countries around the world and to international institutions such as the United Nations, NATO and the European Union, compared to not much more than twenty embassies at the beginning of the twentieth century.

Tony Blair's Labour government began to adopt a more positive attitude towards the Commonwealth, and relations between Britain and its fellow members continued to remain warm. Britain was forgiven for its rapid abandonment of the Commonwealth trade agreement ('Commonwealth preference') as soon as it entered the EEC, and the tolerance of the Commonwealth countries toward one another is such that Britain will doubtless offer its blessings to Australia if and when that country opts to become a republic and replace the British monarch with an Australian president as its head of state.

London endures as a meeting ground for immigrants from both the old and the 'new' Commonwealth (which is a euphemism for the non-white countries), as do the other large cities of Britain, and Britain has become a multi-ethnic society in the years since World War Two. Though people were actively recruited in the 1940s and 1950s from the territories of today's Commonwealth – especially from the Caribbean and the Indian subcontinent – to come to Britain as workers at a time of labour shortages, successive governments made it increasingly difficult for migrants to settle in Britain because of fears of racial integration and urban overpopulation problems.

However, by and large, tolerance remains the keynote of Britain's multiracial society and also of Commonwealth inter-state relations.

More about Britain's contribution to global culture, affecting both the Commonwealth and the USA, as well as many other countries, will be found at the end of the essay.

British-US relations

There can be no argument that North American political institutions and culture were partly derived from British models, and for that reason alone relations between Britain and the USA have remained closer than most since the War of Independence of 1776.

But British-US relations have not always been as warm as they later became. During the nineteenth century the two countries disagreed with each other over many matters and were often suspicious of each other's motives. During the American Civil War of 1861–65, for example, public opinion in Britain tended to side with the Confederacy; much of Britain's raw cotton came from the south, so there was a keen economic interest; and Abraham Lincoln was regarded as a despot for wanting to retain the south by force.

US administrations were primarily opposed to the cause of imperialism, from which their own country had broken away, and, while relations gradually became more correct, the two countries were not enthusiastic about each other until the outbreak of World War Two. This is not to say that cultural exchanges and influences had no positive influence, but the concept of a 'special relationship' did not really arise until King George V visited the USA in the early 1930s, despite the Mayor of Chicago of Irish descent threatening to 'punch him on the snoot'.

The wartime relationship of 1939–45 changed things for the better. President Franklin D Roosevelt warmly supported Britain's solo war effort, and secretly allowed funds to be raised for it, though he needed to assure domestic opinion that such help was in the interests of US national security too. Apart from some descendants of Irish and German origin and those who wanted the USA not to become involved in European squabbles, most US citizens displayed an actively pro-British attitude, as exemplified by Hollywood movies such as *Mrs Miniver* (1942), which portrayed charming English people nobly suffering under the duress of food shortages and Hitler's air raids. As early as August 1941, the two countries penned the Atlantic Charter as a statement of common purpose.

Roosevelt got the green light he wanted when Japan attacked and sank the US Pacific fleet at Pearl Harbour and Germany declared war. From December 1941, the USA became fully engaged as a belligerent against the Axis forces both in the Pacific area and – most notably – in Europe.

US money and material came pouring into Britain, followed by scores of thousands of US and Canadian forces. For the first time Britain was immersed in North American *mores*, and looked with awe at the richer and sturdier young American troops – 'overpaid, over-sexed and over here', as the droll saying went.

Not long after the USA entered the war, it became clear that despite an Atlantic Alliance of equals and a sound working relationship and affection between President Roosevelt and Prime Minister Churchill, the USA would straight away play the leading role among its Western partners, if only because of its overwhelming manpower, weaponry, wealth and aspiration to superpower leadership.

Despite the agreed establishment of a military co-ordination Combined Chiefs of Staff Committee, it was clear that the USA was bound before long to relegate Britain into the second division of military, political and economic influence, not just during the war and its immediate aftermath, but permanently. In fact, as soon as Britain began to be hugely in the USA's debt, the relationship changed in favour of American leadership.

It could even be said that, as early as 1942, the brutal loss of British Singapore to the Japanese saw the beginning of Britain's deflation as a genuine world power. The British General Staff officers were eventually forced to give way to US General Dwight D Eisenhower as Supreme Allied Commander in Europe because the USA supplied three-quarters of the allies' fighting men and much of the money.

Churchill continually talked of 'divergences of view', and behind the scenes disagreement between the two allies was a constant feature of Anglo-American relations. Generally, as in any family, attitudes between the two countries' military and political leaders blew hot and cold. No better illustration can be made than from the diaries and memoirs of Field Marshall Bernard Montgomery and five-star General Dwight D Eisenhower concerning their feelings about each other.

By 1944, the British Foreign Office was hinting at the need for a post-war 'special relationship', a phrase which Churchill articulated for the first time in his famous Fulton, Missouri, speech in March 1946. An internal Foreign Office paper of March 1944 had some interesting if haughty points to make:

> In the long run the nature of the relationship does compel national collaboration between ourselves and the Americans, no matter what friction may occur ... more often than not this means that the Americans follow our lead rather than that we follow theirs ... we have the opportunity and the capacity to guide and influence them. They have enormous power, but it is the power of the reservoir behind the dam, which may overflow uselessly, or be run through pipes to drive turbines.... Many Americans are now thinking for the first time about taking part in world affairs, and to most of them this means collaborating with us.... If we go about our business in the right way we can help steer this great unwieldy barge, the USA, into the right harbour. (Baylis, 1997)

Britain still felt it could play the upper hand in the Anglo-American relationship, despite obvious signs that it could no longer compete with – let alone prevail over – the sheer weight of the United States' global presence in the years after 1941.

From 1945, Labour's Foreign Secretary, Ernest Bevin, had to create brand new policies to cope with new realities, and it was becoming essential for the first time outside of war for Britain actively to secure the constructive support of the USA because it could no longer afford to ignore the combined reality of rising challenges and reduced resources. However, strong tensions and disagreements between these two countries surfaced heatedly from time to time, with differing perceptions about how to deal with east-west relations, the menace of the Cold War and the role the USA should play in the ongoing need to defend Western Europe.

One such mutual disagreement arose over the USA's increasingly militant hostility towards communism – particularly towards Mao Tse Tung's new regime in China – despite which Britain quickly recognised the Chinese regime. Britain believed that it could not be ignored or realistically replaced by Taiwan. It was already stable, and some degree of coexistence with communism would be preferable to mutual antagonism and possible annihilation.

Britain held the same view about Cuba after Fidel Castro's take-over in 1958; Anglo-Cuban relations were normalised as quickly as possible and remained normal, despite relentless US sanctions against Cuba over the decades, the worst threat to peace between east and west during the whole Cold War coming with the Cuban Missile Crisis of 1962.

US forces had become a permanent and overwhelming fixture in Western Europe by 1948, once the Communists had taken power in those countries liberated by the Red Army by the end of the war. Stalin made tensions worse by imposing a land transport blockade to and from West Berlin, and east-west tensions became as taut as they would ever be but for the Cuban Missile Crisis some fourteen years later.

In response at this time, so many US Air Force planes and personnel arrived in Britain that George Orwell, in his 1948 novel *Nineteen Eighty-Four*, saw fit satirically to name Britain 'Air Strip One'. And several years later a retired US Navy Admiral in a BBC TV interview truthfully described the British Isles as 'the USA's advanced aircraft carrier' in NATO, meaning that the USA's military actions from Britain into Europe would ensure that any war was kept as far away from the soil of the USA as possible, regardless of any impact on Britain.

At the same time Britain continued to want an equal partnership with the USA in making global policies, as well as a special relationship in which the USA would take note of Britain's specific interests and share its nuclear secrets with Britain.

Neither Presidents Harry S Truman nor Dwight D Eisenhower showed much relish for Britain's desire to want its cake and eat it too. Eisenhower wrote in his diary in 1953 that 'Prime Minister Churchill has fixed in his mind ... that Britain and the British Commonwealth are not to be treated as other nations would be treated by the United States in complicated foreign problems. On the contrary, he most earnestly hopes and intends that those countries shall enjoy a relationship which will recognise the special place of partnership they occupied with us during World War Two.... In the present international complexities, any hope of establishing such a relationship is completely fatuous' (Lee, 1996).

In a manner considered somewhat perverse by successive US administrations, Britain during the 1950s and 1960s did not want to let go of its Great Power leadership aspirations on the grounds that it was a pioneer of nuclear weapons. Having shared much of its advanced scientific know-how with the USA during the war, it was unwilling to rest totally under the USA's nuclear umbrella. Eisenhower, in particular, wished during the 1950s that Britain would cut its cloth to suit its circumstances and found Britain's pretensions trying. There could be no clearer indication of the changed relationship between Britain and the USA than when Eisenhower's views – backed by threats – prevailed during the 1956 Suez War. On this occasion, Britain – by now a fairly toothless imperial lion – was humiliatingly forced, with its allies France and Israel, to retreat from its last colonial military adventure. Of course, US backing for the Falklands War still lay in the future.

But the USA was quite cheerful about Britain's enthusiastic co-operation in setting up such regional counterparts of NATO as the South East Asia Treaty Organisation, SEATO, established in 1955 (and also including Australia, New Zealand, Thailand, the Philippines, Pakistan and France) to withstand Soviet aggression in Asia; and the Baghdad Pact of 1955, which became the Central Treaty Organisation, CENTO, in 1959 (and included Turkey, Iran and Pakistan).

Thus between 1950 and 1956 the two allies experienced both co-operation and friction: co-operation in the nuclear and defence fields, friction regarding 'the recognition of China, nuclear issues during the Korean War, different interpretations of France's colonial Indochina war, the European Defence Community, and misgivings about the Baghdad Pact on the defence of the Middle East. The worst of these difficulties came with the traumatic clash over the Anglo-French invasion of Suez. Such was the hostility generated by the crisis that the alliance between Britain and the US which had been so carefully built up since the Second World War came close to collapse (Baylis, 1997, p68). Between those years, the Americans regarded the British as a 'pallid ally'.

Throughout the post-war period, both countries fervently maintained their separate and expensive intelligence agencies and operations, sometimes sharing their knowledge and occasionally acting in competition with each other. Britain always felt its Secret Intelligence Service agencies to be more sophisticatedly attuned to global realities than the USA's CIA, but both suffered bad setbacks when pro-Soviet spies were unearthed after having given away or sold much important information. Indeed, the first ten years of the Cold War can be distinguished by spy hysteria on both sides of the Iron Curtain, rising to the 1940s and 1950s treason trials in Stalin's empire and McCarthyism in the USA, a movement regarded by the British with grave mistrust.

Anglo-US relations improved during the Kennedy-Macmillan period of the early 1960s because of their personal friendship, though probably Macmillan mistook Kennedy's care to consult with him over international problems as a more meaningful regard for Britain's Great Power status than was actually the case; or at least Macmillan saw the analogy of Britain as a wise and paternal Ancient Greece to the USA's much more powerful Ancient Rome.

Subsequent presidential-prime ministerial relations were often characterised by propriety rather than closeness. Harold Wilson and Lyndon B Johnson never saw eye-to-eye over Vietnam, and Britain took care not to involve its troops in what it regarded as a foolish Domino Theory adventure that would end in tears for the USA (as it did).

While Britain viewed President Nixon's Watergate predicaments as the USA's internal problem, it looked positively on the USA's withdrawal from South East Asia, and was certainly not averse to East-West détente following Nixon's unexpectedly successful visits to Beijing and Moscow.

Because France did not believe that Britain was fully committed towards Europe – hence its rejection on two occasions of Britain's application to join the EEC – Harold Wilson responded by playing down the 'special relationship' concept, and talked instead of a 'close' rather than a 'special' relationship between the two countries.

Britain under the premiership of Edward Heath was too enthusiastic about joining Europe to get very involved in the Anglo-American alliance. While not regarding himself as anti-American, Heath began instead to dismantle the special relationship as part of his strategy for joining the EEC, travelling in the opposite direction to that of most Western European leaders of the early 1970s who sought to strengthen their relations with the USA. Heath's indifference to the USA turned to outright antipathy when the USA's Treasury Secretary, John Connally, suddenly in 1971 suspended the convertibility of the dollar, thus effectively ending the twenty-seven-year old Bretton Woods dollar-centred international financial system and helping to cause serious repercussions for the British economy for two tough years. [To clarify, the twenty-eight nations' Bretton Woods, New Hampshire, conference of 1944, a Roosevelt initiative, had set up the World Bank and the International Monetary Fund (IMF), but primarily had linked post-war currencies to the US dollar in order to enhance world trade and maintain the value of national currencies, thereby preventing financial crashes of the sort that had marred international relations in the 1920s and 1930s. Britain had benefited greatly from this link.]

The Labour government's regard for Jimmy Carter's policies in the late 1970s was not high, especially his desire to base the United States' external affairs on human rights principles, by which countries with a sound human rights record would receive 'most favoured nation' status in contrast to countries in which human rights were constantly contravened. Britain's attitude to this was that it ignored 'Realpolitik', and could not realistically work. Therefore it is ironic that Tony Blair's Foreign Secretary, Robin Cook, appointed in mid-1997, adopted those principles too in a somewhat delayed reaction. Nor did James Callaghan's Labour government go along with Carter's view that the Soviet intervention in Afghanistan in 1979 should serve to isolate the USSR and end the East-West détente. Carter did however score a success in Britain's eyes with his masterminding of the Camp David Agreement of 1978, which brought a peace accord between Israel and Egypt.

Britain now saw itself as a spokesman for the EEC, and as such sought to find a middle path for US-European relations between hostility and subservience. Callaghan's Labour government preferred to speak in a laid-back way of the Anglo-American alliance as a 'natural relationship'.

Whatever the hot and cold specifics of Anglo-American relations, two factors remained in place throughout the post-war period – Britain's continuing aspiration to be the USA's number one ally, and the British Foreign Office's conviction that Washington was to remain Her Majesty's government's foremost overseas embassy, with more money available for official dinners and receptions than at any other mission anywhere in the world. Prime Minister Callaghan even appointed his son-in-law Peter Jay as Ambassador to Washington in 1977, so highly did he regard the post, and much work and socialising beneficial to both countries was done there.

From the early 1980s, Margaret Thatcher and Ronald Reagan became and remained close allies not only because of personal chemistry but also because their ideologies matched; they were both strong monetarists, were hostile to socialism and were anti-Soviet. Reagan even spoke of the USSR as an 'evil empire'. Reagan and Thatcher fell out only once, and that was in 1983 when the US Marines invaded the Caribbean island of Grenada – a member of the British Commonwealth – to overthrow a left-wing regime without first having the courtesy to inform the Queen, who was Grenada's head of state. In a critical debate in the House of Commons, the prominent Labour Member of Parliament Denis Healey saw the USA's action as ominous: if the Americans would not consult Britain over Grenada, would they do so over the use of their nuclear weapons based in Britain? The Thatcher government could give no convincing answer.

Mrs Thatcher's close friendship with Reagan and her popularity in the USA led her to believe that Britain might once more be an equal partner, especially as she became convinced that it was her influence and ideology that were largely responsible for the 1989 revolutions in Eastern Europe and the downfall of communism there.

In fact Britain paid scant attention to the Communist states of Europe, except for the USSR, once Mikhail Gorbachev became the new president in 1985. He showed himself to be 'a man we can do business with', in Thatcher's words, and he was certainly willing for overwhelmingly adverse domestic economic reasons to find ways to defuse the Cold War and thereby the USSR's crushing defence commitment. Thatcher regarded herself as mediator for the 1987 agreement between the USA and the USSR on the reduction of intermediate range nuclear weapons, though in reality British power never was as authoritative as she believed. The USA always remained the dominant partner, despite Reagan's courteous disposition towards her and Britain.

A mark of this dominance was the American arm-twisting of the British government to allow US planes to fly from British bases to Tripoli, Libya, to try to kill President Gaddafi for allegedly ordering the bombing of a Berlin night-club in which some US soldiers had died. Thatcher was none too enthusiastic about this escapade, but could hardly refuse to collude, especially as Reagan had shown his unstinting support for Britain in its war against Argentina in 1982, and had allowed British military planes bound for the Falklands to be refuelled on and over US territory. The two leaders had, however, created an extraordinarily close alliance between their two countries, and Reagan in his 1982 joint address to both Houses of Parliament talked emotionally of this being 'a moment of kinship and homecoming'.

Undoubtedly the intimate Reagan-Thatcher partnership, to which must be added that of Mikhail Gorbachev, helped to bring a very rapid end to the Cold War. And although Thatcher and her successor, John Major, were not as personally familiar with President George Bush, nevertheless the two countries worked effectively together during and after the 1990–91 Gulf War (though obviously with a much larger US input in men, money and materiél) to contain Saddam Hussein of Iraq. Here again was a case of there being no chink of light discernible between the foreign policies of Britain and the USA. This pleased the USA during a period when there was growing scepticism in Western Europe about the perceived 'gung-ho' nature of American foreign policy.

One big ongoing problem to dampen Anglo-American relations was Ireland. The tendency for US administrations was always to sympathise with the nationalist cause because of a huge Irish Catholic electorate in key cities across the USA, and because of an inherent (though not coherent) tendency to think of Northern Ireland as a British colony, and therefore as a last vestige of British imperialism, rather than as a legitimate province of the United Kingdom. From this point of view, IRA terrorists were freedom fighters, and the accumulation of large sums of money in the USA for their cause and their weapons was legitimate.

President Bill Clinton, with an Ulster Protestant ancestry of his own, was more objective and understood that the Irish problem was a complex one for both countries and both religions. He actually listened to both sides and, on a visit to Northern Ireland and the Irish Republic, pledged his support for a fair peace process rather than for instant nationalist unification.

The Blair-Clinton friendship, like that of Thatcher and Reagan, also led to a strengthening of Anglo-American relations and an almost identical viewpoint about the state of the world and what was to be done about it. At the same time Clinton was shifting the central focus of US foreign policy away from a now potentially peaceful Europe and towards Asia, in particular towards relations with China and the 'Asian Tigers'. Europe in the 1990s, he felt, could take care of itself as it had been unable to in earlier decades; Britain ought to attach itself more strongly to the cause of European unity because a strong Europe could only help the United States, the last remaining superpower. In an address of 1995 to both Houses of Parliament the president summed up his positive view of the Anglo-American relationship: 'Today the United States and Britain glory in an extraordinary relationship that unites us in a way never before seen in the ties between two such great nations.' He emphasised the need for a continuation of their co-operation in order to 'win the peace' in the Cold War era (Baylis, pp246–52).

Undoubtedly the emotional and cultural links between the two countries remained strong, but each had its own national outlook and they did not always coincide. The United States was no longer the first choice for British emigrants. Indeed, of the 200,000 Britons who left for good in 1995, only seventeen per cent went to the USA while nearly fifty per cent went to continental Europe (HMSO, *Annual Abstract of Statistics*, 1995). Each of the two countries was more foreign to the other than most citizens of either realised, but joint traditions and experiences guaranteed an intimate political rapport for a long time to come.

Britain and Europe

Although Churchill had spoken in 1946 of the need for a 'United States of Europe', he did not see the point of Britain being a member of it. Britain also rejected the 1950 Franco-Belgian notion of a European Defence Community, and deliberately refrained from joining the six pioneering countries who formed the European Coal and Steel Community (ECSC) in 1951, the precursor to the European Economic Community (EEC or Common Market) which the ECSC turned into in 1957. Instead, because of its inherent unwillingness to accept the supranational principles of pan-European harmonisation, Britain helped in 1960 to found the European Free Trade Association (EFTA), an organisation existing simply to eliminate tariffs on traded industrial goods without going any further along the path of economic or political integration.

To such (French) founding fathers as Jean Monnet and Robert Schuman, the point of establishing a European union – at first economic and then political – was to eliminate any possibility of future European conflicts by linking together the economies of France, Germany, and any other nearby country that cared to join in; and this would also have the effect of containing German expansionism should it recur. When that was achieved, there would never again be any point to war in Western Europe. British governments understood the essence of that admirable philosophy, but rejected the offer to join the ECSC or its more important offspring, the EEC, because they saw Britain as already being tied into more widespread and perhaps significant global contractual obligations beyond the limitations of Western Europe. So it was left to the initial six without Britain – France, Germany, Italy, Belgium, the Netherlands and Luxembourg – to launch the EEC. In due course the six became the nine (with Britain, Ireland and Denmark), then the twelve (Spain, Portugal, Greece), then the fifteen (Austria, Sweden, Finland), and the doors still remained open for further membership applications.

Britain, despite initially rejecting all forms of European unity, nevertheless began to fear missing the boat, and tried to join the EEC in 1961 and 1967, but its application was twice vetoed by France on the grounds that it was not really enthusiastically European enough, and would act mainly as a Trojan horse for the USA's hegemonic designs over Europe – a conspiracy of Anglo-Saxons, as the then French President Charles de Gaulle might have put it.

Prime Minister Harold Macmillan expressed his government's new-found enthusiasm for Europe in a 1962 radio broadcast, after de Gaulle's first rejection of Britain's application for EEC membership: 'All through our history ... we have been very much involved in Europe's affairs. We can't escape it. Sometimes we've tried to – but we can't. It's no good pretending' (Lee, p293).

Britain finally succeeded in joining the European Economic Community in 1973, a triumph for Prime Minister Edward Heath, as it gradually became transparent that Britain's most important foreign relationship had to be with the EC (so called when the EEC changed its name in 1986, as it did again in 1991 to become the European Union or EU). On joining, Britain immediately withdrew from EFTA, and abandoned 'Commonwealth preference' whereby trade with Britain had been almost tariff-free for countries of the Empire and Commonwealth.

Once Britain joined the Community and confirmed its membership by popular referendum, the linkages between them became irreversibly complex, and by the end of the twentieth century Britain had larger commercial arrangements with smallish Holland across the North Sea than with all of the 'Asian Tigers' put together; and had fifteen per cent less foreign trade with the USA than with Germany.

In fact by 1996, fifty-six per cent of all Britain's exports were to its fourteen fellow EU members, and over two-thirds to Europe in general, while fifty-four per cent of Britain's imports came from the fourteen countries, and two-thirds from Europe overall (*Whitaker's Almanack*, 1998, p601). This reality would serve to tie Britain's future irrevocably to the EU through its economy, but also by way of many other administrative, legal, political considerations that linked the members of the European Union to one another in a resolutely interdependent relationship.

Margaret Thatcher began her term of office relatively well-disposed towards the EEC, but she became progressively more hostile to European integration policies while adopting a more strident tone of popular nationalism, to the annoyance and frustration of her fellow European premiers. Her main and consistent criticism was that the British cash contribution to the EC was too high, largely because the Common Agricultural Policy (CAP) absorbed over seventy per cent of EC budget expenditure, and she saw no need for Britain with its efficient farming industry to subsidise the inept peasant farmers of Western Europe. She failed to acknowledge the huge amounts of EC funding that poured into Britain's more deprived regions, which more than equalised Britain's excess contribution, and she got her rebate anyway largely to keep her quiet on the subject, so that EC heads of state meetings could deal with matters other than Mrs Thatcher's continuing obsession.

Britain could in theory have remained outside of the 'Common Market', as it was called, especially once the discovery of oil in the North Sea ensured its petroleum self-sufficiency, and with this a large slice of wealth, when compared to an average EU member state importation of three-quarters of its energy needs. Norway, another oil-producing country, stayed out after having applied to join but failed to gain the approval of its citizens in a referendum; Switzerland has also not joined as the only other wealthy continental country. However, their relationship to the EU is so close that all their domestic legislation is passed in conformity to EU rules. British Eurosceptics (those opposed either to further integration or to membership of the very EU itself) might have been happy to follow the Norwegian and Swiss pattern. To most analysts this would have been an unrealistic option for Britain's 58 million people of varying degrees of affluence compared to the rich 4.3 million of Norway or the even more well-to-do 7 million of Switzerland.

There have been misgivings among the British public about wholly committing themselves to the EU and its ways, and much suspicion about the machinations of a 'Brussels' determined to undermine the British way of life. No doubt similar fears existed in the other more peripheral member states, but many of those fears were based on a general ignorance of what the EU is, does and stands for: its public relations departments tend to publish a great deal without persuading large numbers of the British public. Consequently the Eurosceptic view prevailed and was gleefully disseminated by the British popular press on all occasions. As always over Europe, Britain continued to hedge its bets and successive governments remained cautious.

Not only had Britain not joined at the beginning when it could have played a key role in drawing up the founding constitution of the Treaty of Rome, it had also failed to act as a constructive partner while usually complaining about the Community's shortcomings. Britain's influence in helping to forge the future union of Europe would have proven invaluable in view of its democratic and pragmatic traditions, and such controversial elements as the Common Agricultural Policy (CAP) could have been made more workable and less costly. Undoubtedly the increasingly integrationist views of the original six members – France, Germany, Italy, Belgium, the Netherlands and Luxembourg – were not to Britain's taste as one of the geographically more peripheral countries in the Community, and it elected to opt out of certain ordinances of the Treaty on European Union (signed at Maastricht in 1991) like the Social Chapter, which, among other things, intended to impose a minimum wage, and the Schengen Agreement, which created open borders among the core member states.

The Maastricht Treaty also undertook to create a system of Economic and Monetary Union (EMU) and a single currency to be initiated on 1st January 1999 and completed by 1st July 2002. Britain balked at joining EMU, having been forced out of the previous EU currency regulator, the European Monetary System (with its Exchange Rate Mechanism) by massive currency market turbulence in 1992; and, stung by this, both the Major and Blair governments pledged to wait and see if EMU could be successful before Britain committed itself to such a huge venture that could well be the first step towards a federal United States of Europe (however differently that might be defined by different European countries and interests). While the commitment to EMU and the abolition of the national currency would be irreversible once proceeded with, there was the risk to Britain that if it stayed out of EMU it would sink into the second division of a two-track Europe – of the fast and the slow, the 'ins' and the 'outs'.

But Britain's historically arm's length outlook towards Europe has always been governed by caution, if not downright suspicion, tempered by the desire to lead Europe in a down-to-earth and sensible direction without becoming too unavoidably involved, admittedly a position of semi-detachment.

Yet because of the huge present economic interdependence of Britain and Europe, this attitude might well have become outmoded and redundant by the end of the twentieth century, and might need to be replaced in future by a more committed European outlook. None of the existing alternatives look anything like as realistic a determinant of Britain's long-term needs. Meanwhile, the arguments about an effective British-EU relationship continue.

Despite persistent suspicions within Britain that the European Union was in danger of becoming a federal superstate, that the Brussels bureaucracy was too powerful and suffered from a 'democratic deficit' without proper accountability, and that national autonomy was being whittled away alarmingly, Britain usually played the game according to the rules and was generally one of the most law-abiding of the member states when it came to accepting the Treaty of Rome and other EU legislation. However, fears about loss of sovereignty remained paramount, not assuaged by the countervailing case for the sharing of sovereignty with other EU partners; and the absence of clear national support was the prevailing government argument against joining EMU immediately.

In fact, for most EU activity, national interests are not relevant, and are anyway promoted by the fundamental policy-makers, the European Council and the Council of Ministers, which consist of political leaders of the member states and their ministers. There the choices are made as to where policies should be carried out between the two extremes of harmonisation (whereby member states follow integrated policies) and subsidiarity (whereby appropriate decisions are made at the lowest possible level of government). British members of the European Parliament (MEPs) have met as a national group one time only, when the Queen invited them to a reception when she was visiting the European parliament in Strasbourg. Otherwise, they remain occupied by pan-European rather than by national affairs.

Unlike Margaret Thatcher, whose leadership of her party and government was extinguished mainly by her overt opposition to Europe, and her successor, John Major, who presided over a Conservative Party and government riven by such divisions over Europe that they became unelectable, Tony Blair trod a delicate line by expressing pro-European sentiments without doing much about them. He promised a referendum when the government had decided that the time was right for Britain to join EMU, and proffered sentiments about the country wanting to be in the vanguard of European leadership when Britain chaired the European Council for its six-month stint in the first half of 1998.

Britain has constantly taken the lead in championing the philosophy that the EU should expand and broaden to include as many European countries as want to join, economic and democratic criteria permitting. The notion of an exclusive, inward-looking club of rich European countries was always anathema to successive British governments, and the poorer countries of Europe – especially the former Communist states – could always count on British support for their applications.

The EU is steadily changing its characteristics and its focus, perhaps bearing in mind the analysis offered by the Franco-Czech academic, Jacques Rupnik, in a public lecture of 1995 that 'the geo-political centre of Europe has moved eastwards, but the institutional centre has moved westwards'. Likewise, the geo-political centre of Germany has also moved eastwards. If Britain can see itself as something of a bridge between Western and Eastern Europe, it will have found itself an important role. Such a vocation is already in place with Britain successfully offering its business, administrative and political know-how throughout the former Communist world and beyond.

Meanwhile Britain has functioned within the EU in a less obvious way – through her regions, which derive aid from the EU rather than solely from the British government. Linkages among many of Europe's adjoining regions are strong, especially economically, and the nation-state's boundaries and borders have become steadily more and more porous. Eventually their practical economic relevance will diminish, and the economy of Britain is well placed to take advantage of this growing regionalism. The EU's own Committee of the Regions has the function of sponsoring regional development notwithstanding the state system.

While EMU has many drawbacks as well as obvious advantages (none of which is easy for lay-persons to understand), it cannot be reversed, and Britain as a major trading nation cannot ignore the Euro whether or not the country is formally joined to EMU. The European Union will thus continue to play a massive role in Britain's future, and all governments understand this fundamental argument though they may feel uncomfortable with it. To ease substantially any discomfort, there is always the fact that the one square mile of the City of London houses more national and international banks and financial institutions than anywhere else in the world, and more people travel to the City every weekday to work than live in the whole of Frankfurt, Germany's key financial and banking city and HQ of the EMU's central European Bank. And as long as Britain's wealth can be substantially underwritten and huge profits made by the City playing a dynamic role in Europe's trading activities, then any misgivings about EMU will be held firmly in check.

Conclusion

Since 1900, Britain's circumstances have changed it from that of the greatest global, imperial, military, industrial and trading power on earth to a middle-size, medium-wealthy, offshore, northern European state with a moderate though still significant international status. The adjustment has not been an easy one, and is an indication of just how different and how much more complex the world has become since 'Britannia ruled the waves'.

Britain can count on many successes since the Second World War, let alone during it; and two of the most important relate to Germany. Firstly, it was thanks to Britain and its functional working relationship with the USA in their post-war West German zones of occupation that a democratic, prosperous and serene Germany was eventually forged, which allowed for the creation of a mostly peaceful Europe. Secondly, Britain was one of the few countries able to acquiesce to and guide the reunification of Germany, and consequently helped bring about the sudden and welcome end to the Cold War.

On a more global scale, the relatively calm decolonisation process whereby the British Empire successfully transmogrified itself into the Commonwealth of Nations must count as one of the finest success stories in the history of imperial decline. Britain has also generally been esteemed as a voice of common sense in unstable international situations, and its long-standing traditions of democratic principles and sound diplomacy are highly regarded within the global system – at least for much of the time. For these reasons alone, Britain can be proud of its past and its calm and rational ability to deal with cataclysmic events.

For the men and women of Britain there has been something of an unofficial trade-off: loss of international power and charisma in exchange for steadily increasing national wealth and individual standards of living. This wealth, while not ideally distributed so as to eliminate poverty altogether, has nevertheless helped to cushion decline.

Indeed, Britain's culture and its national variant of the English language are among the most successful of the country's exports, thoroughly disseminated around the world by the semi-official British Council and over the global airwaves by the BBC World Service, whose reputation as a truthful and reliable broadcaster is second to none, and whose respected example is copied by national radio and television in many countries. Also, British theatrical company tours and British cinema, literary and musical talents remain very much in demand and highly profitable activities.

With good judgement and a positive approach to world citizenship, Britain's relative decline as a Great Power need not lead to any further loss of global prestige. Britain's economy remains one of the very strongest, and Britain's voice in the world will still be heard loud and clear.

References

Annual Abstract of Statistics, HMSO, London, 1995.

Bacon, G W, (ed) *Bacon's Popular Atlas of the World*, G W Bacon & Co, London, 1908.

Baylis, John, *Anglo-American Relations since 1939: the enduring alliance*, Manchester University Press, Manchester, 1997.

The Economist Pocket Europe in Figures, Economist Books, London, 1998.

The Economist Pocket World in Figures, Economist Books, London, 1998.

International Herald Tribune, London, 9th July 1998.

Kennedy, Paul, *The Realities Behind Diplomacy: Background Influences on British External Policy 1865–1980*, Fontana, London, 1981.

Lee, Stephen J, *Aspects of British Political History 1914–1995*, Routledge, London, 1996.

Lloyd, T O, *Empire to Welfare State: English History 1906–1985*, Oxford University Press, Oxford, 1991.

Palmowski, Jan, *The Oxford Dictionary of Twentieth Century History*, Oxford University Press, Oxford, 1997.

Robbins, Keith, *The Eclipse of a Great Power: Modern Britain 1870–1992*, Longman, London, 1994.

Unwin, Peter, *Hearts, Minds & Interests: Britain's Place in the World*, Pinter, London, 1998.

Whitaker's Almanack, Whitaker Press, London, 1998.

Further reading

Britain's twentieth-century history:

Robbins, Keith, *The Eclipse of a Great Power: Modern Britain 1870–1992*, Longman, London, 1994.

British foreign and defence policy:

Young, John W, *Britain and the World in the Twentieth Century*, Arnold, London, 1998.

British-US relations:

Bartlett, C J, *'The Special Relationship': a political history of Anglo-American relations since 1945*, Longman, London, 1992.

Britain and Europe:

Denman, Roy, *Missed Chances: Britain and Europe in the Twentieth Century*, Indigo Books, London, 1996.

General reference:

Gilbert, Martin, *The Dent Atlas of British History*, Dent, London, 1993.

9
British Art since 1945
Carole Machin

In the last ten years the British public has shown increasing interest in home-grown, contemporary art. This has mainly come about through media hype and has resulted in some artists, such as Tracey Emin and Damien Hirst, being catapulted to stardom not so much for their artistic inspiration or skill, but for their ability to shock public sensibilities. Modern art has also become a focus for the leisure and tourist industries resulting in public funding for the lavish remodelling of Bankside power station into a new London gallery, *Tate Modern*, while relaunching the original building as *Tate Britain*.

In common with most current art in the Western world, British art is bewildering and diverse in its use of media, style and presentation. Visitors to exhibitions of British contemporary art are likely to be confronted by preserved sheep, abstract shapes covered in raw pigment, installations (perhaps involving mass-produced objects, video, the written word etc., incorporated into one exhibition space), as well as examples of the more traditional disciplines of easel-painting and sculpture. They may be further bewildered by the fact that the boundaries between sculpture, painting, and performance have broken down, and be tempted to ask the question 'Is this art?' and, further, 'If this is art, what is art?'

The success of the Sensation Exhibition, held in London in 1997, underlined the enthusiastic interest in contemporary art during the last decade. It showed a comprehensive cross-section of experimental British art, or *BritArt* as the media calls it. Pictures and discussion of this exhibition can be seen in the Sensation Catalogue published by the Royal Academy. The very title of that exhibition suggests that its aim was to expose the general public to a more extreme form of art that in this case were the experiments of a number of thirty-something artists who mostly trained at Goldsmiths College of Art, London, in the early eighties. Many of the exhibits, for instance Marc Quinn's self-portrait sculpture, moulded from his own frozen blood, were deliberately made to shock the viewer and, despite the fact most people were repulsed, it proved to be a great crowd-puller. The whole and dissected animals preserved in formaldehyde presented as art by Damien Hirst were also a focus for shock/horror. The most controversial and, for many, the most offensive work was a large-scale painted portrait of the Yorkshire Moors' child murderer, Myra Hindley, which used a jigsaw-like pattern of children's handprints to create her image. Many of the works exhibited, including the two examples given above, are attempts at presenting serious social comments concerning decay, evil and death. Others works were jokey and whimsical, and owed more than a little debt to surrealism (see below). The works displayed demonstrated how far art has removed itself from the traditional idea of a two-dimensional painting, or of carved, cast or moulded sculpture.

The works that were in the exhibition belong to Charles Saatchi, who is an important collector of contemporary art and an example of a modern art patron with the wealth and status to make the reputation of a young artist simply by buying and displaying his/her works. Surprisingly, the exhibition, which was held in the galleries of the normally conservative Royal Academy, attracted greater crowds than any other modern art show in recent years. Did the public go just for the shock value, in the same way that they flock to see the latest disaster movie? And will these works survive the test of time?

Because contemporary art includes multimedia pieces, including video, it poses the difficult – possibly unanswerable – question of how one defines fine art today. *Avant-garde* art of the kind seen at the Sensation Exhibition creates good copy in the media, but the established artists tend to produce less experimental works. Figurative painters such as Lucian Freud, Michael Andrews and Kitaj still put paint to canvas, and abstract artists such as Howard Hodgkin and John Hoyland are no longer controversial in their lack of subject matter. Even now the abstract and semi-abstract sculptures of Henry Moore (died 1986) and the distorted figurative paintings of Francis Bacon (died 1992) are still seen as unacceptably 'modern' by some but, despite this, the general public now gives both men the status of national treasures.

How did this situation in fine art arise?

After photography was invented in the early nineteenth century, the post-Renaissance artist's traditional role, as a mirror of reality, was increasingly questioned by each new generation of artists. This change in attitude also derived from the notion of the artist as an original creative force (genius /creator as distinct from the artist as craftsman) that had arisen during the Romantic Movement at the end of the eighteenth century. Further emphasis was given to the artist's originality when the idea of 'art for art's sake' was floated and voiced publicly in this country by James McNeill Whistler in his 'Ten O'clock Lecture' of 1885.

By the time the twentieth century arrived, the artist was exploring new ways of representing ideas by using visual language and symbols that were not necessarily based on accurate representations of the natural world, giving increasing emphasis to self-expression. This resulted in continuous debate and controversy among the critical establishment and also the art-going public, as to the aesthetic, monetary and historic value of the more experimental works. Probably the greatest difficulty the general public has with contemporary experimental art is that it can be made by virtually any means, incorporating any kind of object and still be considered art if the artist proclaims it so. This wide concept of art has a number of different origins in the early twentieth century, but perhaps the most important of these can be traced back to the French artist, Marcel Duchamp, who first presented a bottle rack as an exhibition piece in 1913, and then a male urinal, which he titled 'Fountain' and signed R Mutt, in an exhibition in New York in 1917. He called these and other pieces his 'ready-mades'. They were mass-produced, functional objects used in everyday life and placed in the context of a gallery as a deliberate challenge and tease, aimed at the art establishment. In 1917/18 Duchamp associated with a group called *Dada*, which was anarchistic and anti-war in its political inclinations and based at first in neutral Switzerland. Dada created what was called 'anti-art' that served partly as a reflection of the group's politics. Perhaps more than any other art movement, Dada was responsible for widening the boundaries of art to include performance art, photomontage and what would now be called conceptual art.

From the opening years of the century one of the common preoccupations of Western art has been to find a modern style to reflect modern times and to place increasing emphasis on originality. We now consider the 'modern movement' as an established part of twentieth-century history, superseded by the concept of 'post-modernism'. Here a distinction must be made between the use of the word modern to mean 'current and progressive' and its use in the term the 'modern movement', which has come to mean a specific style that emerged in the fine arts and architecture in the twenties and thirties. The currently much-used term 'post-modernism' is difficult to define, but refers to the idea that there is no progression in the history of art, only a succession of styles and ideas, and that it is valid to refer to the past in new works in a manner that is not merely reverential but that can be interpreted as ironic pastiche.

Is there a style that can be recognised as culturally British?

The attempt to identify a particularly British style is full of pitfalls. In the first part of the century, Paul Nash's comment in the publication *Unit One* in 1934 summarised an opinion widely held that at that time:

> English art has always shown particular tendencies, which recur throughout its history. A pronounced linear method in design, no doubt traceable to sources in Celtic ornament, or to a predilection for the Gothic idiom. A peculiar bright delicacy in choice of colours – somewhat cold but radiant

and sharp in key. A concentration too, in the practice of portraiture; as though everything must be a likeness rather than an equivalent; not only eligible persons and parts of the countryside, but the very dew, the wind as it passed.

This argument particularly applies to the visionary and literary aspects of British art, as seen in the work of John Piper, Graham Sutherland, Stanley Spencer and others, all of whose working lives stretched from the pre-war period until the 1960s and the advent of pop art (see below). However, the strong modern movement in Britain during the first half of the century, embodied in the work of such artists as Ben Nicholson and Barbara Hepworth, was influenced and reinforced by the many immigrant artists arriving in the country at that time. This modernist approach to art was periodically vilified by the art establishment, for instance, in 1948, when Sir Alfred Munnings, then President of the Royal Academy, criticised its members because 'they feel there is something in this so called modern art ... there has been a foolish interruption to all efforts in Art, helped by foolish men writing in the Press, encouraging all this damned nonsense....'

Ease of travel, and the speed of twentieth-century communication systems, has meant that throughout the century, British art has been closely linked to the artistic developments, not only in mainland Europe, but also in America. Today many of the most prominent artists working in Britain were born elsewhere and have brought with them references to other traditions. Anish Kapoor, who was born in India and won the Turner Prize in 1991, is an example of this. The coinage of the term *BritArt* suggests that it describes a British style, but in reality it refers to an experimental and publicity-seeking attitude to art and the media fostering of young art personalities in the same fashion as pop stars.

The coming of modernism and World War One

Current British art can be baffling without some historic signposts to draw on and these would be easier to identify if twentieth-century British art could be seen in terms of clearly defined movements or styles but this is not the case. However, some signposts can be identified and the following is an attempt to give these some sequence.

Impressionism was still a powerful artistic force at the beginning of the century. It had been pioneered in France by artists such as Manet, Monet and Degas in the 1860s, 1870s, and 1880s, and also had its exponents in England. Whistler, the British/American of the same generation as Manet and Degas trained in France and exhibited with them at the first Impressionist Exhibition in Paris in 1873. He remained closely linked with the Impressionist circle, particularly Degas. Whistler was an influential teacher and his view of 'art for art's sake' was welcomed by many of the younger generation. His pupil and close associate, Walter Richard Sickert (1860–1942), painted in the Impressionist manner until his death. His subjects included urban interiors and street scenes using low-key tones and his work had an important influence on art produced in the middle years of the century. Sickert became leader of the *Camden Group*, formed in 1911, and the *London Group*, both of which continued to exploit impressionist technique until his death in 1942. Even now, his influence can be seen in the work of the highly acclaimed Glasgow School of Painters.

Key figures in introducing revolutionary artistic ideas from mainland Europe in the early years of the century were the members of the *Bloomsbury Group*, so called because they all lived and worked in the Bloomsbury area of London. They were a close-knit group of writers, artists and theorists who produced no group manifesto, nor held any stated intentions beyond acting as an arena for the interchange of ideas. One of its most famous members was the writer Virginia Woolf. The artist members were Roger Fry, Vanessa Bell and Duncan Grant. The group also included the art critic and theorist Clive Bell.

Roger Fry was responsible for introducing the British public to the new, ground-breaking art from France in two important art exhibitions in 1910 and 1912. The first of these, entitled *Manet and the Post Impressionists*, displayed the work of, among others, Gauguin, Van Gogh and Cezanne. The second exhibition, *Post Impressionism*, paid special attention to the work of Matisse and Picasso who, by this time, was working in the Cubist style. Both exhibitions had a great impact on the more experimental art of the day. Bloomsbury artists under the leadership of Fry formed the Omega Workshop, which produced crafts as well as fine art. Examples of this work can be seen in Charleston House in Sussex

Fry wrote *Vision and Design* which, when published in 1920, introduced African and Oriental art to a general public hitherto fixed on Greco/Roman tradition. At about the same time, Bell wrote *Art*, arguing that colour and shape can be aesthetically appealing to the viewer even if the painting has no reference to the natural world. His conception of what he called 'significant form' gave weight to those artists who, like Vanessa Bell and Wyndham Lewis, were already experimenting with abstraction.

Members of the Bloomsbury Group who looked to France for leadership were not alone in finding inspiration in mainland Europe. Much of what we consider avant-garde today was invented, or in gestation, as far back as 1910 and during these pre-World-War-One years Britain was in tune with European experiments to create a modern artistic language. In general terms, 'modernism' is a self-conscious quest to find a symbolic language to represent the spirit of the times. This modernist language developed via Picasso, Braque and Cubism, breaking off from the traditional role of fine art, provided both a message and aesthetic appeal through reflection of the natural world. Cubism's use of geometric-shaped multiple viewpoints, incorporation of lettering, collage and found-object constructions, was of seminal importance in the development of abstraction. The Modernist style was developed in the twenties and thirties and became a recognised style, as distinct from the generic term. Cubism led the way to other important modern movements – Suprematism and Constructivism (in Pre-Revolutionary Russia), De Stijl (in the Netherlands), Futurism (in Italy), Vorticism (in England) and Dada (initiated in Switzerland). If you look at the early work of British artists such as Lewis, David Bomberg and C W R Nevinson in the Vorticist years of 1913 and 1914, you will see how modernist these artists were. Lewis, Vanessa Bell and others produced among the first abstract European paintings for example Bell's *Abstract Painting* (1914) and Edward Wadsworth's *Enclosure* (1915).

The most adventurous of early twentieth-century British artists mentioned above were the *Vorticists*, who were a group of artists and writers inspired by the Italian Futurist Marinetti. He lectured in England in 1910 and again in 1914 when he had a great impact on young artists of the day. *Futurism* was largely inspired by the technological advances of the industrial age particularly the mechanisation of speed that resulted from the inventions of the motorcar and aeroplane. An exhibition of Futurist work was shown in London in 1913. Inspired by this Italian movement and its ideas, Lewis, Wadsworth and Frederick Etchells founded the Rebel Arts Centre in March 1914, which in turn became the Vorticist Group. The style they used was based on Cubism and considered very daring. They produced a manifesto and a publication called *Blast*, of which there were only two issues before the intervention of the First World War. The group ultimately consisted of Ezra Pound, T E Hulme, Jacob Epstein, Jessie Dismorr, Lawrence Atkinson, William Roberts and Gaudier Brzeska. Bomberg, although not a signed-up member, exhibited with the group. Nevinson, who worked in a similar style, proclaimed himself a Futurist. Vorticist and Futurist works can be seen at the Estorick Collection, the Tate Gallery and the Imperial War Museum.

During the war the *War Artists Advisory Bureau* was set up in 1916; this was a government body that commissioned artists to paint the war fronts, its goal being to boost patriotism and the war effort. Many Vorticists were appointed and some like Gaudier Brzeska lost their lives in the process. Their rather brutalist, hard-edged style subsequently became identified with war art, and so lost popularity with the public as well as the artists themselves.

The art that resulted from this was an intensely felt condemnation of the war by artists who depicted the harsh and often horrific realities of trench warfare and was not what the government had intended. Notable examples of these works can be seen at the Imperial War Museum. The modernist art styles, particularly *Vorticism*, based as it was on geometric shapes, became identified with the mechanised industrial world whose products of destruction had caused such enormous loss of life. This sharp rejection of modernism was not, however, echoed in mainland Europe.

The inter-war years and World War Two

There is a view that Britain became somewhat of an artistic backwater for the inter-war period, rejecting the experimental in favour of visionary interpretations of nature. Nevertheless, the inter-war years produced some great artists including Sickert, Spencer, Edward Burra, Nash, and John Piper, whose work is based on nineteenth-century tradition. Alongside this individualistic reinterpretation of tradition there were a number of vigorous attempts to re-align the British art scene with mainland European 'modernism', notably by such artists as Nicholson, Hepworth and Moore, promoted by the art historian and critic Herbert Read. Modernism in England had by this time become equated with abstraction and was seen as a symbol of a new social order where the clean geometric lines of hard-edged abstraction represented a healthy, egalitarian environment – a new order of classless art. This was given added strength in the thirties, when many mainland European abstract artists took refuge in England as fugitives from Nazism, for example the Dutchman Piet Mondrian and the Russian Naum Gabo.

The *Bauhaus* in Germany became a think-tank for modernist ideas in the twenties and thirties in the fields of fine art, design, engineering, and architecture and exerted a great influence throughout Europe. It also developed new methods of teaching art and design, many of which are still in use in art schools today. The Nazis closed down the Bauhaus in 1933, when many of the teaching staff came to Britain, although most of them continued west, eventually settling in America, including Albers who went to Black Mountain College in North Carolina. Significant artistic groups of this period included *Unit One*, founded in 1933 by Paul Nash to incorporate artists and architects in England who were working in the idiom of the modern movement in mainland Europe. In 1935, the *Seven and Five Society*, a group of seven painters and five sculptors in pursuit of modernism via abstraction, mounted the first entirely abstract show in Britain. By this time abstraction was an integral part of the modern movement in Europe.

The *Surrealist Movement* manifested itself in 1924 with the first Surrealist exhibition held in Paris. Surrealists used the power of the unconscious imagination and irrational dreams either through accidental mark-making, or through dream states (sometimes drug-induced) to create works of art. It was championed in England by Read but it was not until 1936 that London launched a major international Surrealist exhibition, where works by Dali, Masson, Magritte etc. were hung alongside their British counterparts including Roland Penrose, Eileen Agar and Nash. It then became an important ingredient of the British art scene and is still influential in art today.

In this politically volatile period, the only group with an overtly political agenda was the Artists International Association, founded in the thirties to promote the working-class struggle through art. By 1935, it became involved with the fight against fascism in Europe. No particularly noteworthy art survives from this association. Meanwhile, other artists such as Spencer, Gwen John and Graham Sutherland, worked in individual styles that defy any specific artistic pigeon-holing. They based their work on the human figure and landscape.

When World War Two broke out, artists were incorporated into the war effort as official war artists and made honorary captains. A War Artists Advisory Bureau was set up, headed by the art historian Kenneth Clark, and a decision was made to concentrate on depicting the home front because the government wanted to avoid the kind of problem it had faced during the First World War when artists had depicted their own all-too-real experiences of the horror of trench warfare. Moore made memorable air-raid shelter drawings, Spencer painted the monumental *Ship Building on the Clyde* and a few, like Edward Ardizzone, travelled to the war zones. The war-time government also set up a Committee for the Encouragement of Music and the Arts (CEMA) that had far-reaching consequences for the course of the arts in Britain in the post-war period.

Post-1945 Britain

A quiet transformation had happened in British society during the war years. The general public became very much more interested in the visual arts and the taste for visiting museums and galleries became more popular. CEMA was adapted in the post-war years and re-named the Arts Council. The Arts Council, founded in 1946, had a brief to 'develop a greater knowledge, understanding and practice of the fine arts exclusively, and in particular to increase the accessibility of the fine arts to the public throughout our Realm'. The Arts Council remains an important public-funding body to this day but, whereas initially it sought to educate public taste, it is increasingly criticised for 'dumbing down' its previously high standards to make the arts more palatable to popular taste.

In 1951, the government made a bid to raise public morale by deciding to sponsor what became known as the Festival of Britain. This succeeded in heralding a renewal of optimism and creativity in the arts of the period. Artists and architects were commissioned to design and beautify the temporary festival area on the South Bank of the Thames, London. Only the Royal Festival Hall survives from this complex. At the same time, some artists were taking up the threads of their pre-war careers. Spencer, whose eccentric personality appealed to the public mood, continued to produce figure paintings of a visionary and individual type. Piper and Sutherland, among others, continued the neo-romantic style of the pre-war period, which centred on intensely felt interpretations of nature, often incorporating more than a hint of the surreal. The painters, Francis Bacon, Freud, Frank Auerbach, Leon Kossoff, and Kitaj were loosely identified as the School of London, connected not by their background (none of them was even born in England), but because they all lived and worked in and around London, a fact that was often reflected in their output. The hard-edged modernist abstraction of the thirties was continued after the war, notably by the painter, Nicholson (died 1982), and the sculptor, Hepworth (died 1975).

During the fifties and sixties, increasing American influence was felt on the art scene in Britain. American Abstract Expressionism had a huge impact on young artists and its effects can be seen in the work of Patrick Heron, John Hoyland and many others. The work produced tended to be on a large scale and suitable only for art gallery or corporate display. The media images of American popular culture that reached this country during this time were a sharp contrast to the period of enormous austerity that Britain (and the rest of Europe) had endured during the post-war years of the late forties and fifties.

Pop Art, inspired by admiration and yearning for the consumerism of America, appeared in theoretical form by 1955, developing from an open forum held at the Institute of Contemporary Arts in which Reyner Banham, Richard Hamilton and Lawrence Alloway and others discussed ways to make contemporary art more relevant to society. It resulted in works based on American advertising and films that were brimming with vitality and appealed to the younger generation, for example Richard Hamilton's *Just What Is It That Makes Today's Home So Popular, So Appealing* (1956). Pop art went on to reflect the mood of 'swinging sixties' London.

Pop Art heralded not only a change in attitude within British art but also its perception by the British public and its international status. Young artists such as David Hockney, Peter Blake and Richard Smith reflected the mood of 'swinging' London, acting as catalysts on the international art scene. Pop art was a major liberator for the young of the post-war generation, encouraging youthful artistic freedom of expression and rebutting the idea of art as the exclusive domain of the privileged classes. Elitism dated back to the art patron and the collector/dilettante, the legacy of those who made the 'Grand Tour' back in the eighteenth century. No artistic education was needed for the layman to understand and appreciate pop art. It allowed young artists to break through the academic, artistic conventions of the Royal Academy, whose conservative ideology had periodically re-surfaced throughout the century.

Typical features of pop art are the use of large-scale simple forms, often borrowed from advertising, the use of primary, sometimes luminous colour, and, above all, works that were instantly recognisable and required no artistic or classical education. They sometimes incorporated the use of real objects, and often broke down the distinctions between two-dimensional painting and three-dimensional sculpture, borrowing heavily from the witty construction sculpture of Picasso at the beginning of the century. Leading pop artists of the sixties included Hockney, Peter Blake and Eduardo Paolozzi. Some of these artists, for instance Gilbert and George, strayed into the realm of performance art. Their 'living sculpture' required them to stand like automata, painted in bronze, and mime to a recording of the popular song 'Underneath the Arches', an art form since adopted by street performers.

Later movements

During the sixties a new type of abstract art appeared termed Op Art, based on tesserae or pattern-making to stimulate the optical nerves, causing visual ambiguity on two dimensional surfaces: Bridget Riley is its best-known British exponent.

Conceptualism was a sixties' phenomenon that continues today, and is perhaps the most baffling art form for the general public to access as it usually involves the spectator in intellectual gymnastics. Artists such as Hamish Fulton and Richard Long, who began their careers in the sixties, are examples of artists who provide the spectator with multi-media installations incorporating written, photographed and material evidence of long walks in the countryside. Their work is presented as document and not based primarily on visual aesthetic pleasure. Many younger artists whose work can be categorised as conceptualist ask the viewer to participate interactively with the work. Confusingly minimalism, land art, performance art and art involving video/film all come under the umbrella of conceptualism. The kind of work produced is often based on perishable components or sometimes simply statements about the visual intention so that the resulting artwork is a non-tradable commodity and, as a result of this, artists must use sponsorship (a kind of updated art by commission system) to maintain themselves. This sponsorship sometimes comes from government arts funding bodies such as the Arts Council, and sometimes through private or corporate funding.

What is the state of fine art in England now?

The public's view of contemporary art tends to be informed not by first-hand exposure but through media hype that loves the controversial and sensational. Every year since 1984, the Turner Prize, which is administered by the Tate Gallery, has had increasing publicity and is probably the single most discussed contemporary art event in England. The prize is £20,000, and the publicity that the winner gets guarantees a prominent career for the immediate future. The winners in recent years have been installation artists but, in 1998, the winner was a talented painter. He felt compelled to incorporate elephant dung onto the surface of one of his canvases; this provoked an artist of the more conventional kind to deposit a load of cow dung on the steps of the Tate Gallery and to stick a placard in it that read 'Modern Art is a Load of Bullshit'. Further outrage was recently provoked when Hirst, also a Turner Prize winner, was discovered to have copied and scaled up a child's toy, which he named *Hymn* and sold to Saatchi for £1 million.

1. David Bomberg (1890 – 1957). The Mud Bath. 1914.
David Bomberg was associated with the Vorticist movement when he painted this picture. The geometrical forms are used as a metaphor for the modern, mechanised world.

2. Francis Bacon (1909 – 1992). Three Figures at the Base of the Crucifixion. 1944.
Bacon's triptych (three-sectioned) work shows the grotesque imagery that Bacon favoured and the influence of Surrealism.

3. Ben Nicholson (1894 – 1982). Still Life. 1945.

At first sight this painting appears to be abstract but in fact it is based on the traditional still-life subject of a table with household utensils. This composition derives from Cubism.

4. Henry Moore (1898 – 1986). Reclining Figure. 1951.

Moore based most of his work on the human figure, taking it to varying degrees of abstraction. Although most of Moore's finished work was in bronze, this one is in plaster.

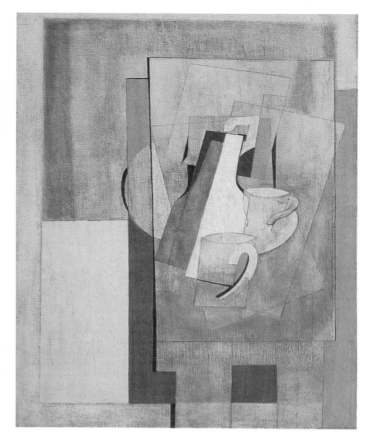

5. Anthony Caro (1924 –). Early One Morning. 1962.
This sculpture has been constructed rather than carved or moulded in a traditional way. It is made of painted metal that has been welded and bolted together.

6. David Hockney (1934 –). A Bigger Splash. 1967.
This sun-soaked evocation of Californian life is painted in strong, flat colour. It follows Hockney's involvement with the Pop Art scene of the Sixties and its admiration for the American consumer life style.

**7. Lucian Freud
(1922 –). Naked
Portrait. 1972–3.**
Much of Freud's artistic
achievement is based
on the traditional
subject of the nude.
However, his interest is
not in ideal human
form but in realistic
human flesh with all its
imperfections.

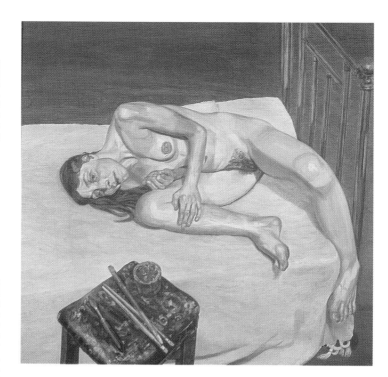

**8. Richard Long
(1945 –). Slate
Circle. 1979.**
This type of sculpture is
often referred to as land
art. The work is made of
slate arranged in a circle
without further artistic
intervention. Long's
works are inspired by
his extensive walks in
the countryside and
sometimes include
photographs, maps and
words.

The public enjoys being shocked by the avant-garde, but its taste is probably more accurately reflected in the sale in 1998 of a painting by Freud, *Naked Portrait with Reflection,* which went for £2.8 million. His work now fetches higher prices than that of any other living artist in Europe. This picture was done in oil on canvas in the time-honoured way and depicts a nude woman on a couch, a subject that has remained a favourite in Western art since the time of the Renaissance. (It should be noted that the female nude as an art subject is itself controversial in this feminist age but is used by feminist artists such as Jenny Saville, whose monumental women challenge the male canon of beauty.)

The increasing prominence of female and feminist artists, such as Rachel Whiteread, Mona Hatoum, Sarah Lucas and Saville, has been a marked feature of the British art scene over the last thirty years.

Unsurprisingly, the public often feels bemused and scandalised, left wondering whether contemporary art is a great confidence trick and whether public money could be better spent elsewhere. Is it all a case of the Emperor's New Clothes? In the last analysis, is public taste an accurate barometer of the art that will be valued in fifty years' time? Only time will tell. But it can be argued that experimental art does inspire new ways of thinking and perceiving the real world. The art debate continues and public interest and opinion is increasingly swayed by careful publicity and marketing by collectors and dealers, like Charles Saatchi.

Selling and buying

The art market is controlled by the commercial gallery system that, by promoting selected artists, can manipulate prices. Traditionally, these galleries have been located in the classy London areas of Bond Street and Kensington, but, as rents have risen and the size and scale of work has increased, more experimental galleries have relocated to the cheaper East End of London, which has also sprouted artist studios converted from abandoned warehouses. Young artists have attempted, often successfully, to go it alone and put on public exhibitions in cheaply rented space, thus cutting out the middleman. But if young artists want to come to the notice of a wide public then they have to ensure that art critics visit the shows and report on them – favourably or unfavourably. Many young artists have deliberately produced works that have a limited lifespan (installations are an example of this) as a protest against art works being valued only as a tradable commodity.

Glossary

Avant garde – art that is experimental and ahead of its time.
Constructed sculpture – sculpture assembled from ready-made or found objects.
Figurative art – art that depicts the natural world.

Environmental art – three-dimensional installation that can be entered by the viewer.

Installation – large-scale temporary construction in a gallery space.

Galleries in London exhibiting British twentieth-century art

Tate Britain (permanent collection and exhibitions)
Tate Modern (permanent collection and exhibitions)
Courtauld Institute of Art (permanent collection)
Imperial War Museum (permanent collection)
Royal Academy of Art exhibitions
Hayward Gallery exhibitions
Barbican Arts Centre exhibitions
Whitechapel Art Gallery exhibitions
Saatchi Gallery exhibitions
Commercial galleries to be found in the Cork Street, Bond Street, and Dering Street areas of the West End of London and in the Hackney region of East London.
Sotheby's Auction House.
Christie's Auction House.

Suggested reading

Sensation Exhibition Catalogue, The Royal Academy, London, 1997.
Buck, Louisa, *Moving Targets: A User's Guide to Art Now,* The Tate Gallery, London, 1997.
Spalding, Frances, *British Art Since 1900,* Thames and Hudson, London, 1987.

The colour illustrations in this chapter are © Tate, London 2000.

10
Understanding British Buildings
Carole Machin

The image of Britain as a land full of castles, cathedrals and thatched cottages is the reason why many visitors and students come to Britain. Pockets of quaint old-world charm still exist, mostly in small country towns, but the reality is a land where cities and towns are overcrowded and where buildings old and new jostle for space.

The built environment lends character and identity to a nation, and has enormous impact on the quality of our lives. It is not only the look of buildings that matters but also whether or not they fulfil the function that they were designed to perform. Materials are fundamental to the look and shape of buildings, and before the days of mechanised transport it was practical to use those materials that were easily available in the location of the building site. The natural building resources of Britain are clay, wood, and stone, including flint. Clay exists in abundance and the Romans left us the art of clay brick- and tile-making even though these skills were only significantly revived in the sixteenth century. Until the sixteenth century, Britain had an ample supply of wood readily available in the great forests that covered the country. Oak was the preferred variety and the timber-framed houses that we associate with Shakespeare's England are examples of its use. Stone is a relatively scarce material in Britain, requires quarrying, is heavy to transport and therefore expensive, and, apart from where it occurs locally was, and is, only used for important buildings.

When we consider the history of architecture, a distinction should be made between grand or public design and ordinary building design based on local tradition. The latter is termed the vernacular and it includes housing, shops, barns, workshops, etc. not designed by architects but by local builders working according to time-honoured tradition with local materials. The real character of the British built environment is formed more by its vernacular architecture than by grand designed building that, until the twentieth century, had been based on the architectural forms introduced by the Romans; these included the arch and dome and the classical orders (the term referring to Doric, Ionic and Corinthian capitals). Most Roman buildings in Britain have long since dis-appeared, but these classical components were methodically revived during the Renaissance and are still part of our architectural language. It was the Victorians who made a conscious effort to create a British style but ironically chose a reworking of the medieval gothic style that had evolved in France. The Houses of Parliament (Fig 19) and St Pancras Station in London are examples of this gothic revival.

One of the problems architects and town-planners face today is the difficulty of blending the old with the new in ancient cities. Merely designing new buildings in imitation of the old is a blind alley and forms no basis for innovation and visual excitement. In addition, there are strict conservation and planning controls concerning areas and buildings of historic interest.

City and countryside alike have winding roads that mostly seem haphazard and illogical; the exceptions are the old straight Roman roads and the new motorway systems. These meandering old roads follow cart tracks, which in turn skirted hills or followed streams, and have resulted in cities that are labyrinthine rather than logically planned. Bath is one of the few exceptions. In the eighteenth century its city council was almost despotic in its clearance of the medieval town to make way for a new, planned town fit for the gentry to visit, take the medicinal waters and, consequently, to enable the towns-people to make money. The result is a harmonious, neo-classical, ordered city with wide streets and gracious squares. London and other cities do have sections that have been laid out according to a master plan. Regent's Park Terraces, designed by John Nash, are an example of a successful attempt to bring harmony and grandeur to a building development within central London. In the later part of the nineteenth century, the more expensive urban develop-ment schemes, such as the Kensington area of London, featured grid-planned roads and communal gardens. Vertical living in apartment blocks did not catch on in Britain until the mid-nineteenth century and these were mostly designed as social housing experiments (Fig 6).

After the Great Fire in 1666, the City of London had a wonderful opportu-nity for radical replanning. Christopher Wren was employed to rebuild St Paul's Cathedral (Fig 10) and many other city churches after they had burnt down in the fire. He also envisaged a new city with wide streets and piazzas reminis-cent of Renaissance Rome. Sadly, the owners of each pre-fire plot of land wanted to reclaim their property and this only allowed for rebuilding along the narrow, winding, medieval streets.

Again, there was a unique opportunity for re-planning many cities after the bombing of World War Two, but the rush to get the population housed and businesses going again did not allow for this. The limited budget available for the rebuilding of Britain prevented much consideration being given to rethinking cities in any profound way. Priority was given to getting buildings constructed as quickly as possible, and many were designed for the short term with the expectation that they would be replaced when the economy recovered. But the recovery was slow to happen. This situation also gave modern architecture a bad name because circumstances required quantity not quality. One of the few distinguished buildings that survives from this immediate post-war period is the Royal Festival Hall on London's South Bank, which was built for the Festival of Britain in 1951 (Fig 20). All the other buildings for this festival were temporary.

In the 1960s, there was a policy to knock down what were seen as slum areas in inner cities. This was well intended but the clearance demolished attractive late eighteenth-century and nineteenth-century terraces without thought of refurbishment as an alternative. Many of the replacement building schemes were tower blocks, which were unpopular as soon as they went up, were soon vandalised and became slum areas in themselves. There have been brave efforts to build new towns and cities in post-war Britain – Milton Keynes, Basildon and Stevenage are examples.

More recently the Conservative government under Margaret Thatcher encouraged the redevelopment of the Thames dock area in East London as an Enterprise Zone. This area had become virtually derelict because of the change to containerised ocean shipping. No planning controls were imposed and there was little overall urban design for the area. The result was a free-for-all where some buildings of merit have gone up, such as Canary Wharf designed by the Argentinian/American Cesar Pelli, but others are of poor quality. This redevelopment of what is now called Docklands has in turn caused the regeneration of the old wharf buildings along the Thames into expensive and much sought after loft apartments.

The rapid outward expansion of British cities has been going on since the eighteenth century, but this was hugely accelerated with the coming of the railways and particularly the suburban and London underground railways in the nineteenth century. The earliest underground system was the Metropolitan Line, which was fully functional by 1863. The result of railway transport was ribbon development circling inner London, which formed inner and outer suburbs. The uniform lines of houses, designed to accommodate the maximum number of people in the minimum amount of space, are typical of this kind of development. This urban expansion accelerated during the 1930s and came to an end with World War Two. By the 1930s, the London County Council was alarmed by this uncontrolled growth and set a limit to the amount of agricultural land that was being swallowed up in Greater London by designating an area of countryside around the city. This area is called the Green Belt. In the 1990s, there was much discussion of where new housing should be developed and the government has been under pressure to develop brown field sites (derelict areas abandoned by industry) rather than eat into the remaining countryside.

The British are, by nature, resistant to the new and organised – during the 1930s the International Style was introduced into Britain, recognisable by its clean lines and uncluttered surfaces as well as its large windows. It was hoped that these light, airy, living spaces would revolutionise their occupants' health and living patterns. The housing developments in this style were mostly blocks of flats, e.g. Highpoint, Highgate (Fig 7), and never really captured the public imagination, which preferred the small mock Tudor semi-detached villas that were being constructed along cities' outer boundaries.

British taste in architecture both in the past and the present is conservative. There are many contemporary British architects, for example, Sir Norman Foster, Sir Richard Rogers and Terry Farrell, who are enormously talented but whose more adventurous designs are only accepted and built abroad, not in cautious Britain. Nowadays most large-scale building schemes are chosen through competitions; the final selection is done by a board specially elected or chosen for the occasion and unwilling to take risks. The Lloyds Building in the City of London (Fig 22) and the Millennium Dome (Fig 23) are examples of innovative design and use of materials.

Recognising building types and styles

Building types can be loosely divided into domestic (Figs 1–7), ecclesiastical (Figs 8–12) and municipal (Figs 13–23). Despite the prolonged Roman occupation, very little building from the Roman period survives. Most of the oldest surviving building in Britain dates back to the Norman Conquest in 1066. The Normans built castles (e.g. the Tower of London) for security and as symbols of power, and they also rebuilt churches on a grand scale as symbols of ecclesiastical authority. These prestigious buildings were generally built of stone, but domestic buildings of the same period were made of wood and thatch except in those areas where stone was plentiful and wood scarce. Obviously stone buildings have more chance of survival and consequently many of these remain but there is very little trace of the wooden buildings of this period. As society changed and became more stable, cities enlarged and building requirements altered. The crafts of brick- and tile-making were revived in the sixteenth century when it was recognised that brick could be a cheap replacement for increasingly scarce wood and it had the added advantage of being less vulnerable to fire. Hampton Court was one of the first large-scale buildings to be built of brick since the Romans had introduced that craft into England in the first century AD. After the Great Fire of London there was leg-islation against rebuilding in the flammable wood and thatch that had constituted most of its buildings and brick was substituted in its place for all but those of major importance.

Wood, stone and brick require traditional building methods and it was not until the middle of the nineteenth century that new materials in the form of cast iron, steel and plate glass and concrete initiated a change to prefabricated building methods and caused a revolution in construction techniques. Buildings of this period and type include railway sheds like those in the main London termini (Fig 18).

Today, in the course of a short walk through the square mile of the City of London, it is possible to see the remains of the 1,800-year-old wall built by the Romans around their city of Londinium and the 1,000-year-old (almost) Tower of London set against the backdrop of buildings from subsequent centuries and dwarfed by contemporary high-tech, high-rise buildings.

Housing

1 Timber-framed house, fourteenth century

This is a timber-framed house of the kind that survives from the fourteenth, fifteenth and sixteenth centuries. The wood most commonly used was oak from the great oak forests that covered Britain at the time. The spaces between the timbers were filled with wattle (woven basket-work screens) and daub (a mixture of clay, water and horsehair). These surfaces were then given a limewash to deter insects. The roof is made of clay tiles but roofs were often thatched with reeds or straw. Note that there is no chimney. Houses at this time had open hearths. The windows had no glass and were closed with wooden shutters at night. This kind of house survives in most areas of Britain but is particularly plentiful in the Midlands and South. The Shakespeare Properties in Stratford are good examples of this building type. The reconstruction of the Globe Theatre is based on the same principles of building method.

2 The Palladian-style villa

Eltham Lodge, Woolwich, Kent, by Hugh May, 1664

Typical of the style favoured by the landed gentry, these large-scale private houses went up in both town and country from the mid-seventeenth century through to about 1800. Based on the designs of Palladio (see Banqueting House, Fig 17), they had imposing entrances marked by the use of pediment and columns based on the classical temple portico. Other examples include Kenwood House and Apsley House, both in London.

3 Late eighteenth-century town house

These late eighteenth-century town houses were designed to maximise land space. Built of brick in rows, they were usually five storeys high. The more upmarket ones were built around squares that had communal gardens in the middle. They had tiled roofs and sash (sliding) windows and had access to piped water but no main drainage. Kitchens were below ground level in the basement. They were heated by fossil fuels and normally had one privy (lavatory), which served the whole house, in the yard at the back. There was no bathroom. Examples include houses around Bedford Square in London and the eighteenth-century stone-built terraces in Bath.

4 Late nineteenth-century town house

This late nineteenth-century suburban terraced house was designed to accommodate the increasing population of white-collar city workers. They were mostly put up by speculative builders and made of clay bricks with tile or slate roofs. They had sash windows filled by large panes of glass and mass-produced, moulded composition stone decorative features around the windows and doors. By this time, there was usually one internal lavatory and bathroom. This type of house can be found in large numbers in the inner suburbs of towns and cities.

5 Family house c1900

This is an architect-designed house of the kind that catered for the middle classes who were able to buy a large plot of land in the suburb or countryside. This example was designed by the arts and crafts architect, C F A Voysey in 1899, and paid lip service to traditional regional houses (the vernacular). It would have accommodated a comfortably off, middle-class family with one or two resident servants. This kind of upmarket house was built in the outer suburbs after the railway age. Examples can be seen in Bedford Park, London.

6 Nineteenth-century social housing

Streatham Street Flats, London, 1849–50

An example of an early social housing scheme financed by the Society for Improving the Conditions of the Labouring Classes. The design encloses three sides of a square and has open walkways between each apartment. Every flat had its own kitchen and lavatory, which was a great luxury for working-class families in the mid-nineteenth century. Individual philanthropists like George Peabody, an American businessman who made his home in England, decided to help 'ameliorate the condition and augment the comforts of the poor' and set up a trust to that end. In 1862, the first of the many Peabody Estate apartment blocks was built in Commercial Road, Spitalfields. Other similar schemes were set up by such groups as the East End Dwelling Company and can be seen in Whidborne Street and Midhope Street, just south of St Pancras Station. By the end of the nineteenth century, local government became committed to funding social housing with public money.

7 1930s modernism

Highpoint, Highgate, 1933–38

Two blocks of apartments designed by the architect Berthold Lubetkin, in the International Style which emphasised minimalist decoration and clean, light, functional forms. This style was linked to the idea of healthy living and its beneficial impact on the morals of society. Other examples include Lawn Road Flats, Hampstead, by Wells Coates.

Ecclesiastical buildings

8 Norman (Romanesque) churches

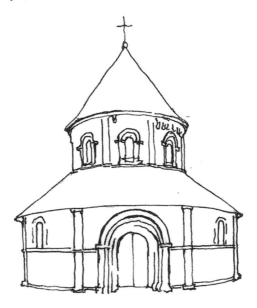

The Round Church, Cambridge, c.1130

The Norman style is distinguished by round arches, heavy, load-bearing walls and small round-headed or round windows. Typical Norman churches were rectangular in shape and variable in complexity and decoration. The style was used for important buildings from the Norman Conquest until the gothic style emerged around 1200. This example is unusual because of its round shape, a feature of those churches built for the Knights Templar, whose lives were dedicated to protecting the Holy Sepulchre in Jerusalem from the Saracens. The only other surviving example of this type of round church is the Temple Church in London. Examples of the rectangular type include St Bartholomew the Great, London, and St Alban's Cathedral.

9 The gothic cathedral

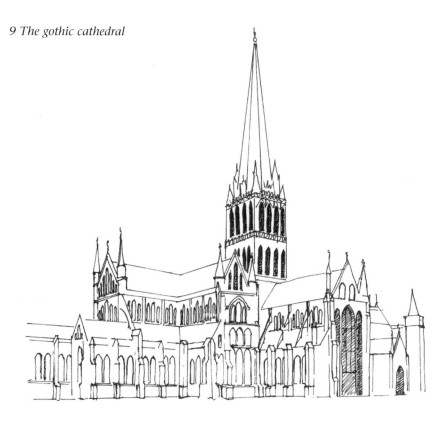

This drawing is based on Salisbury Cathedral, which took almost a hundred years to build but is almost unique in the speed with which it was erected. Usually these medieval cathedrals were built over several hundred years and incorporated a number of different design styles. Gothic is often referred to as the pointed style because its arches are pointed. Fundamental to gothic construction is the use of buttressing (shallow walls at right angles to the main building) to take the weight and stress of the roof so that the walls were no longer load-bearing. Cathedrals and churches could then have large-scale windows which were filled with stained glass, usually dedicated to telling the story of the Old and New Testaments. Examples include Canterbury Cathedral and Wells Cathedral.

10 Renaissance / baroque

St Paul's Cathedral, 1675–1711

Designed by Christopher Wren to replace the old medieval St Paul's, destroyed in the Great Fire of London in 1666. The style is Renaissance with its strict use of classical orders (Doric, Ionic and Corinthian capitals) but the dome, which was the first to be built in Britain, and its use of curved surfaces also identify it as Baroque. Wren also redesigned fifty-one of the eighty-seven City churches burnt down in the Great Fire.

11 Baroque

St Mary Woolnoth, London

Designed by Nicholas Hawksmoor and built between 1716–27, this small square church has an exaggeratedly high, heavy, square tower and heavy rustication (indentation between each stone block) and uses classical forms in an unconventional way typical of the baroque style. Other examples of baroque include Blenheim Palace, Oxfordshire, and St Mary-le-Strand Church, London.

12 Classical revival

St Martin's in the Fields, London

Designed by James Gibbs and built between 1722–26, this church is based on the Greco/Roman temple form with a tower mounted on the pediment. The interior is similar to those designed by Wren and intended for the preaching-based services of the reformed Anglican Church.

Castles, palaces and public buildings

13 The Norman motte and bailey castle

Based on Dover Castle, built in the 1180s, but also similar to the Tower of London in plan, this motte and bailey castle was formed by a series of man-made ditches and banks which culminated in a mound (motte) in the centre on which stood the keep where the main living quarters were located. Ideally castles were built of stone but some temporary ones were made of wood. This design, which included battlements, slit windows, look-out towers and defensive walls, was to gain the maximum amount of security and command of the surrounding terrain. Many other examples survive including Rochester Castle, Kent, and Orford Castle, Suffolk.

14 Medieval barns

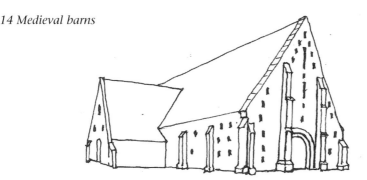

Great Coxwell Barn, Oxfordshire

An important part of the social fabric of medieval Britain, barns were used for food storage. This stone barn, built in the thirteenth century, stored tithes, a levy of one tenth of a community's produce given to support the church and its clergy. Other examples of tithe barns can be found at Bradford-on-Avon, Wiltshire, and at Glastonbury.

15 Medieval hall

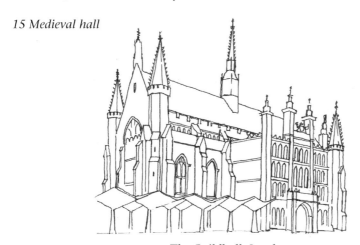

The Guildhall, London

An example of the gothic style applied to a secular building. The hall has served as a civic centre for the City of London since the late twelfth century. The present hall dates from 1411 but had major structural damage during both the Great Fire and World War Two. The stone building has many later additions including the exterior of the porch which is late eighteenth-century and in gothic style. The external post-war arcade or ambulatory was opened in 1974 and is made of moulded concrete and glass. Many halls of this kind, mostly of brick, were built under the Tudor monarchs. Other examples include Middle Temple Hall, London, and the Tudor Hall at Hampton Court.

16 Tudor gothic brick

St John's College Gatehouse, Cambridge, 1516

Dating from the time of Henry VIII, this gatehouse was built of brick with stone dressings at the moment when brick was becoming widely used. It is representative of Tudor gothic with its shallow pointed arch and its casement windows. Other examples include Hampton Court Palace and St James Palace, London, each arranged around a series of courtyards.

17 Renaissance

The Banqueting House, Whitehall

Begun in 1619, this building dates from the time of James I (1603–25) and was finished under his son, Charles I (1625–49). The strict classical orders and emphasis on harmony of proportion and symmetry were principles its architect, Inigo Jones, had studied in France and Italy. He was particularly influenced by the Italian Renaissance architect Andrea Palladio, whose book on architectural theory and design was printed and published in Venice in 1581. An English edition, under the title *The Four Books of Architecture* (1715), had a huge influence. The building was not only intended for court banquets but also for masques, popular court entertainments that combined fancy dress with amateur dramatics. The rich interior has ceiling paintings by the Dutch artist Peter Paul Rubens. It was on a scaffold outside this building that Charles I was executed in 1649.

18 Victorian railway stations

King's Cross, 1850

Designed not by an architect but by the engineer Lewis Cubitt, this is a building that is simple and functional in form compared with the station frontage of neighbouring St Pancras Station, designed by the architect Sir Gilbert Scott, in Victorian gothic style. The train sheds were the most innovative part of the station complex. Built of cast iron, steel and glass, the sheds are early examples of pre-fabricated building construction.

19 Victorian gothic

The Houses of Parliament, London, 1836–68

The Houses of Parliament are also known as the Palace of Westminster. The original palace was established by Edward the Confessor (1042–66) and served as the meeting place for parliament. Westminster Hall is the only section of the original palace to survive the fire of 1834. As the result of a competition, a new parliament building was designed by Sir Charles Barry and Augustus Pugin in perpendicular gothic to match the Henry VII chapel at the far east end of Westminster Abbey, which lies opposite. Other examples of Victorian gothic include St Pancras Station and the Law Courts in the Strand, London.

20 Post-World War Two modernism

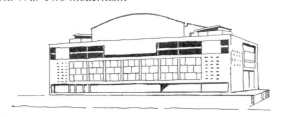

The Royal Festival Hall, 1948–51

Designed by the London County Council Architects Department for the Festival of Britain in 1951, this was a post-World War Two attempt at modernism. Despite post-war austerity, this prestigious building was made of expensive materials including a portland stone-cladding and an extravagant use of wood in its interiors.

21 Brutalism

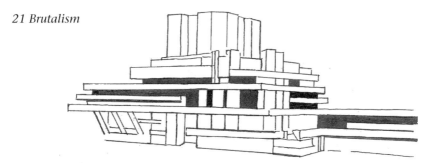

Royal National Theatre, 1967–77

This type of uncompromising use of shuttered concrete is both hated and admired, and was much used in the 1970s when it became known as brutalism. Designed by Sir Denys Lasdun as part of the South Bank Arts complex scheme devised in the 1960s and 1970s, the theatre has three auditoria and an atrium foyer. The Barbican Estate and Arts Centre (1957–84) in the City of London is also designed in brutalist style using shuttered concrete, which weathers badly in a cold damp climate and now looks dark and forbidding. The Brunswick Centre (1962–70) near Russell Square is the product of the same style.

22 High-tech modernism

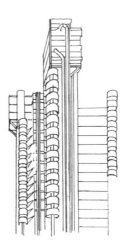

Lloyd's Building, City of London

Designed by Richard Rogers and Partners (1978–86), this stainless steel-clad building is mainly notable for the novel placing of its services (lifts, ventilation ducts etc.) externally.

23 High-tech, limited life-expectancy

Millennium Dome, 1996–99

Designed by Richard Rogers Partnership, this mast and cable, stretched fabric construction was expected to cost £40 million. Built on the tent principle it is a tensile structure using self-cleaning, Teflon-coated, fibre glass fabric and is expected to last twenty years.

Further reading

Pevsner, Nikolaus et al, *The Buildings of England* series, Penguin, Harmondsworth, 1951–.

Saunders, Ann, *The Art and Architecture of London,* Phaidon, Oxford, 1984.

Watkin, David, *English Architecture,* Thames and Hudson, London, 1979.

11
Religion Today: The Church of England and Other Faiths

Alan Walker

Introduction

We acknowledge that the Queen's excellent majesty, acting according to the laws of the realm, is the highest power under God in this kingdom and has supreme authority over all persons in all causes, as well as ecclesiastical as civil.

The Church of England, established according to the laws of this realm under the Queen's Majesty, belongs to the true and apostolic Church of Christ ...

These statements from the Canons or laws of the Church of England, which are part of the law of England, appear to describe a state and a state of affairs very different from that of the United States with its constitutional separation of church and state. The monarch is head of both state and church; and the church in question, the Church of England, is described as the 'established church', which means that the state has accepted a duty to protect and support this church because it is the one that the state considers to teach most truly the Christian faith, which is, presumably, the only true faith.

The reality observed is rather different. The similarities between Britain and the United States are more apparent than the differences. Britain is hardly a Christian country in the sense that some Middle Eastern countries are Muslim. Adherents of all religions are free to practise their faith without interference from the state, and the courts have held that the law is indifferent as to religion. On the other hand, it would appear to be a less religious country than the United States in terms of participation in organised religion, although such a statement would need to be qualified to take into account the differences between the constituent parts of the United Kingdom and the different religious traditions that are now represented in it. For the most part, this essay will examine the situation in England because it is in England that the greatest changes in the religious landscape have taken place in the last half-century, and because if there is one thing that we can say with some certainty about the future it is that it will be characterised by change.

In religious terms, Britain is now a multi-faith society, although not, it has to be said, in a geographical sense, for at present the experience of religious pluralism is largely confined to the major cities and certain institutions such as the universities, but in the sense that education and law and politics must now treat it as such. About a tenth of the population is affiliated in some way to non-Christian religions, while more than sixty per cent would claim some sort of relationship with Christianity, although, as will be seen, rates of participation are quite different. It is not easy to study the non-Christian religions separately from the national and ethnic communities with which they are so closely associated, or to distinguish genuine Christian commitment from traditional Christian values on the part of the host population.

This essay will proceed with an historical overview of the rise of multi-faith Britain, the origins of which go back far further than most would imagine. But whereas in the United States religious freedom was something guaranteed, at least in principle, from the beginning, in Britain religious tolerance was something that was arrived at and only grudgingly conceded. It is also worth pointing out, however, that compared with the tension and violence which until as recently as the last century characterised the relationship between different versions of the Christian faith and community, there is virtually no inter-religious, as opposed to racial, conflict in contemporary Britain.

Just as the status and powers of the monarch provide a convenient and historical starting point for the study of the British constitution, so the status of the Church of England is an appropriate starting point for the study of religion in Britain. In both cases the story is one of a gradual, but decisive, removal of power alongside a continuing, if wavering, respect for dignity and status.

Christianity

Despite the claims of neo-pagans, who have sought to recover ancient beliefs and practices, Christianity is the religion with the longest continuous history in England.

Individual Christians began to settle in Britain during the Roman period from perhaps as early as the late first century, and by the end of Roman settlement at the beginning of the fifth century an organised church had developed and grown to be probably the single largest faith community. The fate of Christianity in the ensuing period, when eastern Britain was transformed into a number of Anglo-Saxon kingdoms, is obscure, but there is evidence that church life continued in the Celtic west, that some contact was maintained with the church on the continent, and that missionary activity, trade and settlement took the faith across the sea to Ireland.

Subsequently the pagan Anglo-Saxon settlers were themselves gradually converted to Christianity by missionaries sent directly from Rome by Pope Gregory I in 597 and by monks from Ireland who were active in the north in the same period. A council held at Whitby in 664 began the process of settling differences of worship and organisation between the Irish or 'Celtic' tradition and that of Rome. Thereafter England was part of a universal church, its religious affiliation unaltered by otherwise seismic events such as the Norman invasion of 1066.

The Church in England was reformed in the sixteenth century when the authority and jurisdiction of the pope were replaced by those of the monarch, and its doctrine and worship were subsequently remodelled under the influence of continental Protestantism. Doctrinally, the Church of England belongs to the reformed or Protestant tradition, but legally it stands in continuity with the church founded in Anglo-Saxon times and retains significant features of its Catholic past. The character of the Church of England owes more to Queen Elizabeth I than to her father, Henry VIII, and reflects her liturgical conservatism, irritation with the fine detail of theological controversy and firm belief in hierarchical forms of organisation. By the end of her lengthy reign, the majority of the population was reconciled to her 'settlement' of religion, but some preserved their loyalty to the papacy and practised their Catholicism in secret and under occasional persecution and consistent suspicion; others sought a more thoroughgoing 'purification' of the English church on the lines of that which had taken place in Scotland, where Presbyterianism had replaced Episcopal ministry and government and a more rigorous doctrinal code had been imposed.

Until the seventeenth century it was generally thought that all citizens or subjects could and should belong to the same church, the only question being 'which church?' But the religious controversies of the era eventually made some kind of legal religious dissent essential. After the Civil War the attempt of the restored monarchy to reinstate 'uniformity' of religion failed, and by the end of the eighteenth century *de facto* freedom of religion had been granted to the non-Church of England Protestants known at first as 'Dissenters' and later as 'Nonconformists'. Roman Catholics achieved legal emancipation in 1829 though some restrictions on their full participation in national life continued, and there remained even into the mid-twentieth century a certain degree of popular prejudice which associated Catholicism with political disloyalty and religious obscurantism. The Catholic population itself was thoroughly transformed in size and character by Irish immigration.

The achievement of freedom to practise religion coincided with the beginning of a declining interest in actually doing so. The census of 1851 showed that only about a half of the adult population attended a church, and that only half of those who did so attended the Church of England. Far from being the majority religion, the established church only seemed to attract about a quarter of the population. The decline was probably largely a consequence of migration from the countryside to the towns and the breakdown of traditional forms of community life. The participation figures do not of course reveal the extent to which the churches were involved in education, welfare and other public activities. Nor should they obscure the fact that in other ways the nineteenth century was an intensely religious era in which, in response and reaction to changes in intellectual life, traditional doctrinal differences became less important than more general conservative, liberal or radical orientations.

If participation in organised Christianity has remorselessly declined since the nineteenth century, the greatest decrease has been among the older Nonconformist denominations, while the Methodists appear to be in virtual terminal decline. This has led to mergers, most notably of the majority of English Presbyterians, Congregationalists and Disciples of Christ into the United Reformed Church in 1972, and official 'conversations' between the Church of England and the Methodist Church, which foundered in 1972, seem likely to be renewed.

Despite the fact that only about a tenth of the population now regularly attends church, the relative share of the Church of England has actually increased – although it has now been overtaken by the Roman Catholic church in terms of total average Sunday attendances. Nevertheless, if allegiance is distinguished from attendance, and statistics for baptisms and marriages are taken into account, it could be argued that the established church still has some claim to the loyalty of about a third of the population. One commentator has pointed out that if this is so, then the most typical way in which loyalty to the Church of England is expressed is by its members not attending church.

The establishment of the Church of England is open to challenge. It retains seemingly anomalous medieval privileges such as the right of its senior bishops to sit in the House of Lords – although the exclusion of its lower clergy from the House of Commons is usually overlooked by commentators. At the same time it remains subordinated to parliament – many of whose members may not even be Christians – even in doctrinal matters, and the appointment of bishops and other senior clergy is still a matter for the 'Crown'.

In reality, the principle of establishment seems more open to criticism than its actual practice. Parliament has delegated most of its ecclesiastical authority to the General Synod of the Church and is unlikely ever again to intervene on matters of worship or doctrine. England, unlike several European states, has no church tax, and the established church receives no direct financial support from the state. The church-state link is very much what the partners make of it: during the premiership of Margaret Thatcher in the 1980s, for example, the church acted almost as an opposition party with respect to social policy. Interestingly, the establishment has been supported by some non-Christians on the grounds that it is better to have a state with some religious dimension rather than a thoroughgoing secular one. It should be noted that the Anglican Church in Ireland was disestablished in 1869, and the Welsh dioceses of the Church of England were disestablished in 1919 and transformed into the 'Church in Wales' on the reasonable grounds that both were minority denominations.

A particular, indeed peculiar, feature of the Church of England is that, whatever its status in its native land, it is also part of the world-wide Anglican Communion, the product for the most part of Anglican missionary endeavour in the former British Empire. The Church of England is the senior member of the Communion but exercises no authority over it. In this, it resembles the United Kingdom in the Commonwealth. The 1998 Lambeth Conference – the ten-yearly meeting of the bishops of the Communion – showed that Anglicanism is not only numerically now strongest in the developing world, but that the bishops from there are increasingly prepared to take the initiative in debates on theological and moral questions. It has been argued that the Church of England is paradoxically the least typical member of the Anglican Communion precisely because its national status requires it to embrace a far broader range of opinion than would be possible for an independent church that was seeking to have a clear identity *vis-à-vis* other denominations.

The two major issues that exercised and divided the Church of England in the last decade of the twentieth century were the question of the ministry of women in the church and the moral legitimacy of homosexual activity. Women were admitted to the priesthood from 1994 but cannot yet be bishops; the bishops have indicated that they remain opposed to the ordination of practising homosexuals. Behind both of these questions lies a perpetual problem that the Church of England has with the nature of authority and decision-making, and the competing claims of scripture, church tradition and 'reason' to be determinative in defining doctrine and morality.

Whatever the difficulties facing the traditional churches, the picture of Christianity in contemporary Britain would be incomplete without reference to the growth of 'independent' Christian churches, which are almost exclusively of an evangelical outlook. It is among such groups that the most rapid growth in the Christian community has been seen in the last decade. Recent years have also seen an impressive growth in the number of Afro-Caribbean churches, although part of the impetus behind these has been a disappointing failure of the traditional churches to respond to the needs of immigrant Christians.

Judaism

After Christianity, the religious community with the longest continuous history is that of the Jews. There were probably Jews in Roman Britain – before there were any Christians – but nothing is known about them. A sizeable community grew up in England after the Norman Conquest and there is archaeological evidence of important centres in London, Bristol and elsewhere. Jews in medieval England did not enjoy rights of citizenship but were protected by the king and were allowed to engage only in certain occupations such as money-lending. They lived in relative peace until the twelfth century when a combination of essentially external factors deriving from their problematic status in Christian theology led to persecution and their complete expulsion from England in 1290. A clandestine Jewish community began to form in the sixteenth century following the expulsion of the Jews from Spain.

The Protestant Reformation encouraged a revival of interest in Hebrew, the language of the Old Testament, and a literalist reading of those passages in the New Testament which assigned a particular role to the Jews in the working out of history. Puritan Christian theological concerns rather than a belief in religious toleration led to the 're-admission' of the Jews to England in the mid-seventeenth century and the modern community has a continuous history since then. It was accepted that there were no legal prohibitions on their residence in England, and Jews were subsequently granted a legal status, which, in areas such as marriage, gave them a better position than non-Anglican Christians. Restrictions on Jews attending university and sitting in parliament were lifted in the nineteenth century. A Sephardi synagogue was opened in London in 1656 for Jews of Spanish and Portuguese origin and this was followed by an Ashkenazi synagogue for those from Central and Eastern Europe. The late nineteenth century saw a major influx of Ashkenazim fleeing from perse-cution in the Russian Empire or seeking better economic opportunities. Others came as a result of Nazi persecution in the 1930s. The Jewish population of Britain peaked at around 450,000 in the early 1950s since when it has declined to about 300,000 partly as a result of emigration, particularly to Israel, and partly because of assimilation, marriage outside the community, and a declining sense of the importance of religious identity.

The presence of the other non-Christian religions in Britain is almost completely the consequence of immigration particularly from the former empire and therefore reflects the character of Britain's imperial adventure.

Islam

Britain's second largest religion is Islam. Muslims have lived in Britain since the seventeenth century when sailors – known as Lascars – recruited on the Indian subcontinent began to be a presence in London and other ports. The first permanent communities consisted of Yemeni sailors recruited in Aden after the opening of the Suez Canal in 1869 who then worked out of British ports and in some cases married local women. By the First World War, they numbered as many as 10,000 and their religious needs were served by several small mosques or prayer rooms. The first – and oldest surviving – British mosque opened in 1889 in Woking, Surrey, where a student hostel for Indian students was established and from where Muslim publications were disseminated.

Through the initiative of a local convert, an Islamic Institute, a Muslim College, and a home for children and orphans were established in Liverpool at the end of the nineteenth century. A weekly newspaper, *The Crescent,* was published there from 1893 to 1908. The first mosque in London, the East London Mosque, opened in Stepney in 1941. In 1944 an Islamic Cultural Centre was opened in Regent's Park, London, and the Central Mosque on that site was completed in 1977. In 1996, there were estimated to be 613 mosques in Britain of which ninety-six were purpose-built.

There are thought to be around a million-and-a-quarter Muslims resident in Britain of whom about half have their origins in Pakistan and another third in Bangladesh. Migration from the Indian subcontinent on a significant scale began in the 1950s, as a result of the post-war labour shortage in Britain. As Commonwealth citizens, the migrants enjoyed full rights of entry and residence. Most settled in the North and the Midlands and parts of London. Cities like Birmingham and Bradford gained substantial Muslim minorities. The first immigrants were mainly men who probably saw themselves as temporary residents, but from the 1960s, and partly because of attempts to control immigration, many were joined by their families and dependants. Immigration policy also contributed to the growth of a Muslim middle class by encouraging the settlement of doctors, teachers and engineers. With the decline of the traditional industries, which originally provided employment, many migrants and their descendants have entered retailing and catering, and surveys suggest that the self-employed status that this often involves is encouraged by and in turn encourages religious commitment.

In addition to Muslims of Pakistani and Bangladeshi origin, there are smaller communities of Turkish Cypriots and of Asians expelled from East Africa. There are also significant numbers of Muslims of Middle Eastern origin residing on a semi-permanent basis as business people, refugees or students, and perhaps around 5,000 converts, many of Afro-Caribbean origin.

The growth of Muslim community organisations and pressure groups reflects and has stimulated the development of a self-conscious Muslim identity – particularly among younger generations – alongside, and increasingly instead of, previous national or ethnic self-definition. Muslim organisations have been particularly active in campaigning for the meeting of educational and social needs. At the same time, there has been concern about the growth of what has been called 'Islamophobia' – the dread or hatred of Muslims deriving from the perception of Islam as 'fundamentalist' and anti-western, of Muslim cultures as monolithic, unchanging and radically different from other cultures, and of Muslims internationally as using their faith for political or military ends. Prejudice against Muslims, mixed with racial hostility towards immigrants, prevents Muslims from taking a full part in British society and makes it harder for moderate Islamic opinion to be heard.

Hinduism

The term Hindu is in origin a geographical one referring to the land bordering the river Indus in northern India. Hinduism is a name given to a variety of Indian beliefs and religious practices bound together by adherence to a number of sacred texts and fundamental concepts. Hindus began to visit and live in Britain as students, traders and professionals from the beginning of the twentieth century, but the present community dates from the 1950s, when at first only men came seeking employment, and from the 1960s when they were joined by their wives and families. The majority came directly from India, but others came from East Africa where Africanisation policies led to the expulsion of communities created in the British colonial period. There are probably about half a million Hindus in Britain today with communities in many of the principal towns and cities. The Hindu festival of Diwali in October-November, celebrated in a carnival-like manner in several towns and cities, is probably the first example of a non-Christian holiday taking on a public or civic character in Britain.

Because Hinduism lacks any central organisation or authority, its adherents tend to associate on the basis of ethnic, caste or sectarian identity rather than that of religious commonality. It has been suggested that those who came from East Africa, and who therefore already had the experience of settlement outside India, had developed a clearer sense of religious identity and sought to express this in the establishment of temples and other religious institutions. Conflict with other religious and ethnic groups, often reflecting tensions in India itself, has also contributed to a greater sense of common Hindu identity.

Sikhism

Sikhism originated in northern India in the fifteenth century. It began as a movement within Hinduism, but developed beyond the boundaries of traditional Indian religion to become the most recent world faith. The majority of Sikhs live in the Punjab, which was an independent Sikh kingdom until conquered by the British in 1849. The Sikhs then became loyal servants of the Crown, and what had been a relatively poor rural community became one of the most literate and educated groups in India. Many served in the British Indian army and supported the Raj against those who called or fought for Indian independence. Former soldiers and others who had gone as workers settled elsewhere in the empire, particularly in East Africa and Canada, and a small number of traders and wealthy families came to live in England. The first British Sikh house of worship was opened in 1911 in Shepherds Bush in west London. Small communities of Sikhs grew up in East London and Glasgow during the 1920s and 1930s, consisting almost entirely of men engaged in selling clothing, but the greatest migration, like that of Hindus and Muslims from the Indian subcontinent, took place in the 1950s and 1960s, with others arriving from East Africa in the 1970s. There are now between some 350,000 and 500,000 Sikhs living in Britain in the largest community outside of India.

Many of the first post-war male immigrants abandoned some of the distinctive features of the Sikh religion, in particular the uncut hair and beard and the wearing of the turban. Although this was done reluctantly to escape discrimination and other elements of religious observance were maintained, it was only with the arrival of their families in the 1960s that the number of worship centres increased from a handful. There are now around 200 in Britain. The arrival of educated and better off co-religionists from Africa encouraged the return to traditional customs, the abandonment of which had any case made little difference in terms of attitudes of the host population. A number of legal cases in the 1970s dealt with the issue of turban-wearing in situations where non-Sikhs would be required to wear uniform headgear or to remove their covering. In 1976, Sikhs were given a special exemption from the law requiring the wearing of a crash helmet when riding a motor-cycle, and in 1983 the House of Lords declared that Sikhs constituted a separate ethnic community and therefore their customs were protected by race discrimination legislation.

Jainism and Zoroastrianism

In addition to the three major groups mentioned above, there are also two other religious communities that have been established principally through immigration from the Indian subcontinent between the 1950s and 1970s. About 25,000 Jains have settled in Britain, mainly in London and Leicester, and have established four temples. Although Zoroastrianism began in Iran, where a small population still exists, adherents began to migrate to India from the ninth century and became known there as Parsis. They have a continuous history in Britain since the nineteenth century and established their first community organisation in 1861. The first Asian member of parliament was a Parsi, elected in 1894. A small number of Iranian Zoroastrians settled in England after the fall of the Shah in 1979 and the community now numbers between 5,000 and 10,000 with one permanent place of worship.

Buddhism

Buddhism in Britain differs from the other faiths of Indian origin in that it became established for the most part outside its homeland in countries that did not become part of the British Empire and from where as a consequence there has been little immigration. Some Buddhists from Ceylon (Sri Lanka) and Burma have settled in this country together with Chinese from Hong Kong who incorporate some Buddhist features in their syncretistic religious faith, but the history of Buddhism in Britain begins with academic study by British scholars and intellectuals in the nineteenth century and the translation of the texts of the southern or Theravada school of Buddhism. From these, an ideal picture of Buddhism was constructed which was then contrasted with the 'degenerate' form of the religion as it was actually practised in the Orient. Buddhism was portrayed more as a 'way of life' or a 'philosophy', a rational 'scientific' religion, less vulnerable than Christianity to the challenges of modern thought.

A Buddhist Society was founded in 1907 and a number of 'missions' from Ceylon and Burma were received. The first residence housing monks from Ceylon was opened in London in 1928 and there are now a number of centres providing teaching about Buddhism and the practice of meditation. Many of these founded since the 1970s have belonged to one of the Tibetan schools, although most of the other traditions of Buddhism are also represented in Britain as well as new, distinctively western traditions. The large audiences attracted to hear the Dalai Lama on his teaching visit to London in the summer of 1999 demonstrate the extent of interest in Buddhist spirituality at the turn of the Christian millennium.

New religious movements

In addition to the historic or traditional religions, a considerable number of new religious movements are represented in Britain. These can be divided in the first instance on a chronological basis into para-Christian groups, such as the Christian Scientists, the Mormons and the Jehovah's Witnesses, which arrived from the United States in the nineteenth century, and those of oriental origin which appeared in Britain in the wake of the social revolution of the 1960s. In contemporary Britain, there are always a considerable number of new religious movements of various forms and origins, the majority of which will not survive or see any significant growth. Studies show that the number of people who have any kind of contact with these movements vastly exceeds the number who develop any kind of commitment to them. New religious movements often face considerable opposition from the friends and relatives of members who believe that unethical means have been used to recruit or hold on to members. Hostility also comes from Christian and other groups who believe that many, if not most, new movements are inauthentic cults which are exploiting their members for financial or other ends. Movements which have proved particularly controversial include the Unification Church (the 'Moonies'), the Church of Scientology, and the International Society for Krishna Consciousness ('Hare Krishna').

As well as new religious movements which require various degrees of committed membership from their adherents, there are a considerable number of New Age groups, agencies and individuals that provide what might be called services to clients without demanding any formal allegiance. Such services would include astrological readings, 'alternative' therapies, and the sale of objects and literature, which, it is claimed, help to bring desirable goals such as spiritual health, growth or insight.

Freedom of religion

Given the considerable diversity of religious belief and practice which exists in contemporary Britain it is of interest to enquire whether all forms of religion enjoy the same freedom and rights. The Church of England continues to enjoy a privileged position not always shared with other mainstream religions. It still, for example, has access, either by right or tradition, to universities, hospitals, prisons and the military through the appointment of chaplains. At the same time, a number of such institutions have introduced policies restricting access by certain new religious movements to their premises. No religions are proscribed in Britain, and the United Kingdom is a signatory to international treaties guaranteeing freedom of religion, but there is no law against religious discrimination and entry to the country has been prevented in the case of certain members of the Unification Church and the Scientologists on grounds of public policy. English law in several important areas appears to favour some religions over others, and for obvious historical reasons treats Christian traditions as normative. The law, for example, makes it difficult for small, poor or exclusive religious groups to be registered for marriages. The state educational system supports distinctive Christian and Jewish schools but until recently made no provision for similar Muslim schools. Most notoriously, the courts have held that the law of blasphemy protects only the Christian religion from ridicule and vilification.

The future of religion

Religion obviously has a future in Britain, although some religions would appear to have more of a future than others. Most people still claim to have some kind of religious belief with only about a quarter of the population declaring itself to have none at all. However, the latter outnumber those who actually participate in public expressions of religion. In other words, religion in the United Kingdom – with the possible exception of Northern Ireland – is increasingly thought of as a private matter and for most people, and for the most part, consists of a general outlook on life rather than any doctrinal or ethical system. It is not easy to see what difference such belief makes either to the lives of the individual or the nation. It is precisely those forms of organised religion which make fewest demands on their members in terms of commitment, and which have therefore colluded with the trend towards individualism, which have seen the most rapid decline. Religions that demand little from their adherents tend to receive little in return. On the other hand, it is unlikely that those which make greater demands in the face of such a trend will achieve anything more than limited success as regards the population as a whole, although their share of the religious market is likely to increase at the expense of the more liberal bodies.

Most practising Christians in the future will belong to conservative denominations, and those, such as the Church of England, which have traditionally encompassed a wide range of traditions will become increasingly conservative. The same is probably true of Judaism, with the added dimension that the decline of participation in the public life of the community leads individuals outside of the community altogether. The reaction of the more recent immigrant religious communities to the tendency towards a more private expression of belief will depend upon the fate of these communities in the Britain of the twenty-first century. In the immediate future, religious identity is likely to assume a greater importance as it replaces national and ethnic identities among new generations who speak only English and perceive themselves to be primarily British. But in the longer term it may be that for most their religious identity will be part of their cultural 'heritage' and their beliefs will be 'their own', while a small core follow conservative and traditional forms, and a smaller body develops a westernised form of the faith. Islam is likely to be an exception here, and the future form that it takes in Britain will depend on the more general world situation.

It has been suggested that there is likely to be more religion around in the future than there has been in the immediate past, that in a free society creativity is in the nature of things, and so the creation of new religious possibilities will be the norm. These, however, are more likely to enrich private religion than significantly increase public participation in any one faith. There is likely to be a greater awareness of other faiths; educational programmes – and religious education remains compulsory in British schools – will no doubt encourage this, and it is to be hoped that this will promote religious tolerance and dialogue. It remains to be seen how the religious communities of the future will relate to one another, and how they will negotiate internal changes, as they go through whatever transformations face them.

Further reading

Davie, Grace, *Religion in Britain since 1945: Believing without Belonging,* Blackwell, Oxford, 1994.
Gilley, Sheridan and W J Shiels, *A History of Religion in Britain,* Blackwell, Oxford, 1994.

12

The Formation of the British State: 1525–1945

David Smith

The following essay attempts to guide the reader in a chronological fashion to some of the key issues in the process of the formation of the British state, from the Tudors to the end of World War Two. Clearly such a brief survey is incomplete and provides a very selective view of Britain's past. There has been a conscious choice to focus on mainly important political developments at the expense of an interpretation drawn from social history.

The following six themes are presented concurrently throughout the essay.

1   The changing role of monarchy is traced from the consolidation of monarchical power in the sixteenth century to the establishment of a limited monarchy by 1688. This change was accompanied by the growing assertiveness of parliament that challenged and redefined the role of monarchy in the seventeenth century. By the eighteenth century, the Crown had begun to act as a constitutional monarchy using patronage to gain the co-operation of the aristocratic élite.

2   Growing parliamentary power was linked to the political and economic strength of the landed aristocracy. By the eighteenth century, landowners dominated the political parties in parliament and local government in the counties. This power was only effectively challenged in the late nineteenth century and relinquished in the twentieth century.

3   The growing influence of the middling classes in British politics and society who, under the impact of the industrial revolution and the rise of modern political parties, were able to challenge the monopoly of power held by the landed élite. It was this class that spearheaded political reform in the nineteenth century and by the twentieth century played the leading role in charting the course of British political life.

4   The impact of the labouring classes is traced from their role as rioters and radicals in the eighteenth century and their quest for democracy and economic justice in the nineteenth century. The growing power of the trade

union movement and the Labour Party in the twentieth century reinforced the new forces that emerged in British politics. The quest for democracy failed to include women, who struggled for the vote in the late nineteenth century but received full political rights only in the twentieth.

5   The essay stresses England's determination to subjugate Scotland, Ireland and Wales and bring them into a political union within a United Kingdom. The struggle to bring Scotland into Great Britain continued into the eighteenth century while that to retain Ireland lasted until the twentieth. The creation of the United Kingdom was accompanied by a growing British imperial presence throughout the globe. The British Empire was increased in the eighteenth century and its expansion culminated in the late nineteenth century. Britain entered both world wars of the twentieth century as an imperial power.

6   A central theme of the essay is to trace the function and size of the state. Government in the eighteenth century was still relatively small and intruded little in the lives of the population. With the increase of urbanisation in the nineteenth century, the responsibilities of the state grew and programmes of social reform were inaugurated. It took, however, the challenge of the two world wars to escalate state activity to the point that it supervised many aspects of daily life. Social welfare and some intervention in the economy had become a reality by 1945.

Monarchy in the sixteenth century

Henry VII

If one looks at the balance of power between monarchy and the aristocracy there is no better place to start than the reign of the first Tudor king, Henry VII. One might think that Henry, who won his right to the throne on the battlefield in 1485 with little support from the aristocracy, would have found it difficult to reassert the power of monarchy after a long series of civil wars spanning the fifteenth century. In fact, he was a very active monarch and controlled the aristocracy by asserting the feudal and judicial rights of the Crown. The estates of rebels were confiscated and private armies of the nobility were limited. More importantly, Henry VII built up the Crown's finances by cutting down on royal expenses and he refused to get embroiled in costly foreign wars. Henry's re-establishment of royal authority and the more effective use of the royal administration was not very novel as he used institutions developed in the Middle Ages. He also needed the overall support of the aristocracy. Like other strong medieval monarchs, Henry VII reduced the power of individual nobles by the use of prerogative courts and strengthening the powers of the Justices of the Peace (JPs) who carried out the wishes of the Crown throughout the country.

Henry VIII and the Reformation

Henry VIII (1509–47) strengthened the power of the monarchy and the state by resorting to new methods of support and control. He found the opportunity to gain and exercise authority in the political effects of the religious reformation. Because his wife, Catherine of Aragon, was unable to provide Henry with a male heir he wanted a divorce. The Pope was unwilling to grant Henry an annulment of his marriage as the papacy in 1529 was controlled by Henry's rival, the Emperor Charles V. The impasse led Henry to reject papal jurisdiction over the English church. This radical step towards independence was stated clearly in the preamble to the Act of Restraint of Appeals (to Rome) in 1533:

> This realm of England is an empire, and so hath been accepted in the world, governed by one supreme head and king having the dignity and royal estate of the imperial crown of the same.

England for the first time claimed imperial status: an empire that was self-sufficient and free from any external jurisdiction. Just as importantly, Henry felt he needed the support of propertied classes in his break with Rome so the legislation, which dissolved ties with Roman Catholicism, was carried out by the king in parliament through statutes that established the sovereignty of law made in parliament. Henry, in 1534, with the guidance of Thomas Cromwell, by the Act of Supremacy became the 'Supreme Head' of the English church. The term 'majesty' appeared in the statutes that reinforced the idea that church organisation and practice were under the control of the monarchy and everyone was to obey its dictates. Although Henry – conservative in his theological ideas – was averse to any move away from the Catholic faith, the removal of papal authority in England inevitably stimulated a movement towards Protestantism in the 1530s. All religious issues became political ones; dissent became a challenge to the Crown. For example, Sir Thomas More, who refused to swear an oath demanded under the Act of Succession and opposed Henry's divorce, was executed for treason. The new Treason Act of 1534 applied to anyone who spoke against the Crown and denied royal supremacy over the church. This new-found power of the monarchy over the church was evident in the first translation of the Bible in English that was dedicated to Henry, where he claimed 'the word of God' supported his claim of royal supremacy. The Crown demanded that this new Bible be placed in every parish church in the country.

The assertion of royal jurisdictional control over the church was extended, between 1536 and 1540, when monastic properties were transferred to the Crown. This action was very unpopular among the population and led in 1536 to a serious revolt, known as the Pilgrimage of Grace, which was crushed by troops loyal to Henry. The wealth of monasteries could have served as the basis of a permanent income for the Crown and hence a source of enormous power:

a monarch with an independent income would not be forced to seek extra revenues from parliament. However, Henry let this opportunity slip away as he embarked on a series of very expensive wars both with France and Scotland. As a result, the Crown was forced to *sell* church property both to the established aristocracy and gentry and to some new supporters. Therefore it was, ironically, the landed élite that profited from this transfer of 'chute' lands for it provided them with the wealth and power in their struggle with monarchy in the next century. This aristocratic social and political power, as we shall see, was to survive until the late nineteenth century in England.

The Tudors and the extension of government to Ireland, Wales and Scotland

Henry VIII not only brought the Church of England under the control of the state, but with other Tudor monarchs extended its power to the more distant parts of the country and enforced national policies there. The national changes that the religious reformation demanded impelled the Crown to take much stronger control over the localities, placing even greater responsibility on the local élite who were employed as unpaid Lord Lieutenants and Justices of the Peace. This élite was willing to implement these changes: but the Crown was to face a challenge if the aristocracy and gentry opposed the royal policies and refused to co-operate.

The Crown was determined to extend the reformation into Wales, and between 1536 and 1543 various Acts of Union brought it directly into the English governmental system. Power was taken from the Marcher lords, who had ruled Wales in a semi-autonomous fashion, and a uniform system of government was set up. Counties and Justices of the Peace were introduced and the legal language was to be English, although Wales had its own court system that lasted until the nineteenth century. Even though the Welsh were given legal equality with the English, there was a concerted effort to destroy their customs: all important positions were filled by English-speaking and English-educated Welsh gentry or by Englishmen. These landowners gained more wealth and power from the dissolution of the monasteries in Wales as they bought, like their English counterparts, these properties from the Crown. The progress of the reformation in Wales was aided by the willingness of the Tudors to permit the translation of the Bible and Prayer Book into Welsh, which now became the official language of public worship. The acceptance of Protestantism by Wales meant that it was less feared by the English than Ireland, which continued to support Catholicism, and so was spared the repression and persecution suffered by the Irish.

Ireland rejected the Protestant reformation and the Tudors, starting with Henry VIII in the 1530s, attempted to bring the country under English control. Parliament officially acknowledged Henry as 'Supreme Head' of the Irish church and, in 1541, the Irish parliament accepted him as 'King of Ireland'. Subjugation began with the plantation of English settlers in areas close to those under

English control, an unpopular policy that involved dispossessing Gaelic landowners, and led to military occupations and rebellions throughout the reign of his daughter Elizabeth. The most serious uprising occurred in the 1590s under the able Hugh O'Neill, Earl of Tyrone, who was not overcome by the English until 1603. The English gained control over the whole island and more Protestant settlers were sent from England and Scotland to occupy more land, mostly in Ulster, confiscated from the Catholic Irish. By 1618, there were 40,000 Scots and English 'planted' in Ireland.

In the sixteenth century, the Tudors waged intermittent war against Scotland because they saw France as her ally. Unlike Wales and Ireland, Scotland was not easy to conquer and the Scots were determined to assert their independence. However, in 1560, the Scottish Protestants turned to Elizabeth for support against Mary Stuart ('Queen of Scots') their Catholic monarch. This paved the way to an eventual union between the two countries. The Protestants deposed Mary, first in line to the English throne, and she fled to England to be held prisoner. She remained there until 1587, a centre of intrigue and conspiracy, until she was eventually executed, with much reluctance, by Elizabeth. In 1603, Mary's son, James VI of Scotland, inherited the throne as James I of England, Wales and Ireland: for the first time one person ruled throughout the British Isles.

Weak and unpopular Tudors

The strength of the Henrician monarchy was seriously undermined when his young son Edward VI (1547–53) came to the throne as he was dominated by two 'Protectors', the Dukes of Somerset and Northumberland. Serious protests and rebellions plagued the period that the monarchy could only put down with the co-operation of the social élite. In 1549, Kett's rebellion, (against economic discontent and the rapid movement towards Protestantism), posed the most serious challenge to the Tudor establishment of the century. Nevertheless, by 1552, the pious and haughty young king and his advisors had virtually eliminated Catholic doctrine and practice. A thoroughly Protestant Second Prayer Book, devised by Thomas Cranmer, was mandated for adoption in all churches. Ironically it was not the spread of Protestantism that further weakened respect for the Crown. The decision by Mary Tudor (Mary I, 1553–58), Edward's successor and older sister, to reintroduce Catholic doctrine into England may not have been a disaster in itself, but Mary became very unpopular when she married Philip of Spain, conducted an unsuccessful war with France, and created martyrs by burning 280 Protestants for their faith. This fanatical policy of persecution of Protestants brought sympathy to the heretics. More significantly, the landed classes were defensive about the possibility of having to hand back church lands they had acquired, and they resisted in parliament Mary's attempt to restore church property. Her policies all helped to identify

Protestantism with an anti-Spanish, English patriotism in the minds of the English people.

The achievement of Elizabeth

The strength of the Tudor monarchy was most evident during the long reign of Mary's younger sister, Elizabeth I (1559–1603). She instinctively understood and shared the hopes, fears and prejudices of her people. She brought respect and reverence to the Crown that profited by her wise choice of servants and energetic use of the Privy Council. Elizabeth employed her power to promote the unity of the country rather than pursue personal polices. The queen was parsimonious and able to keep factions at court under control by her wise distribution of patronage. The will of the Crown was felt throughout the country as she relied, like her father, on unpaid Justices of the Peace to carry out the wishes of the monarchy. Forty justices were active in each county, meeting every three months to deal with civil and criminal affairs at Quarter Sessions. These were more like local parliaments, and the Crown needed the co-operation of their landowner members for they could, if disaffected, sabotage central authority

Elizabeth's force of personality, political skill and unwillingness to marry brought stability to the country after the unwelcome changes in the 1540s and 1550s. Her refusal to marry meant the likely successor after the execution of Mary Queen of Scots was James VI of Scotland, a Protestant who was acceptable to the country. Elizabeth did not share the religious convictions of her sister and supported a religious settlement that was Protestant in doctrine though less radical than that of 1552. She supported ceremonies and the use of clerical clothing so that congregations did not feel the wrench away from the practices of the old religion. In the last quarter of the century, Elizabeth was determined to keep royal control over the church, the bishops and doctrine. She refused to support the Puritans who demanded further reformation of the church by abolishing bishops and setting up a Presbyterian system. The Queen warned them they had no right to question religious matters either inside or outside of parliament.

Elizabeth was equally determined to preserve peace at home by crushing Catholics when they plotted and revolted against the Crown. In 1569, in the wake of a conspiracy to place Mary Queen of Scots on the throne, there was a serious rising led by the Catholic élite in the northern counties who wanted the re-establishment of Catholicism. A royal army defeated the rebels and although the ringleaders were let off with fines, over 450 rebels were hanged as an example. The efficient crushing of this rising proved that royal government was stronger than the vestiges of northern feudalism. Despite the continued infiltration of Jesuit priests into England and a number of plots against the Queen's life, the Catholic threat was extinguished and their numbers were by 1600 reduced to 35,000. At the beginning of her reign most Englishmen and women were believing Roman Catholics but forty-four years later they were overwhelmingly Protestant. This explains why most of the country rallied to English Protestant nationalism in the war with Catholic Spain.

This war and the defeat of the Armada (a Spanish invasion force of 1588), although it boosted national pride, had been very expensive and that caused difficulties for Elizabeth in her last years. Unquestionably the Queen enhanced monarchical power, but she failed to address its fundamental financial weaknesses. Her frugality had prevented her calling parliament regularly, but the Crown had not been able to generate enough revenue to meet expenses incurred in wartime. She was forced to seek additional money from parliament, imposed very unpopular taxes and sold monopolies on certain manufactured goods or by granting certain individuals the sole right to sell particular items. In 1587, this unpopular policy led to bitter disputes between the Crown and parliament, particularly as Puritan members felt it was their right to demand changes in the church before they would support the Crown. In 1597 and 1601, parliament continued to oppose Elizabeth and refused to grant her enough money to support her foreign policy. These were bad omens that foreshadowed the contest between monarchy and parliament of the next century.

The conflict between crown and parliament in the seventeenth century

James I and Charles I in conflict with parliament

The union of Scotland with the rest of the British Isles under James I (1603–24) was relatively successful. Scotland remained suspicious of a complete union, however, and was not joined administratively to England, retaining its own Privy Council and other institutions. Though intelligent, James lacked the charisma of Elizabeth and failed to gain the trust of England, which he never understood. His choice of unpopular favourites, such as the Duke of Buckingham, and his heavy expenditure on extravagance at court brought him continual criticism from parliament. James did his best to govern without a parliament that was unwilling to grant him any funds until he had recognised their grievances. In 1610 and 1614, it declared his increased customs duties ('impositions') illegal. Tensions between the Crown and parliament became so heated that in 1621, James dissolved parliament when the Commons asserted the right to debate any topic. By 1624, parliament had succeeded in linking the redress of grievances to the financing of foreign policy, a major step that signalled its determination to play a role in political decision-making. It also asserted its independence from the Crown by passing an Act of Monopolies that forbade the King to grant a monopoly to a private individual.

The political tensions between Crown and parliament continued in the reign of Charles I (1624–49), who was obstinate and unwilling to compromise with his adversaries. Charles was unpopular because he also relied on favourites, conducted an expensive and unsuccessful foreign policy that forced the monarchy to seek unpopular financial expedients without reference to parliament, and turned to questionable legal means to secure income. In 1628, parliament protested against what it considered an illegal use of royal power in the Petition of Right. This document, regarded as a triumph of liberty, declared that arbitrary imprisonment and taxation without parliamentary consent was illegal. The Petition asserted that there existed a public liberty and general rights enjoyed by all of the population that could not be touched by the government. Parliament by this stage considered itself the champion of the liberties of property owners and was clearly challenging royal control, no longer trusting the Crown to defend national interests.

In 1629, Charles, who held an exalted view of the nature of kingship, decided to rule without parliament; tensions mounted as the king was forced to seek what many thought to be illegal measures for raising income. Ancient feudal rights, customs duties and monopolies were exploited and ambiguous powers were exercised by the government. In 1635, for example, Charles imposed Ship Money on inland areas in order to support the navy, and John Hampden, a wealthy landowner, refused to pay. At his trial, Hampden's attorney argued that the king's prerogative was always bound by the law, but the judges' ruling (by only seven to five) upheld the king as an absolute monarch unrestrained by any other power. The Crown also followed a very unpopular religious policy. Charles married a Catholic and was tolerant of Catholics at court. More importantly, in 1633, he strongly supported William Laud as Archbishop of Canterbury. As an Arminian, Laud believed in church ceremony, ritual and free will, tenets many felt were a reversal of Protestantism. Puritan nobles were angered by his desire to control the appointment of their personal chaplains, and the gentry at large were offended by the use of prerogative courts to discipline those who disobeyed the doctrine and practices of the church.

The conflict moves to civil war

However bitter relations between Crown and parliament became in the 1630s, the landed classes sitting in parliament were not considering the overthrow of the monarchy. Most believed that the constitution needed to be re-balanced: a divinely instituted monarchy would exercise considerable prerogative powers while at the same time respecting the liberties of its subjects. It must be remembered that the constitutional struggles in the seventeenth century were not over the issue of sovereignty: that is the location of supreme power in the nation. Most of the political nation believed in the mixed government of Crown, Lords and Commons that had functioned so well under Elizabeth. The differences lay over an interpretation of the extent of the prerogative powers of the Crown (the monarch's lawful powers) and who should declare its extent. It was assumed that the prerogative was checked by fundamental law that was seen as part of the Common Law. Parliament by the 1630s felt it was the highest court in the land, and assumed it possessed the authority to declare what the law was and when the king was beneath it. But what was unthinkable for many in the 1630s became a reality by 1645. Power rapidly collapsed at the top. The problem lay in the fact that the Crown, once it had sold off church property in the sixteenth century, never found an alternative source of revenue and without a standing army could not create the institutions necessary for an absolutist regime. Charles faced bankruptcy and was still dependent on the goodwill of the gentry in the counties to carry out his policies in the midst of the crisis that erupted in the late 1630s and early 1640s.

The outbreak of the Civil War was the result of a political crisis caused by rebellions in Scotland and Ireland between 1638 and 1641. In 1639, Scotland rose in revolt against Charles after he tried to invade it in order to impose bishops on the Church of Scotland, despite rejection of such a proposal by a National Covenant. In April 1640, after two unsuccessful military campaigns against the Scots, Charles was forced to summon parliament in search of more funds. Because parliament refused to vote any money until grievances had been met, Charles dissolved it. However, by November, he was forced to call parliament back as the Scots had occupied northern England and demanded a daily payment before they would leave. After hotly contested elections, parliament met, impeached, and executed key royal ministers. (Laud followed them later.) Parliament also abolished the prerogative courts and moved to limit the financial power of the Crown. In an attempt to make parliament a permanent part of the constitution, it was decided that it should meet every three years. There was unity on these issues: Lords and Commons wanted a monarchy that respected Protestantism and provided a role for the aristocracy in government through parliament and in the Privy Council. However, by June 1642, the issues arose that divided the élite, and two parties, driven by determined minorities on both sides, had emerged that were willing to fight each other.

Perhaps the most important issue in the events that led up to the outbreak of the Civil War in 1641 was Charles' reluctance to accept the role of a limited monarch. He refused to consult leaders in parliament like John Pym. This situation led to increased suspicion and tension, so in the summer of 1641, when there was a serious rebellion in Ireland, parliament feared that if he gained command of an army raised to suppress the Irish it may well be used against them. In order to save their own skin, parliament passed a Militia Bill that transferred control of the army away from the Crown. Meanwhile, Charles attempted to carry out a military coup by sending armed officers into parliament to arrest five leading members. These leaders had fled but, to protect themselves, parliament demanded control direct control over the militia.

Religion also played a part in dividing the parties. In December 1640, the citizens of London presented a Root and Branch Petition to parliament that called for the abolition of bishops. A royalist party, supportive of the need to preserve the Book of Common Prayer and bishops, appeared in reaction to these radical Puritan demands. When these religious issues were debated in the House of Commons as part of a list of demands in the Grand Remonstrance, the members were sufficiently divided that it was only carried by eleven votes. By the summer of 1641, the king had gained considerable support in parliament: 302 members were loyal to parliament, but 236 sided with the Crown. The political nation was divided, but parliament had more support in the south and east of England, the major ports and in the navy. London and Bristol also gave strong support.

By May 1646, parliament, after the reorganisation of its forces into the New Model Army was victorious in the field and Charles I had surrendered to the Scots. The collapse of royal power was partly due to them as the union of the crowns had intertwined the political destiny of the two countries. Parliament paid for a Scots army to enter England and help defeat royal forces at Marston Moor in 1644. Charles was returned to England in 1647 to the custody of Oliver Cromwell, the zealous and very successful parliamentary general in the Civil War. In January 1649, after Charles had rejected various proposals, and after Cromwell's soldiers had purged parliament, the King was tried in Westminster Hall and convicted of treason. He was executed on the balcony of the Banqueting Hall in Whitehall.

The Republic and return to monarchy

The successful parliamentary army and its greatest general, Cromwell, dominated the politics of the Commonwealth up to 1660. Divisions soon appeared within its ranks between Grandees, officers that identified with the gentry, and Levellers, who espoused radical and democratic political and social ideas. In October 1647, the Levellers debated their ideas, which they presented in 'The Agreement of the People' with Cromwell. They advocated republicanism, equality before the law and recognition of the sovereignty of the people by granting all freeborn Englishmen the right to elect the House of Commons every two years. Although the Levellers were not opposed to private property, the Grandees feared they aimed at the levelling of estates and society, and, in 1649, Cromwell suppressed them after a mutiny. The Diggers, a smaller group who supported the communal cultivation of land, were also promptly suppressed by the army generals.

The Commonwealth could not feel secure until the different governments in Scotland and Ireland had been overthrown. By 1653, Cromwell, believing that he was acting as a direct agent of God's will, had entirely conquered Ireland. Catholics were slaughtered in a brutal campaign: their land was confiscated and given to Protestant soldiers and adventurers. The previous year he had conquered Scotland, which had supported the cause of Charles' eldest son Charles II. After he had subjugated the British Isles, Cromwell ruled the nation as a military dictator. He purged parliament, which now had representatives from Ireland and Scotland, not elected but chosen by army officers. After 1653,

Cromwell practically did without parliament and was named Lord Protector, and in 1655, the country was ruled by major-generals who kept order and attempted to uphold a godly regime. Puritan officials deprived immoral clergy of their positions. Theatres were closed and popular leisure, like cockfights and maypole dancing, was suppressed. Radical Puritanism was imposed unwillingly on the Welsh, where commissioners deprived Anglican clergy of their livings and Puritan preachers were appointed in their place. Cromwell was committed to the toleration of all Protestant religious sects, and compulsory attendance at the parish church was abolished. This resulted in the proliferation of religious sects during the Commonwealth. Congregations of Seekers, Ranters, Baptists and Quakers sprang up, often rejecting Calvinist assumptions of predestination and the saving power of God's grace.

By the time Cromwell died in 1658, the nation, which was basically inclined towards conservatism, and whose élite was too attached to their parliamentary liberties, and too afraid of religious toleration, no long wanted the Commonwealth to continue. They hated the high taxes imposed by authoritarian major-generals who had replaced the gentry, considered to be the natural rulers in the counties. Cromwell's son, Richard, was unable to command respect and feelers went out to Charles II, the legitimate claimant to the throne. It was again the Scots army under George Monck that played a pivotal role by marching south and ordering new elections that produced a moderate royalist parliament. In 1660, this new 'Convention' parliament, restored the House of Lords and Charles II (1660–85). It is important to remember that 'the English restored their parliament before they restored their king' (Roberts, p382).

The restored monarchy enjoyed fewer powers than it possessed before 1640, as prerogative taxation and courts were abolished. Charles II was granted an allowance but it fell some £200,000 short of what was needed even in peacetime: once again the Crown had insufficient regular income to be independent from parliament. This was intended to be a parliamentary monarchy, which was evident as soon as Charles II tried to build an Anglican settlement that would incorporate a broad range of Protestants and provide toleration for Roman Catholics. Parliament responded with the Corporation and Test Acts that excluded Catholics and Dissenters from public office. In 1662, it passed an Act of Uniformity that made certain only Anglicans and not Presbyterians filled clerical positions. Clearly parliament had learned to rule during the Civil War and jealously guarded its right to define the Church of England and avoid the instability caused by the toleration of sects during the interregnum.

Charles II was very unhappy with this religious settlement as he was sympathetic towards Catholicism, so much so, that in a secret treaty with Louis XIV of France he promised to declare his conversion to Catholicism and restore the faith to England. In return for this pledge, Charles received funds from

France with the promise England would support France against the Protestant Dutch. As a result of his religious views, and those of his brother James, the heir to the throne and an avowed Catholic, Charles was not trusted. He was determined to maintain control over the military, and it was feared a Catholic monarch would aim at establishing absolutism with a standing army. This conflict saw the beginning of political parties: the Whigs, a group of aristocrats, wanted to exclude James from the succession while the Tories stood for the hereditary right of monarchy.

In 1678, the uncovering of an alleged 'Popish Plot' to assassinate Charles II led, in a climate of frenzy and zeal, to a number of show trials (and executions) of Catholics. Charles could still dissolve and summon parliament at will and he retained his strength in the House of Lords so he resisted the exclusion of his brother. The exclusion crisis of 1678–81 resembled the situation of 1640–42. Parliament stripped James, the Duke of York, of the succession and threatened him with treason if he returned to England from his exile in Scotland. In 1681, the Commons resolved not to grant any funds until an Exclusion Bill had been passed, so in response Charles II dissolved parliament. He was not as foolish as his father and did not attempt a coup against his enemies, preferring subtlety and patience. He could afford to do so because the funds from Louis XIV allowed him to dispense with parliament for the rest of his reign.

James II and the glorious revolution

Charles had preserved the throne for his brother but it was a struggle. James II (1685–88) succeeded despite a very serious rebellion led by his brother's bastard, James, Duke of Monmouth. But he soon alienated the country: he put Catholic officers in charge of an enlarged professional army, and prorogued parliament so it never met again during his reign. Moreover, he worked towards granting civil and religious equality to Catholics and relied on his prerogative powers to do so. Roman Catholic justices were appointed and filled the Privy Council. Finally, James alienated Anglican bishops by ordering them to support the reading in all parish churches of a Declaration of Indulgence that publicised the grant of full equality of religious practice to all Protestants and Catholics. In 1688, the birth of a male heir crystallised fears of a permanent Catholic regime.

This threatening situation led a cross-section of the aristocracy to invite William of Orange, the Dutch Protestant monarch married to James's daughter Mary, to protect English liberties. James failed to repulse William's invasion and, after being deserted by the nobility, went into exile. This bloodless coup was to be known as the 'Glorious Revolution': parliament declared that James II had abdicated and the vacant throne was offered to William and Mary as joint monarchs.

The development of limited monarchy

Politics in the wake of the glorious revolution

Parliament made sure that William (1688–1702) and Mary (1688–94) ruled as limited monarchs so that it would not have to face the difficulties it experienced under Charles II and James II. It stipulated that there was to be no interference with petitioning before elections, and the Crown lost the power to suspend or dissolve. Indeed the Triennial Bill of 1694 ensured that a new parliament was called every three years. Neither could the Crown control a standing army in peacetime without parliamentary consent. By an Act of Succession, which dictated that only a Protestant monarch could reign in Britain, the Stuarts were excluded from the throne (James's younger daughter Anne was, like her sister Mary, a Protestant). The Whigs regarded (and their later historians interpreted) this revolution as the foundation of political liberalism and parliamentary supremacy; other historians have suggested that it was merely a coup engineered by an élite. Whatever the case, William soon wanted to preserve the strength of the monarchy by asking for customs to be granted to the Crown for life. The Commons, on the other hand, not wanting to lose any power, were only willing to grant customs revenues for four years, quite inadequate to meet the Crown's needs even in peacetime. A bitter William threatened to return to Holland.

We can see that, by 1688, there had been a permanent shift in the balance of power between the monarchy and parliament. The monarchy acting as the executive remained the central institution of government but there had been an important change in the constitution. Parliament had to be summoned every year and was now a permanent part of the political life of the nation. Because the Crown could no longer dissolve parliament it had to be constantly managed in a more subtle way. Monarchy had survived the crises of the seventeenth century, but its new contractual form had lost some real power. It has been suggested that the decline of this power was masked by the fact that national power in the eighteenth century was growing so fast: a limited monarch in this united country had more power than the quasi-absolutist monarch in a weak and divided country.

The Glorious Revolution in Scotland and Ireland

The Whig interpretation of the Glorious Revolution did not make much sense to the Irish and Scots who suffered from the invasions of William as he moved against the Stuart rivals to the throne. In April 1689, James, in his attempt to regain the throne landed in Scotland, where he had considerable support but was unsuccessful militarily against a Dutch and English army. The throne in Scotland was offered jointly to William and Mary, but this was conditional on the abolition of the episcopacy and the firm establishment of the Presbyterian system. James, with French support, now used Ireland as a stepping stone for his return. While the Irish wanted independence, they were careful not to grant him absolutist powers: parliament was called in Dublin, an Act of Attainder named some two thousand Protestants and the land settlement was reversed. William invaded Ireland, and in July 1690, overcame a Jacobite (Stuart supporting) and French army at the Boyne. Over the next three months, the Protestant army defeated the Jacobites who surrendered at the Treaty of Limerick (1691). This was a disaster for the Irish as more land was taken from the Catholics and they were prevented from freely acquiring it. Protestant landowners often did not reside in Ireland and allowed the rural economy to decline. Catholics lost the right to vote, sit in parliament and hold offices of state. Mixed marriages and Catholic schools were banned.

The Glorious Revolution therefore led to English domination of the British Isles aided by Anglicans in Ireland and Presbyterians in Scotland. In 1707, because politicians in Scotland and England were afraid of Jacobitism in an independent Scotland, they promoted a union between the two countries. The Scots were now represented in the parliament at Westminster and received commercial equality with England. There was no union between England and Ireland, and Dublin still retained a Protestant parliament until the Act of Union in 1800. After the union, Scotland retained its own local government, system of education, legal system and national church. However, the élite in both Ireland and Scotland adopted English language, customs and habits. Wales remained very conservative and Anglican at the end of the seventeenth century, and its gentry often intermarried with the English. Because they were often educated in England, they became closely linked to a British sense of identity. The Welsh language went into decline among the élite, but it was still spoken by ninety per cent of the population and provided them with a clear sense of identity and difference from the English. Both the Scots and the Welsh upper classes helped play a role in the expanding Protestant empire in the eighteenth century and played a large role in building a sense of British nationhood.

The threat of Jacobitism

Jacobitism threatened the Whig ascendancy and the Protestant succession until the middle of the eighteenth century. William and Mary were succeeded by Anne (1702–14) but the Protestant queen produced no children that survived into adulthood. The Act of Succession meant that George I (1714–27) from the German house of Hanover succeeded Anne on her death in 1714. This led to a Jacobite uprising in Scotland in 1715, headed by James's son, the 'Old Pretender' James Stuart (James III). His army marched south as far as Preston, but they were defeated by the government and James was forced once again into exile. Another attempt to reinstate the Stuarts was made in 1745, by Charles Edward ('Bonnie Prince Charlie'), the eldest son of James III, who again invaded England through Scotland. The Jacobites this time reached Derby but decided to retreat, although such was the panic among the English élite that they might have captured London if they had pressed south. In 1746, the British army eventually defeated Charles and the Protestant succession was finally secured. The impact of the '45 rebellion was devastating for the Scottish Highlanders who had supported the Jacobites. They were brutally suppressed and their clan system was broken up. This repression was carried out not only by the English but by Scottish (mainly Lowland) Presbyterians who supported the Protestant Succession. A relationship between England and Scotland became established that was cemented with the willing co-operation of the powerful Lowland Scots who were attracted to the patronage offered by the new British state. This process obviously sped up the movement against political autonomy in Scotland.

Oligarchy and the people in the eighteenth century

Aristocratic politics in the eighteenth century

The role of limited monarchy in the eighteenth century can be best understood by an examination of the relationship between the ruling élite and the central government. The élite consisted of the peerage, landed gentry and leading figures in the towns. The central government was the monarch and a small group of advisors and officials. In a pre-industrial society the government could not intervene effectively in the localities and neither did it aspire to promote plans for domestic policies; much authority was therefore decentralised and many functions were carried out by social élites. For example, education and poor relief was administered by the local parish under the eyes of the gentry, while the regulation of commerce was left to town governments. Most importantly, as we have seen, the administration of justice was in the hands of local gentry and nobility acting as JPs and lord lieutenants.

The key to political stability was to ensure that the local élite governed in accordance with the wishes of the centre by issuing them orders that agreed with their ideology as property owners. The British aristocracy in the eighteenth century also wanted to make sure they received a fair share of the patronage offered by the Crown. This élite dominated the House of Commons, where they tried to avoid radical changes and supported social stability. The building of a large number of stately homes and their impressive gardens are testimony to the enormous wealth and power of the land-owning class in the decades after 1688.

Therefore, Britain in the eighteenth century operated as a constitutional monarchy in which parliament controlled supply and the armed forces; meeting annually, it was now a central feature of political life. There were frequent elections to the Commons, and the Crown had to cultivate parliamentary majorities in order to carry out the policies of the executive. The first minister had to have the confidence of the king and to have support in the Commons. Sir Robert Walpole, effectively Britain's first prime minister, remained in power from 1721 to 1742, because he could manipulate monarchy and was good at managing the Commons. However, in 1742, George II (1727–60) had to accept Walpole's resignation after being defeated numerous times in the Commons. This policy and technique continued when George III (1760–1820), unable to find a minister acceptable to the Commons in the 1760s, settled with Lord North between 1770 and 1782 and Pitt the Younger from 1783 to 1801. In 1761, however, George III had been forced to accept the resignation as prime minister of his tutor Lord Bute, whom he was completely dependent upon, because he was regarded with suspicion by parliament.

Party politics in the eighteenth century

The Whigs and Tories were active up to 1715, deeply divided by questions of religion, the Protestant succession and the continental wars waged during Anne's reign. After 1715, with the failure of the Jacobite rebellion, the Tories, tainted with disloyalty, were excluded from power by both George I and George II. A long period of Whig hegemony stretched into the 1760s, and Tory seats in the Commons had by 1750 shrunk to 100. The dominance of the Whigs rested on their increased control of small 'rotten' boroughs that had few electors. The actual number of borough seats controlled by aristocratic patronage increased, as did the cost of contesting elections, which again helped Whig grandees secure their dominant position in parliament. It has been estimated that forty per cent of the members of parliament were controlled by the aristocracy.

Despite the dominance of the aristocracy in parliament, the Crown, because of its ability to reward office holders, was able to rely on supporters in the Commons. Offices were recommended only by those in power and their bestowal provided an important supplement to the income of the aristocracy. Patronage was particularly useful in purchasing the political support of members from smaller boroughs. The number of appointed positions grew with the expansion of the empire and because of the constant involvement of Britain in wars throughout the century. The need to administer a growing bureaucracy, particularly in the revenue departments, meant that there were jobs for contractors, military officers and various placemen that could be used to increase the political power of the executive in the Commons. However, the government could never gain a majority on the strength of patronage alone because it needed in addition to gain the support of the aristocracy in the small boroughs and the independent minded country gentry in the counties.

Aristocratic and court patronage relieved parliament from succumbing to electoral pressure but this oligarchical system was not immune to forces outside the House. Politicians were exposed to criticism in the growing number of daily newspapers that played to public opinion. By the 1750s London had four daily papers and thirty-two were published in provincial towns, their circulation embracing many readers beyond the élite. Voters in the open boroughs in large cities, which often had a fairly large electorate, were also able to make their influence felt in elections that were contested with more regularity. These voters believed that their chosen MP was a delegate and should carry out the wishes of his constituents.

Popular politics in the eighteenth century

Crowds were also able to help undermine the system of patronage and bring attention to the numerous causes that concerned the population. Food riots were frequent throughout the century; market towns were taken over by the poor demanding that JPs establish a just price for bread. These riots, which assumed there was a 'moral economy', often made successful appeals to the paternalism of the justices. Plebeians could also jeer and intimidate the wealthy and powerful at national celebrations and rioting took place through the 1720s by Tory mobs in opposition to the Hanoverian regime. The public mood, more patriotic and Protestant in the 1740s, showed its dislike for Walpole's ministry between 1739 and 1741. They demanded a more aggressive policy towards Spain and were responsible for his eventual resignation. Historians have noted that this robust political culture could mobilise forces against the government and compromise the certainties of formal oligarchical politics. Attacks were made on Pitt the elder in 1775–76 for his failure to defeat the French navy and the loss of Minorca. However, his eventual success as war minister brought him great popularity and support from the electorate he cultivated in the City and metropolitan London.

The pressure of political forces outside of parliament on the ruling élite became stronger after 1769, intensified by the impact of the American and French revolutions. New methods of mass petitioning and extra parliamentary clubs, associations and debating societies appeared and transformed national politics. Such developments reflected the growing impatience with closed aristocratic leadership. The Association movement, led by country gentry in 1779, demanded the elimination of rotten boroughs, the introduction of a secret ballot and the extension of the franchise. There was more than a hint from the Association that if these reforms were not made, parliament could be superseded by delegates from the counties. After 1775, even more newspapers appeared and concentrated on political issues.

These new techniques and forces were evident in the popular support given to John Wilkes in the 1760s. Wilkes, a critic of government policy in the American colonies, was arrested for seditious libel against government policies expressed in one of his papers. He identified himself with the ordinary citizen and became the champion of popular liberties. The Wilkite movement received enormous support from some business and professional men, small property owners, artisans and seamen when he trumpeted his right of freedom from arrest and of the press after pro-Wilkes newspapers had been shut down. He also became a spokesman for the freedom of all electors once his election and subsequent re-elections for Middlesex had been declared invalid by parliament and he was banned from sitting in the Commons. The movement was able to hold festivals and large gatherings drawn from his constituency, which had a large electorate.

The support given to Wilkes reflected the wider transatlantic dimension: radicals on both sides of the Atlantic were in contact. There was considerable sympathy for the claims of the American colonists, often based on the seventeenth-century belief that there should be no taxation without representation. They rejected as ridiculous claims by the British who argued that the colonists had adequate representation in parliament. This argument was made in defence of an unlimited sovereign parliament backed by the unbounded legal authority of the Crown. Thus, the American Revolution in the 1770s, as well as opposition to the slave trade, mobilised the political nation outside of parliament: mass petitions against government policy containing millions of signatures circulated throughout the whole country.

Radical ideas were stimulated by the French Revolution, directed against unjust oligarchical politics. Often led by Dissenters (Protestants who did not support the Church of England) in provincial towns, radicals fought for civil equality, and in their attack on the patronage system endorsed the democratic principles espoused in the French Revolution. Thomas Paine's *The Rights of Man and Citizen* (1791–92), which sold 200,000 copies in 1793, was the most widely read book in working-class homes. Paine's ideas were discussed among artisans and shopkeepers in political societies that sprang up around the country. These radical societies, the most important being the London Corresponding Society founded by the shoemaker Thomas Hardy, were a great concern to the authorities. Property owners found Paine's republicanism, welfare reforms, anti-clericalism, advocacy of natural rights and plans for a radical change in the tax system, very threatening. Riots and a wide range of popular protest broke out during the French Revolution and revolutionary cells were formed with connections to Irish rebels in the North of England. In the 1790s, plans were hatched by radicals to carry out a *coup d'état* and assassinate the King. United Irishmen and United Scots made plans to dismember the British state by proposing the establishment of independent republics in Ireland, Scotland and England. In response to this revolutionary atmosphere, conservative landowners and the government encouraged loyalist associations that asked the people to support King and Country. These loyalist associations, exploiting the appeal of nationalism, may not have contained as many committed followers as the press suggested. People were attracted to attend loyalist events, not out of principle, but because they had been forced to do so by their social superiors or because they were bribed by the beer and food offered at these celebrations.

Protest and repression

During the wars with revolutionary France and in the 1820s, the government attempted to crack down on radicalism. Radical societies, infiltrated with spies and government informers, were forced underground and their leaders were punished under more comprehensive treason and sedition Acts. In 1795, meetings of more than fifty people were prohibited. The war, by increasing the anxiety of the oligarchy in face of radicalism, accelerated the demise of paternalist legislation. In 1799, the Combination Act banned collective bargaining by trade unions and allowed owners of factories to prosecute workers for trade union activity. These measures and the appeal of conservatism prevented the outbreak of revolution during the war, and as a result, the élite in Britain came out of the war in a stronger and more secure position than the aristocracy in the rest of revolutionary Europe.

The policy of repression, however, did not prevent the development of working-class consciousness and the widespread strike activity that occurred in the harsh years after the final defeat of Napoleon in 1815. The loss of life in the French wars was on a scale proportional to losses during the First World War and the poor faced heavy taxation and the difficulties of demobilisation. In 1813–14, the government committed to a *laissez-faire* economic policy, abrogated paternalism when the regulation of wages was repealed. However, in 1815, parliament, dominated by the landowners, passed the Corn Laws, which protected the price of British grown wheat against foreign competition and kept bread prices high for wage earners. These circumstances led to an outbreak of industrial violence where workers smashed textile machinery in the Midlands and Lancashire. These machine-breakers, known as Luddites, linked their industrial concerns to the need for a political revolt and a general uprising. In this post-war period, plagued by under- and unemployment and low wages, enormous bitterness was felt against the political regime by those excluded from it. Discontent was not restricted to urban areas; in the 1820s 'Captain Swing' riots spread in agricultural areas where farmers were the object of arson and animal maiming by discontented agricultural workers.

Historians have suggested that the pattern of protest between 1815 and 1832 was carried out on a national scale and it represented a new sense of working-class consciousness based on economic exploitation and political exclusion. A working-class presence backed by a mass platform was now part of the political landscape and was very threatening to the élite. Although only a small minority were revolutionaries, most working-class radical leaders used the persuasion and pressure of public opinion at mass demonstrations and through newspapers to promote their cause. National movements to reform parliament led by Orator Hunt demanded male household suffrage, and annual parliaments that meant working-class grievances would be met with the advent of democracy. Once more, combinations were prohibited and special taxes were imposed on the popular press. Under the Six Acts passed in 1819, public meetings were controlled by magistrates and radical leaders were harassed by the legal authorities. Troops were often used to back up the civil authorities and on one occasion in 1819 in St Peter's Field, Manchester, the yeomanry killed eleven demonstrators when they broke up a large political meeting. The loss of life, at what was called 'Peterloo' in ironical contrast to the British victory over Napoleon at Waterloo, added to the hatred of the government. Nevertheless, the authorities failed to stifle popular agitation that held the political oligarchy's corruption and inefficiency responsible for the harsh economic conditions. In the same period, George IV as Prince Regent (1811–20) and as king (1820–30) was extremely unpopular for his political conservatism and his attempt to divorce his wife and exclude her from enjoying royal status. The public enthusiastically took up her cause and the king lost all respect when he was able to deny Caroline a coronation.

Discontent in Ireland and the Act of Union

Concern that the French Revolution had radicalised Irish discontent and the chance that the French might support rebellion in Ireland led to the improvement of the legal position of Roman Catholics. Although Ireland had, from 1783, its own parliament, power remained in the hands of the lord lieutenant and executive decisions were made in London. In 1793, Pitt, against the wishes of the Protestants, granted Catholic freeholders the vote and allowed them to sit on juries, bear arms and hold minor political offices. Catholics were still barred from parliament. These concessions were not enough to satisfy the United Irishmen, an organisation composed of both Protestant and Catholics led by Wolfe Tone. In the climate of the French Revolution, the United Irishmen, now forced underground, became increasingly more Catholic and revolutionary to accomplish manhood suffrage and annual parliaments. The situation became more tense in 1793, when Britain went to war with France and there was the immediate fear of invasion and revolution in Ireland. The French made an abortive invasion attempt in 1796, followed by a 1798 rebellion led by the United Irishmen and linked to another French invasion. Despite the swift defeat of the rebels, these events made the Protestants in Ireland feel they could not maintain stability so they turned to the British in support of a union. The Act of Union in 1800 abolished the separate Irish parliament and one hundred Protestant Irish MPs sat in Westminster. This legislation completed the structure of the United Kingdom of Great Britain and Ireland that was to last up to 1921.

The expansion of the British Empire in the eighteenth century

It must not be forgotten that the expansion of Britain as a maritime and colonial power was one of the most important developments in the eighteenth century. By 1750, Britain governed some 15 million persons outside of the British Isles, mainly in India, the West Indies and North America. The British had a large share in the slave trade from West Africa to the Caribbean and the southern American colonies to work the plantations that produced sugar and tobacco. These stirrings of empire brought commercial rivals France and Britain into conflict in the Seven Years War (1756–63) that expanded into a general European struggle. Britain's impressive victories were reflected in the Treaty of Paris in 1763 whereby she secured control over a number of West Indian Islands, Canada, Cape Breton Island, and Florida, and the East India Company virtually ejected the French from India. These gains should be balanced against the loss of the thirteen American colonies some fifteen years later. The British failed to appreciate the slow development of colonial self-identity and often ignored American public opinion, as when George Grenville attempted to impose higher taxes and customs on the colonists in order to pay off the National Debt after the Seven Years War. Once the war had started, the government failed to understand the extent of colonial opposition or the type of war they faced. This failure to conduct the war effectively resulted in defeat and independence for the colonists.

Politics, the state and empire in the nineteenth century

The middle classes and political reform

The dual impact of the Industrial and French Revolutions did not accelerate the desire of the radical labouring class alone to reform the oligarchical and corrupt political system. As industrialisation accelerated in the late eighteenth and early nineteenth centuries, there was a corresponding growth of class-consciousness among the owners of commercial and industrial wealth. They saw themselves as responsible for the creation of wealth, power and progress of the nation. Consequently, this emerging and more self-confident middle class wanted to be included in the national government and exercise power so they could tailor the state agenda to their interests. These leaders of capitalist enterprises disliked the inefficiency and corruption of patronage politics that served only the interests of the landed élite. Many middle-class Nonconformists were excluded from parliament, local government offices, the civil and armed services. They joined the movement for parliamentary reform to remake a political structure that would respond to their growing social and economic power.

This middle-class agitation for the reform of parliament continued unabashed during the Napoleonic wars and the 1820s. They put pressure on the wealthy landed aristocracy to change a system that only represented one in forty-two males, and where fifty per cent of the boroughs returned candidates with less than three hundred electors. But, while the middle class supported a political system that was more open to promote its interests, it feared democracy. It envisioned parliamentary reform that extended the franchise only to responsible and independent males based on a property qualification; hence universal manhood suffrage demanded by working-class radicals was out of the question, and women were not eligible to vote. Therefore, we can see that the working- and middle-class reformers found it difficult to co-operate with one another as they had such different aims and motives. Only in certain parts of the country, such as Birmingham, where factory production was on a small scale that more often produced a closer and more harmonious relationship between owners and workers, did middle- and working-class radicalism fuse together.

From the last quarter of the eighteenth century, the idea of modest reform to include industrial and commercial wealth in the constitution gained the support of number of aristocratic Whigs in parliament. They reasoned that if moderate to middle-class reform was not conceded there might be a revolution that could entirely destroy aristocratic predominance in politics and society. They were also willing to oppose the monopoly of the Church of England at a time when Anglicanism was assumed to be the protector of the institution and part of the state. With Whig support in 1828 and under strong pressure from Nonconformists, the Test and Corporation Acts were repealed so almost all Protestants possessed equal civil rights. Ironically, it was the Tories under the leadership of the Duke of Wellington and Sir Robert Peel, who granted similar rights to Roman Catholics. In 1829, the government, faced with a very strong movement led by Daniel O'Connell in Ireland for the emancipation of Catholics and fearing a violent civil war if it was refused, passed the Emancipation Act that allowed Catholics to participate fully in political life. Because the Ultra Tories felt so betrayed by their leaders, they created circumstances in 1830 whereby the Whigs, who supported parliamentary reform, were elected. The Whig leader Lord Grey, afraid that the extra-parliamentary movement for reform might spill over into revolution, believed it was now prudent to attach the middle classes to the constitution. It has been suggested that the pro-reform rioting, which took place in large towns such as Bristol and Nottingham, and incendiary statements from middle-class reformers frightened the Whigs into an exaggerated perception that revolution was imminent. But Grey had other motives for pushing through a Reform Bill. He thought that a reformed parliament would strengthen the legislature at the expense of the executive and shift the balance of power towards the Commons away from the Lords.

In June 1832, the Whigs, promised by King William IV (1830–37) that he would create enough pro-reform peers for the measure to pass through the House of Lords, passed the first Reform Bill. The bill met many of the demands of the middle classes as parliamentary seats were redistributed to meet the growing population in the large industrial towns. Manchester and Birmingham, for example, for the first time had representatives in parliament. Many of the rotten boroughs with small electorates were eliminated, but county represen- tation increased as the Whigs, great supporters of the independent county MPs, did not want the land-owning interest to suffer. They wanted to preserve the power of the country gentry, feeling assured that the electors, drawn from forty-shilling freeholders, often tenant farmers of larger landlords, could be relied upon to support their social superiors. The vote was extended as a result of these changes to include ten-pound householders uniformly in urban areas: that increased the electorate by fifty per cent, giving one in five adult males in Britain the vote. Despite the concessions to the landed interest, and the retention of many anomalies in the system, the Reform Bill brought most middle-class males into parliamentary politics. The property franchise, however, excluded almost all of the working class from a participation in the constitution and they, as we shall see, were disappointed with what they felt was a very limited movement towards reform in 1832. The passing of the Municipal Corporations Act in 1835 was as important to the middle classes as the measure of parliamentary reform three years earlier. Under the act, towns were to elect borough councils that came under the control of the business and professional classes. Consequently, these councils, invested with the responsibility for a growing number of urban issues, were now responsive to their middle-class, and often Nonconformist, electorate.

The working classes and political movements

Working-class dissatisfaction with the extent of political reform in 1832 was soon expressed in the Chartist movement that demanded universal suffrage, annual parliaments, a secret ballot and equal representation from equal districts that they hoped would liberate the working class. In the late 1830s and 1840s, the Chartists rallied at massive meetings, conducted membership drives and supported radical newspapers like the *Northern Star*, edited by Feargus O'Connor. Ordinary working people, in the 1830s, were clearly angry and felt cheated out of political reform at a time of economic depression and distress. Linked to this political agitation was the demand for a ten-hour working day in factories and hatred of a new centralised Poor Law that consigned paupers to workhouses. The Chartists had very little support from the middle class and they were divided among themselves over whether to use physical violence or not. Although the movement provided the working class with a sense of identity and pride, it failed: many Chartist demands were not met until later in the century and some not at all.

By contrast, the middle classes were successful in forcing parliament to repeal legislation, promoted by the landed classes, that protected the price of home-grown wheat against imports from aboard. The Anti Corn-Law League launched a very well organised and financed campaign that claimed the end of duties on wheat would lead to a revival of the economy. This movement was bitterly opposed by the Chartists who thought cheaper imported wheat would lead to manufacturers paying lower wages. The League's argument convinced Sir Robert Peel, now prime minister, that free trade would lead to prosperity. In 1846, he repealed the Corn Laws at the cost of splitting his Conservative Party and alienating the aristocracy. The success of the campaign demonstrated the arrival of new political power of the middle classes, who had prevailed over the monopolistic and arrogant aristocracy.

The growth of modern political parties

The growing impact of the middle classes on parliament caused the formation of the Liberal and Conservative parties in a modern form that acknowledged that general elections could only be won by the efforts of party organisation outside parliament. The Liberal Party was based on the promise of reform, while the Conservative Party, still the organ of the aristocracy and gentry, hoped to attract the middle classes by offering them stability. These parties operated in a political system that was far from democratic, but the cry for further political reform was kept alive in the Liberal Party throughout the 1850s. William Gladstone, the future Liberal prime minister, became convinced that responsible and respectable working men could be awarded the privilege of the vote because they would not exercise it on class lines. Such reformers were not moved by the fear of social revolution but by the relative social peace that prevailed in the mid-Victorian period. Even the working-class leaders who spoke for the respectable and prosperous artisans were opposed to universal suffrage. By the 1860s, reform was inevitable so both parties wanted to take the credit for extending the franchise and to attach the new voters to their respective parties. In 1866, the Liberals introduced a bill, but it was defeated by the Conservatives led by Benjamin Disraeli, the latter hoping to introduce a measure himself to secure his leadership and to confer victory on his party. In 1867, the Liberals lost office, and Disraeli, in an effort to outbid his rival Gladstone, accepted a more radical bill that gave the vote to all urban householders, doubling the electorate. The redistribution of seats meant that urban interests for the first time balanced rural constituencies. Just as important reforms came in 1872, when the secret ballot was introduced and, in 1883, legislation was passed to check the amount of money spent in bribing voters. Finally in 1884, the Third Reform Bill extended the franchise to all householders, which meant one in six males in the UK had the vote, but introduction of universal manhood suffrage would have to wait until 1918. Throughout the last quarter of the nineteenth century, women actively sought the vote that was being extended to their male counterparts. Parliament resisted this movement, even after 1905 when suffragette protests led to violence and the imprisonment and forced feeding of their leaders.

Up to the 1880s, the majority of the working class, especially trade union members, was loyal to the Liberal Party. Class-conscious working-class voters wanted their own independent MPs like Keir Hardie, a Scottish coal-miner who continued to wear his cloth cap once he was elected to parliament in 1892. An Independent Labour Party was formed in 1893 but its members were too socialist to attract the majority of British workers who were wedded to trade unions.

The trades unions, however, were sympathetic to the project of a Labour Party which could defend them against legal attacks from employers, so in 1900, they joined with socialists to found the Labour Representation Committee, later the Labour Party. Therefore, between 1906 and 1914, the Liberal Party had to compete with the new Labour Party for the allegiance of the working class. The number of Labour MPs had risen to forty-five by 1910, supported by a larger number of unions which in turn were becoming more militant. Rising prices and declining wages created violent disputes with employers between 1911 and 1914. Troops were deployed to quell disorder during miners', dockers' and railwaymen's strikes. The government was forced to sponsor legislation for the payment of MPs, to allow trades unions to contribute funds to the Labour Party, and to provide a minimum wage for coal-miners.

The Victorians and social reform

The long reign of William IV's niece Victoria (1837–1901) saw massive social change. Parallel to the reform of the aristocratic political structure and the advent of liberal and democratic system in the nineteenth century was the growing responsibility and intrusion of the state into the lives of its citizens. As Britain became more urbanised and industrialised, a plethora of social problems emerged that had not been appreciated or experienced before. Moreover, knowledge of these problems became widespread as the government issued very detailed and graphic reports on a range of social ills. Conditions from child labour in factories to the state of prisons were brought to the attention of the public. Society was informed about the rising crime rate, the neglect of inmates in the poor houses and insane asylums and the terrible conditions facing emigrants on passenger ships that left for America. These reports of the ills of unregulated capitalism touched the humanitarian spirit of and infused fear into the middle classes who felt some action had to be taken by the state. In the past JPs, town councils and the parishes had been responsible for the relief of poverty, the provision of water and sewerage and establishing law and order on a local level. This system of local government was usually carried out inefficiently, by unpaid and often self-appointed officials.

In the 1830s and 1840s, parliament appointed inspectors responsible to the central government to enforce regulations that excluded young children from factories and limited the hours of work of young adults and women. Inspectorates were set up to report on the state of prisons, accidents in mines and on railways and passenger ships. These inspectors were few and their powers were fairly restricted, but their appointment does represent a desire to strengthen a partnership between central government and local government. A new Poor Law in 1834 placed the supervision of elected guardians in 500 new-formed Poor Law Unions under commissioners responsible to parliament. This legislation aimed at the eradication of pauperism by encouraging the poor to apply for relief only in the last resort. Therefore, because conditions for paupers seeking relief were to be worse than those experienced by the independent poor, the Poor Law mandated that paupers be supported in workhouses. These workhouses were strictly disciplined and inmates were not allowed any luxuries. In the 1840s too, a system of new rational and efficient penitentiaries under the control of the central government was constructed for convicted prisoners. This system was devised to accommodate the larger numbers of prisoners held because of the shift away from capital punishment for most crimes, and the refusal of the Australian colonies to accept any more British prisoners.

The first half of the nineteenth century saw the establishment of a professional police force whose purpose was the prevention of crime. Robert Peel established the Metropolitan Police in 1829, and this force became the model for the other forces adopted in the boroughs and counties between 1835 and 1860. These forces, at first strongly resisted by the working class, slowly gained acceptance as they provided protection and order in the cities and countryside and crime rates declined. Although the forces possessed local autonomy, they were increasingly regulated and supervised centrally by the Home Office.

Despite the growing acceptance, in the nineteenth century, of the expanding role of the state, its resources were to be used only in co-operation with, and often in a subordinate position to, voluntary effort. It was assumed that philanthropy should act as the main source of relief for the poor, and consequently, the era saw an explosion of charitable activity. Middle-class women, in particular, ran the innumerable charitable organisations, devoting their energy to raising funds and distributing them to the less fortunate members of society. Education was left in the hands of religious organisations that were often in competition with each other. Anglicans and Nonconformists disagreed about the allocation of state funding. As a result of this conflict, comprehensive elementary schooling was adopted in Britain only in 1870, after the élite had concluded it was necessary to educate the growing electorate. A compromise was made to satisfy the religious groups: state schools were to be built where voluntary schools were found inadequate. In 1880, elementary schooling was made compulsory for children under eleven years old.

The attempt of the state between 1830 and 1870 to address social ills that arose from urbanisation and industrialisation has been named, perhaps with some exaggeration 'the Victorian Welfare State'. In fact, much of the legislation passed during this period was permissive: local government had the option to adopt measures, and legislation that improved public health or working-class housing was not mandatory. However, after the election of 1906 the Liberals, aware of the threat of Labour, initiated a progressive programme of social reform. School meals were provided for poor children, the state provided small old age pensions and Labour exchanges were set up to help the unemployed find jobs. In 1909, the Liberals intervened in the economy and fixed wages in the 'sweated' industries like tailoring and lace-making. However, the most important burst of social legislation came in 1911 with the National Insurance Act pushed through parliament by David Lloyd George, the radical Welsh Chancellor of the Exchequer. This act provided protection for workers suffering sickness and unemployment through benefits funded by contributions from workers, employers and the state. This legislation was impressive in that the state launched a programme to relieve social suffering, but it fell short of constructing the welfare state. Social insurance was far from comprehensive and only workers in certain industries qualified; the particular circumstances of female poverty were ignored. The Liberals wanted to provide more for the working class than the Poor Law but turned away from tackling the issues of unemployment, poor wages and affordable and decent housing for them. However, it is significant that in 1909, Lloyd George produced a budget in which these social programmes would be financed by imposing inheritance, income and land taxes on the aristocratic landed élite. This budget was passed by the House of Lords with great reluctance and only after they had accepted the verdict of the electorate in the two general elections of 1910.

Ireland, Wales, Scotland and the empire in the nineteenth century

The Irish experience in the nineteenth century was defined by the potato famine in the mid-1840s. Eight hundred thousand died of starvation when a blight infested the potato that had become the mainstay of the Irish diet. The government provided little relief for the unfortunate population, many of whom emigrated, mainly to the United States. However, by 1860, three per cent of the population of England and Wales was Irish-born. These immigrants, concentrated in London, Newcastle and Liverpool, were very poor and forced to live in the worst conditions. The Irish in England took the lowest paid jobs and were subjected to prejudice, because they were Catholics and they often undercut English workers.

It is well to remember, however, that Ireland's political life, after the Union of 1801, was closely tied to that of Britain. The Irish economy developed as part of the growing imperial economy with considerable economic interdependence on Britain. Legislation enacted between 1860 and 1903 reduced the power of landlords, and farmers increasingly owned their property. Local government shifted from the old Anglican oligarchy to the Catholic population, a shift that ushered in the political decline of the land-owning class. Despite these changes that linked Britain and Ireland closer together, there was throughout the century a growing nationalist movement in Ireland. The Fenians, founded in 1858, wanted to promote a rebellion in Ireland by the use of violence. They carried out a number of dramatic terrorist attacks in the last quarter of the century. But most Irish nationalism was non-violent. In the 1830s and 1840s, Daniel O'Connell led a party that wanted to repeal the Act of Union, and as a result of this pressure, the government in 1867 and 1884 increased the number of Catholic voters who then used the franchise to back home rule for Ireland. The Home Rule League, led in the 1870s and 1880s by Charles Parnell, wanted an Irish parliament to control all matters except defence and foreign policy. Parnell with as many as eighty-five Irish Home Rule MPs was able to use their power to influence the political agenda throughout the United Kingdom, although *three* Home Rule bills failed to pass through parliament in the years before 1914.

Changes in nineteenth-century Wales centred on the rapid industrial expansion, based on coal-mining, of southern Wales that by 1900 contained the majority of the population. This led to a decline in the importance of agriculture and rural Wales. Nonconformity was popular in Wales: Dissenters outnumbered Anglicans and gave support to the Liberal Party and a growing national feeling. Welsh identity was represented by Liberalism that triumphed in Wales. The Conservatives, representing the Anglican and landlord interest, were defeated by the fusion of Nonconformity and Liberalism. In 1881, Welsh Nonconformity was strong enough to secure legislation that closed Welsh pubs on Sundays. Radical Liberals took on Welsh national issues that included the disestablishment of the Anglican church in Wales and land reform to abolish tithes and lower rents. Liberal Nonconformists were bitterly opposed to Anglican church schools subsidised by public funds.

In the 1830s and 1840s the transformation to industrialism caused a violent response among Welsh workers who joined in Chartist protests and Rebecca riots in South-west Wales. These riots, directed against toll gates, unfair rents, the loss of common lands and workhouses, were regarded as very threatening to landlords and mine owners. However, this violent protest did not erupt into revolution and worker solidarity was restricted to quite limited objectives. Riots occurred again in the 1880s against landlords but the level of violence was low, and the Welsh always wanted to differentiate themselves from the bitter nationalist and agrarian struggle in Ireland.

Industrial growth in south Wales attracted immigrants from Ireland and England, which meant the Welsh language was not used as much in the centres of greatest economic and political power. Moreover, English language was increasingly used by the Welsh middle class as it was the language of commerce. In reaction to the encroachment on the Welsh language, there was a Gaelic revival that supported home rule, the importance of Welsh poetry and choral singing. A stronger sense of cultural and national identity can be seen in the revival of the eisteddfod (a national cultural festival) and the establishment of a Welsh national university, library and museum.

Nationalist feeling in politics were less prominent in nineteenth-century Scotland as it identified closely with the idea of Britain and the British Empire. Scotland did not seek political independence through a home rule party and Scottish nationalists were a distinct minority. Scotland, like many areas of England and Wales was transformed by growing industrialisation and urbanisation, especially in central Scotland. Change also affected the more rural and remote Highlands and Islands: the Gaelic language declined and the population was displaced by the 'clearances' to make way for commercial agriculture and the hunting preserves of the rich. Poor economic conditions forced large numbers of Highlanders to emigrate and resistance to these changes came from a Land League that emulated Irish opposition to economic exploitation. By the 1880s, legislation protected some of the crofters' rights and checked the clearances.

These developments within the United Kingdom have to be placed alongside the continued expansion of the British Empire particularly between 1870 and 1914. Areas that had been part of the informal empire came under formal rule and new lands were annexed. This expansion was so rapid that by 1900 the empire contained 400 million people spread over 12 million square miles. Many colonies were acquired during the scramble for Africa in the 1880s. Politicians, aware that annexation was expensive, preferred informal to formal control, but none opposed the empire and all agreed that British interests around the world should be secured.

From 1870, the British developed an ideology of imperialism based on national pride in British institutions to justify these new acquisitions. Politicians of both parties believed the colonies should be tied closely to Britain in order to bring religion and progress to backward peoples. The élite saw themselves as part of a superior race carrying out a mission of noble trusteeship to less civilised parts of the world. Thus imperialism was seen as a duty by the upper middle classes who were sent out to govern the empire, which in turn became profitable for the officials and soldiers who administered and protected it. Investors and businessmen were also beneficiaries of colonial annexation, but with the exception of India the cost of the empire was detrimental to the tax payer at home The acquisition of colonies was also promoted and justified by their value in the rivalry between Germany and Britain. Ironically, the British were able to reach agreement with Germany over annexations in Africa but clashed bitterly with the French in the 1880s and 1890s over control of Egypt and Sudan. Therefore, colonies were often annexed for strategic reasons based on the concern that the other European powers might step in first and secure future economic and political advantages. Britain wanted to appear to be a great power with colonial possessions and sought to establish economic self-sufficiency through empire. The most serious colonial war was not, however, with a European nation but with the 'Boers', the white Dutch settlers in South Africa. The British wanted control over the Dutch republics of Transvaal and the Orange Free State, where gold had recently been discovered. The Boer War (1899–1902) was only won by Britain after a long and brutal guerrilla war that tarnished the military reputation of British troops.

Many supporters of imperialism were Social Darwinists who felt that the British had to achieve greater 'social efficiency' to defeat her global competitors. Often these apologists were supporters of social reform in Britain because the working class had to be strong and healthy in order to support imperial designs and become victorious in the racial struggle. These ideas led to the ambiguous assumptions that the urban poor as a result of interbreeding were becoming degenerate, while the Anglo-Saxon race was superior to all others. This imperialist ideology lay behind the cult of sports in the public schools, the Boy Scouts and was transmitted to the population in mass circulation newspapers, cheap literature that catered to children and in history textbooks in the schools.

From the First World War to the Second

World War One

With the outbreak of war in 1914 the tensions and conflicts inside Britain subsided very quickly: the issue of Home Rule for Ireland was suspended for the duration of hostilities and the Trade Union Congress (TUC) suspended strikes. The nation felt it was fighting against Germany for the highest moral principles and volunteers enthusiastically joined the armed services. However, as the trench warfare on the Western Front produced a stalemate, the horrific conditions produced an aversion to war that was to affect a whole generation. The British suffered 60,000 casualties on the first day of the battle of the Somme in July 1916 alone. During the course of the war, 750,000 were killed and another 2.5 million were wounded. Pacifists and 'War Poets', who had experienced the war first-hand, suggested that the population had turned against the military commanders whom they held responsible for the carnage. This, however, does not seem to have been the case as most troops even in the worst conditions acted with resolution and humorous tolerance of the terrors that faced them.

The war was popular because it involved the whole population in its cause. The state took over control of the economy, agriculture and key industries. The Ministry of Munitions led by Lloyd George saw to the production of arms and ammunition and made an impact on welfare, housing and the status of women. Ironically, the war initiated more activity in social reform than had been urged by the unions and humanitarians throughout the previous century. In 1918 the Fisher Act extended free elementary education and secondary education and initiatives were made in public health and subsidised local-authority housing. The government negotiated an agreement with the trades unions that forbade strikes but instituted the process of guaranteed collective bargaining so union leaders now had access to government. Industrial peace did not last throughout the war and official strikes in 1915 broke out in South Wales. Between 1916 and 1917 unofficial strikes on Clydeside and in Sheffield showed that wartime consensus was not unanimously accepted by war workers. However, for the majority of the workforce, conditions improved and real wages increased. Women were the short-term beneficiaries of the war as they found employment opportunities in a wide range of occupations previously reserved for men. In 1918, women over thirty were rewarded for their patriotism with the vote. But, once the war was over, women were forced out of the workforce back to the home as male veterans returned to jobs reserved for them.

The First World War was responsible for great political changes. It was a disaster for the Liberal Party because the impact of total war had discredited liberal values in general. Moreover, H H Asquith, the Liberal leader, provided poor leadership when, in 1915, the party divided over the issue of conscription. By 1916, the Liberal Party was being criticised for not waging the war effectively and for being unable to resolve the Irish question. As a result, Lloyd George emerged as the leader of an all-party coalition that included Labour ministers but deeply divided his party in parliament. The Labour Party, a surprising beneficiary of the demise of the Liberals, doubled its membership during the war, and in 1918 profited from an increase in the working-class vote with the extension of the franchise to all men of twenty-one and over. However, the Conservatives, now the majority party, became the real winners. Led by and representing business and manufacturing interests, the party used the post-war elections to usher in an era of right-wing domination.

The circumstances of the war led to great changes in Ireland, where any consensus truly broke down. The Easter Rising of 1916, staged by fewer than 2,000 nationalists, was brutally repressed by the Liberal government. This action led by 1918 to widespread support of republicanism in the twenty-six southern Irish counties by nationalists who now rejected Home Rule. In 1919, a new national assembly declared independence from Britain, precipitating a brutal civil war that ended in 1921 with the partition of Ireland. In the south, the Irish Free State was declared an independent nation within the British Empire (which they finally left in 1937) and six out of the nine counties in Ulster became Northern Ireland, which remained an integral part of the United Kingdom. The partition was rejected by the Irish Republican Army (IRA), which conducted a terrorist war in both the north and south of Ireland. The IRA was defeated by Free State republicans in 1923, although many of its followers continued to fight for a united Ireland. Protestantism remained the dominant political and social force in Ulster that contained a significant Catholic minority.

The idea of empire was taken very seriously during the war and the dominions made sizeable contributions to the military effort. Britain, as a result of secret peace treaties and mandates, ended up in 1919 with a larger empire than ever before. New territories, important for their oil reserves and strategic position, were acquired in the Middle East and the Persian Gulf with partition of the Turkish Empire. However, in the 1920s the constraints of empire were evident when nationalist revolts in Egypt and Iraq forced the British to grant them independence. The empire continued to face serious problems in the 1930s: the Indian National Congress continued to campaign for independence rejecting British attempts to offer a modicum of self-government. Revolts took place in Palestine with the Arabs protesting against Jewish immigration. Despite these setbacks, it would be a mistake to assume Britain lost interest in imperialism between the wars. Economic links between the empire and Britain were strengthened and Empire Day was an important event on the patriotic calendar. British commitment to the imperial idea was demonstrated by the construction of a large new naval base in Singapore for the defence of the Far East. The concern to preserve the empire lay behind the British policy of appeasement in the 1930s as Prime Minister Neville Chamberlain felt the country could not fight a war on two fronts against the Germans and the Japanese in the Far East. Indeed, during the Second World War, Britain continued to behave as an imperial power with a strategy devised to retain the empire even after Japan had forced the surrender of Singapore, Malaya and Hong Kong. India was threatened by the Japanese invasion of Burma. Only with great reluctance did the United States restore the British colonial presence in the Far East after war with Japan had ended. In North Africa, the British fought to preserve access to the Suez Canal and the oil fields of the Middle East.

Britain between the wars

Britain remained a great power in 1919: but with a weakened economy and after the devastating experience of the Great War she was not interested in maintaining a large military force. A 'Ten Year Rule' was established by which the armed forces were to assume each year that there would be no major war in the next ten years. The strength of the navy and army was reduced to a bare minimum, at a time when the country still had a large empire to defend. In Europe after the war, Britain wanted to act as a mediator between France and Germany while encouraging the restoration of the latter to a normal role on the continent. Britain felt that Germany had legitimate grievances in the 1920s and, for the good of all Europe, its economy had to be revived. By the 1930s, this 'appeasement' mentality faced a new challenge in the shape of Adolf Hitler's aggressive foreign policy. With domestic public opinion strongly pacifist, the government began to support rearmament only in 1934. Chamberlain, prime minister from 1937, believed that he could deal with Hitler and reach an agreement over border issues in Central Europe that would avoid a war with Germany; this was now also the policy of the French government. The continuation of appeasement policy in 1938 convinced Hitler, after his annexation of Austria went unopposed, that Britain was weak. Later that summer another international crisis broke when Hitler cast his eyes on Czechoslovakia. Chamberlain, after twice flying to Germany to appease the demands of Hitler, joined the French to pressure the Czechs to grant autonomy to German nationals living inside Czechoslovakia (since they wanted to rejoin Germany this effectively was a policy to dismember the country). Hitler was furious because the war he sought had been avoided, while Chamberlain received accolades from a relieved British public which dreaded another conflict. Chamberlain's policy was opposed by the Conservative dissident Winston Churchill, who realised the danger of German aggression to Britain and her empire and regarded the deal over Czechoslovakia as a national humiliation. However, British opinion and policy did change in March 1939 when Hitler invaded the rump of Czechoslovakia and Britain began actively to prepare for war. On 3rd September, after Hitler invaded Poland, even Chamberlain was convinced that Britain, which had committed herself to protect Poland's frontiers earlier in the year, should declare war on Germany.

On the domestic front throughout the 1920s and 1930s, Britain suffered from a range of economic ills that emerged at the end of World War One. The country was faced with a huge national debt and massive unemployment that rose to over a million workers in the older industrial areas. Coal exports, in particular, took a sharp downturn and the miners launched a number of serious strikes to save their jobs and to protest lower wages. The cycle of industrial decline led to social bitterness that erupted in the general strike of 1926. The government refused to subsidise the coal-mining industry and for nine days the unions brought the country to a standstill. In the end, the unions were defeated, but the industrial unrest showed the depth of solidarity within the working class although social divisions did not erupt into physical violence. The older industrial areas, especially in the north and north east of England, industrial South Wales and Clydeside in Scotland, never recovered between the wars. Most agricultural areas suffered from the fall in the price of farm products and rural depopulation continued throughout the decades. Unemployment reached a peak in 1932 with the slump in world trade during the Depression.

However, there was considerable prosperity in southern England, London and the Midlands. There was employment in light industries that produced consumer goods and a building boom provided an increase in private home ownership in the new suburbs. Those in work were able to profit from low inflation, cheaper housing and a wider range of consumer goods. The contrast between the living and health standards of the prosperous south and the 'depressed areas' grew, but there was little revolt or protest from a resilient working class. Attitudes of hopelessness and despair permeated the ranks of the unemployed who had to survive on meagre assistance from the government but their political activism rarely went beyond hunger marches to protest at their condition.

Prolonged Conservative rule was punctuated by two brief Labour governments, but in 1931 the second of these split over the measures deemed necessary to resolve a massive financial crisis: it was succeeded by a National, but Conservative-dominated, administration with unchallengeable parliamentary power. Despite political divisions, the country remained united in support of the monarchy under the popular George V (1910–36) (though his son who reigned briefly, in 1936, as Edward VIII was forced to abdicate by the élite who objected to his proposed marriage to an American divorcée); patriotic mass entertainment and an interest in sport transcended class lines. Little was done by the National and Conservative governments to solve the problems of long-term unemployment. The old Poor Law was virtually abolished and some assistance was given to special areas, but little attempt was made to redirect investment into the depressed areas.

Britain and the Second World War

The first year of the war was not led resolutely by Chamberlain, who was forced to resign in May 1940. He was succeeded by Winston Churchill, who had opposed Nazism in the 1930s and had not been tainted by appeasement. From the beginning of his tenure, Churchill, leading a new national government that included the union leader Ernest Bevin as Minister of Labour, was an energetic and able war leader. He mobilised the nation at a time when Britain stood alone after the Germans had defeated France and forced the British Expeditionary Force to retreat from Dunkirk. His aggressive leadership and oratory, often broadcast on the BBC, was particularly effective in August and September 1940 during the Battle of Britain. The invasion of the island was thwarted when the Royal Air Force gained air supremacy over the Luftwaffe. Churchill also helped maintain morale and instil a sense of patriotism despite massive German bombing attacks on British cities (the 'Blitz') that killed over 60,000 civilians – and left many more homeless – during six years of war.

After the US entered the war in December 1941, the British became heavily dependent on their stronger ally in both the European and Pacific theatres. In the Pacific, US support came only after the loss of all British colonial posses-sions in the Far East to the Japanese. In February 1942, the fall of Singapore constituted the greatest defeat in British military history, and, by May, the British had retreated into India. That November, however, a combined British and American force defeated the Germans and Italians in North Africa at El Alamein; indeed, the British had held Egypt and the Suez Canal against the Germans and Italians since 1940. In 1943, Allied co-operation defeated a German U-boat campaign that had threatened the vital war supplies and food from America on which Britain's successful prosecution of the war depended. Churchill persuaded the Americans to launch a joint – and ultimately successful – invasion of Italy in July 1943 to protect imperial lines of communication in the Mediterranean: but they were unable to expel the Germans until 1945. The Americans and Russians pushed Churchill into agreeing to a massive invasion of Normandy in France launched on 'D-Day' (6th June 1944). British and American troops fought a hard campaign together for the next year in France, the Low Countries, and finally in Germany to defeat the Nazis. Anglo-American efforts also brought defeat to the Japanese: the British recaptured Burma, but it was the overwhelming strength of the United States that brought victory over the Japanese forces with the eventual dropping of the atomic bomb in August 1945.

Britain mobilised its entire adult (over-eighteen) population, including women, towards the war effort. Civilians and soldiers pulled together, unified in part by the common experience of the German air raids, and for a while it seemed that class divisions were less important than the need to defeat the enemy. There was a spirit of egalitarianism and a mood of 'fair shares' as everyone faced hardships equally. The classes were thrown together in the Blitz and when working-class children from the cities were evacuated to middle- and upper-class homes in the smaller towns and countryside. National unity was enhanced by the royal family led by George VI (1937–52), who chose to remain in London during the bombing. The British from all walks of life shared contact with the millions of US servicemen training in Britain before the Normandy landings. Some resented the Americans but many friendships were formed and thousands of British women became GI brides.

The power of the state expanded dramatically as the economy was planned and regulated to increase output of goods and armaments. Food was rationed, the state ran the mines and railways and the government sponsored many scientific activities. The British were forced to make many sacrifices during the war, as transport was scarce, and food, clothing and fuel were strictly rationed. Ironically however the standard of living and health of the majority *improved* during the war.

The government provided a wider range of social services for civilians drawn into the war effort. For instance many children and their mothers were evacuated to rural areas and hospital services had to be made available free of charge to all victims of bombing. Unemployment had begun to fall in the late 1930s with the increase in armament production; this trend continued with the massive demand for planes and other war goods once war had broken out. As a result of full employment and long working hours, the working classes had more money to spend than they had had in the depression years.

All this was paid for by increasing taxes, liquidating Britain's overseas assets and creating a huge national debt. To avoid inflation caused by an increased demand for a limited amount of consumer goods, the government encouraged savings and increased taxation. The shared experience of war produced a spirit of egalitarianism and there emerged a mood of unity and equality of sacrifice that many people felt should be reflected in government policies. Nevertheless, much war material was provided by the United States under the 'lend-lease' programme. The Ministry of Labour had the power to draft workers into any industry and Bevin successfully gained the co-operation of the trades unions, though there were some strikes that disturbed the consensus of government and TUC. Real wages, union membership and employment all increased in the war years.

A combination of the growth of government planning and the need to demonstrate to the people that victory would bring them benefits made post-war reconstruction the goal. Those improvements that were to take place sprang from the active involvement of the government in the economy and the lives of its citizens. The wartime mood of equality of sacrifice also influenced a radical shift in public policy. Accordingly, when William Beveridge published a report in November 1942 that set the agenda for social reconstruction it was greeted with great enthusiasm. Beveridge called for a single comprehensive scheme for the social services. All social classes would receive benefits paid in part by employers, the employee and the state. The entire population would have the right to a minimum standard of living provided by full employment, unemployment insurance, social security, family allowances, old age pensions, and a free national health service. Public support for a basic welfare state ensured that it eventually came to fruition in 1945 under a Labour government. Plans were also made in the war years to revitalise the depressed areas and to use Keynesian policies to promote full employment. Policy papers suggested government management over demand and investment and the nationalisation of key industries.

In 1944, social reconstruction began with an Education Act that provided secondary education for all up to the age of fifteen. The legislation introduced the '11-Plus' examination that decided which pupils went to grammar schools and which to the less educationally elevated secondary modern and technical schools. Reconstruction was deep-rooted as it matched the radical movement of the public during this the 'People's War'. This rapid shift towards the political left was soon reflected in the general election of July 1945 that focused on housing, health and full employment. Many feared that victory for the Conservatives, who were not as committed to social welfare and government economic intervention, might mean a return to the hardships of the 1930s. The result was a landslide for the Labour Party (they held 394 seats to the Conservatives' 210). Clement Attlee, the Labour leader who had served as Churchill's deputy during the war, replaced him as prime minister.

Further reading

Black, Jeremy, *A History of the British Isles,* Macmillan, Basingstoke, 1997.

Heyck, Thomas, *The Peoples of the British Isles,* 2 vols, Wadsworth, Belmont, CA, 1992.

Morgan, Kenneth O, ed, *The Oxford History of Britain,* vols 4 and 5, Oxford University Press, Oxford, 1992.

Roberts, Clayton and David Roberts, *A History of England,* 2 vols, Prentice Hall, London, 1991.

Afterword
'Soft you, a word or two before you go' ...
on Shakespeare
Jean Elliott

No introduction to Britain would be complete without a word or two on Shakespeare, Britain's greatest poet and dramatist. Why bother with Shakespeare? Well, because he *is* the greatest poet and dramatist, and this is his country.

Shakespeare was born, grew up, and died in the very heart of England's countryside in Warwickshire, though he spent much of his working life, and found fame and fortune in the heart of England's capital city, London. Incidentally, you should ignore all those various conspiracy theories that suggest that Shakespeare's plays were written by Queen Elizabeth, Christopher Marlowe, Ben Jonson, the Earl of Oxford and/or a creature from outer space. There are numerous cures for these delusions, but I will recommend Ian Wilson's *Shakespeare: the Evidence* (Headline Book Publishing, 1993) as a clear, concise and very readable treatment. Shakespeare did exist, and his works are a fact of life.

'Familiar in his mouth as household words'

The average 'Brit' has no especial reverence for Shakespeare. He's just *there* – a perpetual balding presence, a resident relative, part of the furniture, fixtures and fittings. Shakespeare is in the water we drink and in the air we breathe.

Shakespeare is woven into the fabric of our language, to such an extent that he is regularly quoted, half-quoted or misquoted by English speakers who rarely realise that they are quoting Shakespeare at all. His words are used with the ease and casual indifference of long familiarity by a range of English writers, and his lines are to be found in advertisements, newspaper headlines, editorials and soap operas. Quite apart from obvious lines like 'Romeo, Romeo, wherefore art thou, Romeo?' or 'To be or not to be, that is the question', or 'Friends, Romans, countrymen, lend me your ears', there are countless phrases which have passed into common usage: the sound and the fury, to beggar all description, in one fell swoop, poisoned chalice, salad days, cold comfort, vanish into thin air, to the manner born, more in sorrow than in anger, bag and baggage, let slip the dogs of war, and many, many more.

'Unwillingly to school'

Virtually everyone in Britain will have read and/or seen some Shakespeare at some time in their lives. The British have all been inoculated early. As a consequence, many people are, alas, effectively cured of Shakespeare forever. They did him at school, they will tell you, and then solemnly quote, word perfect, 'a speech of some dozen or sixteen lines' before concluding that, yes, they hate Shakespeare. He has long been an integral part of the British education system, and, in recent years Shakespeare has been enshrined in the National Curriculum (i.e. the government's regulations on national education standards). Thus, every schoolchild in the country has the interesting (and perhaps dubious) privilege of being forced to study at least two Shakespeare plays, starting at the age of about eleven or twelve. The state, with well-meaning fervour, demands that all children should display 'knowledge, understanding and appreciation' of Shakespeare by the time they reach fourteen years of age. Different examination boards will select different 'set texts' by Shakespeare, and children grapple gamely with the texts of plays written by an adult for adults. They do not study translations, nor are they given bite-sized chunks or edited highlights or anything of that sort. They plough through the whole text, again and again, line by line and word by word.

Recommended classroom activities also include acting out scenes, reporting the murder of Duncan as though for a popular newspaper, interviewing Julius Caesar and the conspirators as though for a television talk show, and so on. Touring children's theatre companies will turn up at the school in a battered van to do Shakespeare Workshops, followed by a five-man version of *The Taming of the Shrew*, or *Hamlet*, or whatever happens to be the school's set texts. Every theatre company will check out which of Shakespeare's plays are on the current year's English syllabus and adjust their programme accordingly.

All children between the ages of twelve and sixteen will be 'doing' Shakespeare, and huge parties will be bussed out to see productions at nearby theatres. This fact explains the notoriously bad behaviour of young audiences. Compulsory activity of any sort is deeply resented at that age – and to be sitting through three hours of Shakespeare when the vast majority of them would rather be watching television or playing computer games inevitably leads to restlessness, irreverence and occasional rioting. The rest of us in the theatre must console ourselves with the thought that Shakespeare himself had to endure his noisy 'groundlings' (the ones who paid a penny to stand in the yard of Shakespeare's theatre and who were known, brutally, as 'penny stinkards'). It is the experienced actor Shakespeare who is really speaking when Hamlet sneers at the groundlings 'who for the most part are capable of nothing but inexplicable dumb-shows and noise'. Somewhere in the theatre will be a few, perhaps even several, children who will be silenced and amazed and entranced by the magic of the play. And it is the philosophical Hamlet who concludes that the opinion of just one 'judicious' member of the audience must 'o'erweigh a whole theatre of others'.

Regardless of whether junior groundlings ('the beast/With many heads') emerge like butterflies to become judicious admirers of Shakespeare, all will have been exposed to him in some way. All will have 'caught' the Shakespeare, like measles, and something of him is there in the blood forever. ('God help the noble Claudio!' says Beatrice, 'If he have caught the Benedick.') America, with its less regimented views on education, can and sometimes does, send its students out into the world without their ever having read a word of Shakespeare.

'I understand a fury in your words,/But not the words.'

Having taught Shakespeare to thousands of visiting American students, I have frequently encountered those who solemnly assure me that they don't understand a word of it! ('All those "thees" and "thous"', they say, with a shudder.) Quite why something as ordinary as 'thee' should be set up as an insurmountable hurdle, I do not know. It just means 'you'. In some parts of northern England people still say 'thee' and 'thou'. I don't know why it is not more generally used nowadays. French, Italian, German and Spanish all still use two forms of 'you'. It is perhaps significant that most English and American-English speakers have dropped the 'intimate' form in favour of a universal formal 'you'. Are we all afraid of getting too close to someone? Anyway, it's just a question of getting used to it, in the same way visiting Americans quickly adapt to translating from American-English to English-English. It may be slightly disconcerting at first to be asked if you've got a fag, or to be told that there's a queue for the loo, but you will soon work out from the context that you are being asked for a cigarette, or told that there's a line for the bathroom.

It may be a comfort for you to know that Shakespeare invented about 2,000 words. Not only would his own audience have been baffled from time to time, but so would his actors! Shakespeare was writing at a time when the English language was just beginning to flourish and blossom. There were no dictionaries, no fixed rules of spelling, grammar or punctuation. The Elizabethans were discovering a 'brave new world', both geographically and culturally, and seemed generally to have been 'snappers up of unconsidered trifles'. They actually *liked* hearing new and unfamiliar words! The only other age that has created so many new words since has been our own. Every day we encounter new words, to do with science, medicine, technology, psychology. Consider only the 'computer' words we have newly created. If we don't know the meaning, we ask, or work it out from the context, or get by without knowing. I can still use a computer without knowing what a megabyte is. You don't leave a computer in its box because you don't understand every word to do with computers. No, you get it out and play with it, make mistakes, look up the odd instruction only when you get stuck. The same applies to Shakespeare.

You might also like to know that Shakespeare seems to have spoken American quite fluently. He uses words like 'trash', 'garbage' and 'gotten' – all considered loftily as American words over here, and, in the case of 'gotten', condemned as being grammatically incorrect. Moreover, there are many scholars who argue that his accent would have been more recognisably American than English. So you see you have a head start on all of us.

'I will hear that play.'

Shakespeare was writing for an audience. 'Audience' comes from the Latin *audire*, to hear, and thus his audience went to hear a play. Nowadays we go to see a show, which is rather different. No one in his audience would have read the script before they went. Nor would they have been able to read it when they got home. Scripts were very rarely printed at all and no one would dream of reading a play script anyway unless they were a theatre manager or the prompter. The publication of all the plays of Shakespeare in one volume was an extraordinary and rare event, and even that didn't happen until seven years after his death. The fact that his plays were collected and printed together is, by the way, a useful reminder of how popular Shakespeare was in his own day. Francis Meres, a Cambridge scholar and literary man-about-town, was praising him as a great dramatist in 1598: 'As Plautus and Seneca are accounted the best for comedy and tragedy among the Latins, so Shakespeare among the English is the most excellent in both kinds for the stage' (*Palladis Tamia, Wit's Treasury*). This observation was made before Shakespeare had written some of his greatest plays: a few years before *Othello* and *Macbeth, The Winter's Tale* and *The Tempest*.

'Pyramus, enter! Your cue is past; it is "never tire."'

Not even Shakespeare's actors would have read the script, as they were given only their parts and a few cue words. The quality of listening and concentration on Shakespeare's stage must have been phenomenal. The audience had to listen carefully too if they were going to understand the play. Quite apart from the newly minted words, they had only the words to tell them where the play was set (there was no scenery), and what time of day it was (plays were performed at two o'clock in the afternoon and there were no lighting effects). So characters have to 'announce' the scenery, effects and lighting changes as they go along: 'So this is the Forest of Arden', 'Welcome to Cyprus', 'This is Venice', ''Tis bitter cold', 'The moon is down', 'How sweet the moonlight sleeps upon this bank', 'But look, the morn in russet mantle clad/Walks o'er the dew of yon high eastward hill', 'But soft, what light through yonder window breaks?'

The more poetical the description, the greater was the stage effect, provided, of course, the audience would 'with patient ears attend'.

'On your imaginary forces work'

Shakespeare had to rely on his audience's willingness to listen to the words, and, moreover, on his audience's ability to imagine the scenes he was creating with his words. 'Think, when we talk of horses, that you see them', implores the Chorus in *Henry V*. Again and again in his plays, characters describe in vivid detail moments and scenes that the audience's imagination has to create. 'I will tell you', says Enobarbus, launching a vision of the beautiful Queen Cleopatra on a decorated golden barge with perfumed purple sails coming up the Nile; a woman so sexy that 'she makes hungry,/Where most she satisfies'. This is especially necessary when the Cleopatra we see on stage often acts like a spoiled teenager and, in Shakespeare's day, was male. Notice that Shakespeare creates the smell of perfume to go with the picture. Here he has a particular advantage over anything that can be done today. Lady Macbeth is obsessed with not only the sight, but also the smell of blood on her hands: 'Here's the smell of blood still: all the perfumes of Arabia will not sweeten this little hand.' In *Hamlet*, Claudius says, 'O my offence is rank, it smells to heaven.' If something is 'rank', it is rotten and is usually applied to rotting meat. Hamlet uses this word several times, most vividly to his mother when he reprimands her for living 'In the rank sweat of an enseamed bed'. 'Enseamed' means saturated with grease, so this is not a pleasant smell nor a pretty picture! A modern audience may crave realistic effects, but it would surely want to draw the line here.

All this talk of pictures is a useful reminder that were Shakespeare alive today, he would be making movies. Television sometimes, perhaps, but definitely the movies. Shakespeare loved big pictures! He thought in pictures, and he yearned for his audience to see pictures too. Limited by the available resources, he made a virtue of necessity and used words instead, inventing or adapting them to suit his purpose. Out of hundreds of possible examples, I will give my own favourite 'picture' which comes from the play most full of moving pictures, *Macbeth*. (This is the play that refers to horses eating each other, not to mention a suckling baby being snatched from its mother's nipple and having its brains dashed out. Picture that, if you can!) Macbeth has just murdered the king and is left alone while his superbly confident wife plants the blood-stained daggers on the guards who are to get the blame for the murder. Contemplating his own blood-stained hands he says:

Will all great Neptune's ocean wash this blood
Clean from my hand? No, this my hand will rather
The multitudinous seas incarnadine,
Making the green one red.

If you don't know that Neptune was the god of the sea it doesn't matter, because we all know what an ocean is. If we are listening properly we will stumble our ears against that clutter of multisyllabic consonants 'multitudinous seas incarnadine', which is at once 'translated' for us into the simple words, 'Making the green one red'. With that set of words, we can at once create exactly the right filmic picture: a close-up on a bloody hand frantically being washed in the sea. The camera closes even tighter so that we can see with horror that the blood, instead of coming off the hand simply spreads, with the water around getting redder and redder. And the fantastic climax is a wide-angle shot of an entire ocean stained the colour of blood. At that precise moment, just as we have gasped in shock, Shakespeare skilfully cuts to the re-entrance of Lady Macbeth proudly announcing that 'My hands are of your colour; but I shame/To wear a heart so white'.

We are brought up on pictures nowadays: not just television and film and illustrated papers and magazines, but we can also easily understand icons on a screen without thinking that we are doing anything especially clever. Thus we are so close to Shakespeare's mind, if only we knew it!

'The play's the thing'

Of course there have been some fine films made of Shakespeare's plays, quite apart from the wonderfully absurd fantasy of *Shakespeare in Love*, and many people discover Shakespeare through this route. But I would urge you all to make the most of your opportunities here to see Shakespeare in the theatre. He was, when all is said and done a playwright, a 'maker' of plays. And he was an actor. He began his stage career as an actor and he went on acting even after he had found fame and fortune as a playwright. As a manager of the Globe, he took a share of the box office receipts, and he was certainly wealthy enough to buy one of the grandest houses in Stratford-upon-Avon later in life. When his two friends and fellow actors John Hemmings and Henry Condell put together the collection of plays now known as *The First Folio,* they included the names of 'the Principall Actors in all these plays' and they put the name of William Shakespeare first. In fact, the real principal actor was Richard Burbage, and his name comes next. Obviously Hemmings and Condell, whose names feature somewhat lower in the list, had decided that it would be a gracious compliment to put Shakespeare's name first, but it does remind us of why all actors yearn to play Shakespeare. Having been an actor himself, he knew what *worked* in the theatre. He was very good to his actors and he wrote them the most wonderful parts. Even a minor character will usually have his 'moment'.

Certainly, Shakespeare expected his plays to be performed in a theatre and not read in a study, so take yourself off to whatever Shakespeare productions happen to be on offer. There's bound to be something on somewhere (all those 'set texts'!), and go prepared to listen, go to *hear* the play. The Royal Shakespeare Company performs in both London and in Stratford-upon-Avon. They also tour their productions to the further reaches of the country, from Newcastle in the north to Plymouth in the south. In London Shakespeare is to be found (occasionally) in the West End, but also in unlikely places like converted film studios, a warehouse, or a room above a pub. Some of the best Shakespeare productions I have ever seen, and heard, have been presented in fringe venues like pub theatres, and some of the worst in grand respectable theatres including (I'm sorry to say) in the Royal Shakespeare Company's own grand London house, the Barbican. But almost any Shakespeare performed is better than reading his plays in a library. In London during the summer months Shakespeare is performed, optimistically, in the open air: at the theatre in Regent's Park and, more recently, at the reconstruction of Shakespeare's Globe Theatre on Bankside, a theatre that owes its existence almost entirely to the enthusiasm and dedication of an American, Sam Wanamaker.

'Why do you dress me in borrowed robes?'

Go prepared for anything. Theatres have been playing Shakespeare in this country for well over three hundred years. He is performed so often that it is considered quite the normal thing to put characters in modern dress or Victorian costume or, often, a wild medley of costumes from various times and places (to show that he is relevant and universal and so forth). It is not unusual to see *Macbeth* in modern battle fatigues, *A Midsummer Night's Dream* set in a hippy commune or *The Winter's Tale* in an African village. It doesn't always help, but at least it's different. Occasionally American visitors are deeply shocked, assuming that, in Britain at any rate, they would be sure to see Shakespeare performed in 'traditional' dress – whatever that might be.

But for us Shakespeare has been around so long, has grown along with us, that we are perfectly happy to dress him any way we please. It goes back to my opening remarks: we don't revere Shakespeare, he's just one of the family. We can even suggest from time to time that he doesn't have to be studied at all being, as he is, a dead, white, patriarchal male. There's a ripple of naughtiness about the suggestion, like not inviting an elderly relative to the Christmas party. Responses to such an idea range from guilty glee to high moral indignation. Common sense prevails. Even if we don't invite him, he'll come anyway.

However we dress him up, chop him up, push him around and shove him into the corner or into the bed nearest the door, he still gets up and speaks to us. Despite (or because of?) being force-fed Shakespeare at school, the British did vote him into first place as their 'Man of the Millennium'.

'a local habitation and a name'

So this is Shakespeare's country, his own 'local habitation', and his works live on as his friend Ben Jonson so confidently predicted they would all those years ago:

> Thou art a monument, without a tomb,
> And art alive still, while thy book doth live,
> And we have wits to read, and praise to give.

The 'Sweet Swan of Avon' (Jonson again) has his grave in Stratford-upon-Avon, the town where he was born, a town at the very heart of England. He might well be astonished to find it now given over to the Shakespeare industry; he would certainly be delighted to find his plays are still good 'box office' (he was ever a shrewd observer of public tastes); and perhaps not too surprised to find his words being plundered by sellers of t-shirts, mugs and towels, and flourished by journalists, politicians and smart ad-men in search of a nifty half-familiar phrase. It was, after all, Shakespeare who wrote that 'it was always yet the trick of our English nation, if they have a good thing, to make it too common'.

Index

Compiled by Martin Upham